INSPIRE / PLAN / DISCOVER / EXPERIENCE

PARIS

PARIS

CONTENTS

DISCOVER 6

EXPERIENCE 64

NEED TO KNOW 306

Left: Looking over the Seine from the top of Notre-Dame
Previous page: The city of Paris at springtime

DISCOVER

WELCOME TO
PARIS

Sweeping, tree-lined boulevards and beautifully manicured parks. World-class museums and cutting-edge haute cuisine. The inspiration of countless artists, writers and philosophers, Paris is a city that speaks to the soul. Whatever your dream trip to Paris includes, this DK Eyewitness Travel Guide is the perfect travel companion.

1 Admiring art in the Musée du Louvre

2 Irresistible macarons, a pâtisserie favourite

3 The cobbled streets of Montparnasse

4 Taking a break in the Square Jean XXIII

The birthplace of the French Revolution, Paris is steeped in history. From the Gothic magnificence of Notre-Dame, through the Napoleonic opulence of the Opéra Garnier to the elegant modernity of the Eiffel Tower, the city's landmarks are a testament to its enduring status as a political and cultural powerhouse. Art is everywhere: lose yourself in the galleries of the Louvre and marvel at the Impressionist masterpieces in the Musée d'Orsay, or visit Belleville to view the ever-changing street art on Rue Denoyez. Paris's renowned food scene is equally rich, with an enticing array of boulangeries and bistros that reflect each neighbourhood's local flavour. Stalls overflow with fresh produce at the Marché d'Aligre, while La Cuisine offers the opportunity to learn to cook your own French classics.

The city's charms extend beyond its centre and it's well worth heading to Versailles to experience the royal splendour of the palace and gardens. Alternatively, escape the crowds and play *flaneur* for the day at the Bois de Vincennes or Bois de Boulogne, exploring their winding trails, stately châteaus and serene boating ponds.

Compact enough to travel easily around, Paris can still overwhelm with the volume of unmissable sites on offer. We've broken the city down into easily navigable chapters, with detailed itineraries, expert local knowledge and comprehensive maps. Add insider tips, and a need-to-know guide that lists the essentials to be aware of before and during your trip, and you've got an indispensable guidebook. Enjoy the book, and enjoy Paris.

REASONS TO LOVE
PARIS

It's soaked in history. It's steeped in culture. It's a gourmet's delight. Ask any Parisian and you'll hear a different reason why they love their city. Here, we pick some of our favourites.

1 **EIFFEL TOWER**
The most iconic symbol of Paris. Some people scale its full height while others view it from a distance, but no one forgets the first time they see the Iron Lady *(p200)*.

COFFEE AND CAFÉS *2*
Parisians caffeinate in style. Centuries-old cafés are the place to sit and stir the perfect espresso as you smell the caramel scent of roasters wafting through the city.

3 **PLAYING FLANEUR**
Parisians invented the concept of the *flaneur*, an aimless wanderer. Whether it's the Seine's footpaths *(p210)* or the boutique-laden Marais *(p84)*, there's always a reason to put one foot in front of the other.

MUSÉE DU LOUVRE 4

Home to the *Mona Lisa*, the Louvre *(p184)* houses over 30,000 works from across the ages. It's easy – and recommended – to get lost in its seemingly endless galleries.

NOTRE-DAME 5

This massive cathedral *(p70)* is a textbook example of Gothic architecture. The dramatic twin bell towers dominate central Paris, while inside light floods through its celebrated rose windows.

CLASSIC FRENCH CUISINE 6

French food is unrivalled, and eating in a restaurant is a total experience, where service is an art and every server can recommend a stellar wine.

VERSAILLES 7

Built to wow the world, Louis XIV's epic château and gardens are true marvels. Find yourself awed at every turn by the opulent display of wealth and grandeur *(p296)*.

RIVER SEINE 8

Paris's identity flows from its beloved river. Car-free paths on both banks offer romantic strolls or cycle rides past eye-catching street art and historic landmarks *(p210)*.

9 PÂTISSERIES AND BOULANGERIES

Baguettes and pastries fuel Parisians, and a daily trip to the bakery is routine for most. A buttery croissant anywhere else will never compare.

10 MARKETS

Rain or shine, Paris's street sellers spring to life each day. Bustling food markets colour nearly every neighbourhood, while the flea markets brim with hidden treasure.

OPERA AND BALLET 11

France raised the bar on ballet and opera under the Sun King. Savour the spectacular fruits of that legacy in the ornate Opéra Garnier *(p172)* and the modern Opéra Bastille *(p106)*.

HAUTE COUTURE 12

Paris is a fashion capital, and its designer stores are veritable temples to couture. Marvel at the dazzling displays that elevate clothing into fine art.

EXPLORE
PARIS

This guide divides Paris into 15 colour-coded sightseeing areas, as shown on the map below. Find out more about each area on the following pages. For areas beyond the centre see p290.

Cimetière de Montmartre

Place de Clichy

MONTMARTRE AND PIGALLE
p152

Parc Monceau

OPÉRA AND GRANDS BOULEVARDS
p168

Opéra National de Paris Garnier

Place de l'Opéra

Arc de Triomphe

CHAMPS-ÉLYSÉES AND CHAILLOT
p214

Place de la Concorde

LOUVRE AND LES HALLES
p180

Jardin des Tuileries

Musée du Louvre

Palais de Chaillot

La Seine

Jardins du Trocadero

Musée du Quai Branly-Jacques Chirac

Musée d'Orsay

Eiffel Tower

EIFFEL TOWER AND INVALIDES
p196

Parc du Champ-de-Mars

Place Joffre

Dôme des Invalides

ST-GERMAIN-DES-PRÉS
p234

Place de Breteuil

Jardin du Luxembourg

MONTPARNASSE AND JARDIN DU LUXEMBOURG
p278

Cimetière du Montparnasse

Place Denfert Rochereau

WESTERN EUROPE

UNITED KINGDOM

NETHERLANDS

BELGIUM

GERMANY

Lille

PARIS

Rennes

Strasbourg

Atlantic Ocean

FRANCE

SWITZERLAND

Bordeaux

Lyon

ITALY

Toulouse

Marseille

SPAIN

Mediterranean Sea

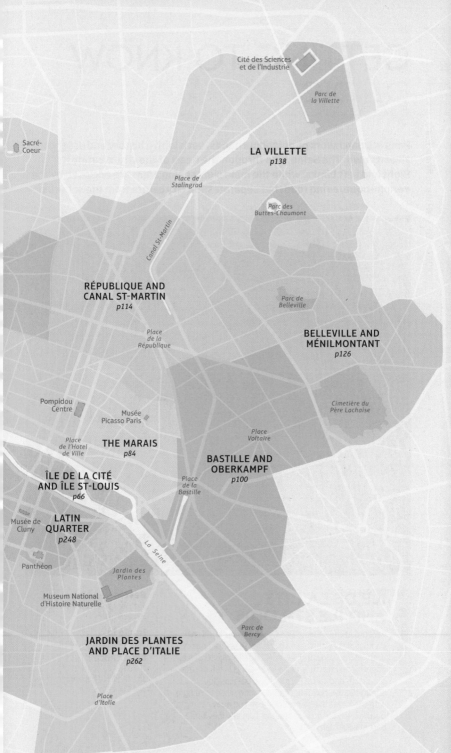

Cité des Sciences
et de l'Industrie

Parc de
la Villette

Sacré-
Coeur

LA VILLETTE
p138

Place de
Stalingrad

Parc des
Buttes-Chaumont

Canal St-Martin

**RÉPUBLIQUE AND
CANAL ST-MARTIN**
p114

Parc de
Belleville

Place
de la
République

**BELLEVILLE AND
MÉNILMONTANT**
p126

Pompidou
Centre

Musée
Picasso Paris

Place
de l'Hôtel
de Ville

Cimetière du
Père Lachaise

THE MARAIS
p84

Place
Voltaire

**ÎLE DE LA CITÉ
AND ÎLE ST-LOUIS**
p66

Place
de la
Bastille

**BASTILLE AND
OBERKAMPF**
p100

Musée de
Cluny

**LATIN
QUARTER**
p248

La Seine

Panthéon

Jardin des
Plantes

Museum National
d'Histoire Naturelle

Parc de
Bercy

**JARDIN DES PLANTES
AND PLACE D'ITALIE**
p262

Place
d'Italie

0 metres   800   N

0 yards   800

GETTING TO KNOW
PARIS

Paris is a patchwork of neighbourhoods, each with a history and essence all of its own. The Seine runs through the heart of the city, creating its Right and Left banks, while the main sightseeing areas are enclosed by the Périphérique, a ring road that separates the city centre from the suburbs.

PAGE 66

ÎLE DE LA CITÉ AND ÎLE ST-LOUIS

Located at the heart of Paris, these two islands are cornucopias of must-see sights. Île de la Cité houses both Notre-Dame and Sainte-Chapelle, masterpieces of gothic architecture, while Île St-Louis is full of cute boutiques and cafés. Former royal palaces double as administrative buildings, but it's not a place to mingle with the locals unless picnicking on the quays at night. Both islands are an essential, and usually inevitable, part of a Parisian excursion.

Best for
Sightseeing and strolling along the river

Home to
Notre-Dame, Sainte-Chapelle

Experience
The awe-inspiring Gothic architecture of Notre-Dame and Sainte-Chapelle

PAGE 84

THE MARAIS

Full of fashionable boutiques and restaurants, the Marais is the neighbourhood visitors return to over and over again. Its noble origins are apparent in the Renaissance mansions repurposed for the likes of Chanel and the Musée Carnavalet. Along Rue des Rosiers, the scent of freshly fried falafel wafts through the air while the city's best Jewish bakeries prepare poppy seed pastries. Parisians spend afternoons mingling at the Place des Vosges, with its leafy green trees set against the rosy bricks of a former palace.

Best for
Shopping, dining, history, architecture, LGBT+ life

Home to
Musée Picasso Paris, Pompidou Centre

Experience
The trendy boutiques and the scenic Place des Vosges

PAGE 100

BASTILLE AND OBERKAMPF

Gritty and lively, these areas east of the Marais make up for a lack of major tourist attractions with stellar dining options. Upstart coffee shops, independent boutiques and innovative bars draw a younger, multicultural crowd from across the city. *Flaneurs* can enjoy the elevated Promenade Plantée for a bucolic stroll above the streets, or wander the markets at Aligre and along Boulevard Richard Lenoir – both sell fresh flowers and mounds of seasonal produce. Those looking for a taste of local life will find it here.

Best for
Nightlife and restaurants

Home to
Place de la Bastille

Experience
The magnificent July Column and a stroll along the elevated Promenade Plantée

→

PAGE 114

RÉPUBLIQUE AND CANAL ST-MARTIN

These areas have recently transformed into exciting, somewhat quirky destinations. Characterized by the *bobos* (bohemian-bourgeois Parisians) who helped gentrify it, the canal is a hotspot for daytime coffee dates and evening picnics, fuelled by an extensive selection of cafés. Shoppers should head to the pockets of boutiques specializing in homewares, clothing and jewellery. This is the side of Paris that few visitors see but are exceedingly happy to find.

Best for
Coffee lovers and getting off the beaten track in style

Home to
Canal St-Martin

Experience
The Musée des Moulages medical museum and a pizza picnic along the canal

PAGE 126

BELLEVILLE AND MÉNILMONTANT

Far from the beaten path, Belleville and Ménilmontant are local enclaves that are little visited by tourists. Artists toil away in their galleries and in the streets, turning thoroughfares such as Rue Denoyez into open-air masterpieces, while Asian restaurants and shops attract locals who want a break from duck confit. Hipsters and international residents have made their home in these characterful areas, which offer a rewarding glimpse into everyday Parisian life.

Best for
Ethnic food and experiencing local life

Home to
Cimetière Père Lachaise

Experience
A hunt for the tombs of famous figures such as Edith Piaf and Oscar Wilde at the Cimetière Père Lachaise

PAGE 138

LA VILLETTE

On the city's northeast edge, the canal cuts a broad path through this green park that's as family-friendly as it is cultural. The city's stunning Jean Nouvel-designed Philharmonie towers like a spaceship while the science centre and playground across the water provide endless entertainment for kids. Joggers and cyclists appreciate the traffic-free pathways, and in spring and summer concerts and outdoor movies soundtrack the evenings. Parisians of all ages head here, to while away the time with a glass of rosé as the clinking of their *pétanque* games echoes over the water.

Best for
Music lovers and getting some fresh air

Home to
Parc de la Villette, Cité des Sciences et de l'Industrie

Experience
Playing pétanque *along the canal or taking in a show at the Philharmonie de Paris*

PAGE 152

MONTMARTRE AND PIGALLE

Although the area around the Moulin Rouge is still dotted with sordid "love" shops and seedy bars, Montmartre and Pigalle have become fashionable destinations for diners and shoppers. Pigalle's red lights have given way to some of the city's best pastry shops, boutique hotels and designer stores. Visitors still love browsing the art at Place du Tertre and soaking up the view of Paris from atop hilly Montmartre, where the cobbled streets and quaint houses retain a 19th-century village feel that few other districts reproduce.

Best for
A night out and great views

Home to
Sacré-Coeur

Experience
The sound of buskers on the steps in front of the Sacré-Coeur while watching the sun set over the city

$\rightarrow$

PAGE 168

OPÉRA AND GRANDS BOULEVARDS

Studded with theatres and crowned by the Opéra Garnier, this district epitomizes Baron Haussmann's plans for Paris, with monuments at every intersection. Its broad avenues, lined with exquisite churches and wallet-emptying department stores, are filled with bustling crowds of Parisians. This is the place to stroll, shop and repeat, whether it's for rose-flavoured macarons from Ladurée's original shop or a luxury bag from Printemps.

Best for
Shoppers and theatre-goers

Home to
Opéra National de Paris Garnier

Experience
Shopping for perfume under the Art Nouveau cupola at Galeries Lafayette, before heading next-door to Printemps' rooftop café

PAGE 180

LOUVRE AND LES HALLES

Paris's former royal palace and central market are as lively as ever. The Musée du Louvre, with its infamous glass pyramid and *Mona Lisa*, needs no introduction. The stately manicured gardens of the adjacent Tuileries house cafés and other art galleries. Les Halles was historically the hub of food distribution in the city, and the smells of ripened cheeses and fresh baguettes still tempt shoppers along Rue Montorgueil. It's all about cuisine here, from fine dining to street food, and wine bars and cocktail clubs shake up the nights.

Best for
Shopping, dining and history

Home to
Musée du Louvre

Experience
Coming face to face with the Mona Lisa before sampling pastries along Rue Montorgueil

EIFFEL TOWER AND INVALIDES

This corner of town is grandiose and ornate, with the gold-topped Dôme des Invalides soaring against the skyline. Full of history and artifacts, it plays second fiddle to the neighbourhood's real star: the Iron Lady herself, the Eiffel Tower, rises at the edge of the river. Away from the chaos of tours and elevator lines, this district also offers quaint streets such as Rue Cler where colourful, buttery pastries await. Some of the city's top restaurants aren't far. If Michelin stars are out of the budget then a picnic on the Champ-de-Mars underneath the tower will do, with the appropriate bottle of oaky red wine, of course.

Best for
Sightseeing and fine dining

Home to
Eiffel Tower, Dôme des Invalides, Musée du Quai Branly–Jacques Chirac

Experience
Stunning views from atop the Eiffel Tower before bowing to Napoleon at his tomb at the Invalides

→

PAGE 214

CHAMPS-ÉLYSÉES AND CHAILLOT

The world's most beautiful avenue still has a shine to it. Although its shops are mainly frequented by tourists, it's worth a visit for the iconic stores and the monumental Arc de Triomphe. Well-heeled Parisians do live nearby, more likely to be found at one of the museums at the Palais de Chaillot. Luxury shoppers will revel along the Avenue Montaigne and the area's palace hotels are the perfect place for a ritzy afternoon tea or evening cocktail.

Best for
Window shopping and Michelin dining

Home to
Arc de Triomphe, Palais de Chaillot

Experience
A dip into the Petit Palais exhibition hall before splashing out on a terrace coffee on the Avenue des Champs-Élysées

PAGE 234

ST-GERMAIN-DES-PRÈS

Cafés line the streets and squares of this iconic district – the chocolates and pastries are some of the city's best. Shoppers delight in the boutiques and art galleries found here – Le Bon Marché in particular captivates shoppers who walk through its perfume-laden halls. A smattering of museums and centuries-old churches attracts tourists, but locals continue to lay claim to this bohemian enclave. There's no better place to rub elbows with true-blooded Parisians than in one of the neighbourhood's endless supply of cafés and bars.

Best for
Strolling and people watching

Home to
Musée d'Orsay

Experience
Local life at one of the legendary cafés while nibbling macarons

LATIN QUARTER

PAGE 248

From Romans ruins to Hollywood backdrops, the Latin Quarter is beloved by Parisians and travellers alike. Café crowds are decidedly younger than most, filled with university students from the Collège de France and La Sorbonne. Every block seems to have a bookstore, from obscure academic shops to the bursting shelves of the famed Shakespeare and Company. Peppered among the tiny twisting streets are crêpe stands and dive bars, all offset by the grandeur of stunning sights such as the Panthéon, Musée de Cluny and St-Étienne-du-Mont church.

Best for
Budget travel and history lovers

Home to
Panthéon

Experience
Shopping for a picnic at the Marché Maubert and discussing philosophy with students around the Sorbonne

→

PAGE 262

JARDIN DES PLANTES AND PLACE D'ITALIE

Many people stop at the Latin Quarter, leaving this corner of the Left Bank less busy than the rest. The flowering Jardin des Plantes is home to natural history galleries and a zoo, and is a popular spot with Parisian families at weekends. A stroll along Rue Mouffetard delights with cheese and pastry shops, while architectural surprises such as the mosque or the national library make an exciting break from the traditional Parisian cityscape.

Best for
Family days out in any weather

Home to
Muséum National d'Histoire Naturelle

Experience
Sipping mint tea at the Grande Mosquée de Paris after visiting Europe's second-oldest zoo

PAGE 278

MONTPARNASSE AND JARDIN DU LUXEMBOURG

Old and new Paris come together in this lively area, where traditional cafés nestle alongside modern tower blocks. The gorgeous Jardin du Luxembourg attracts Parisians looking for a bit of fresh air, while in-the-know visitors head to the Tour Montparnasse and the Catacombs. Locals still congregate at the *belle époque* brasseries, where the appetizing smell of lentils and sausages is accompanied by the sound of clinking beers.

Best for
A day at the playground and belle époque dining

Home to
Cimetière du Montparnasse

Experience
The cavernous underground Catacombs before ascending the Tour Montparnasse for a unique perspective of the city

BEYOND THE CENTRE

Beyond the Périphérique (Paris's ring road),
two natural parks act like the city's green lungs.
The Bois de Vincennes and Bois de Boulogne offer
lakes for boating, paths for strolling and châteaus
for exploring, as well as attractions such as the
contemporary Fondation Louis Vuitton art gallery
and an innovative zoo. Disneyland® Paris grants
families another daylong escape, while history
buffs will enjoy an outing to the palace and
gardens at Versailles, a 17th century Disneyland®
in its own right.

Best for
Getting out of Paris

Home to
*Bois de Boulogne, Bois de
Vincennes, the Palace and
Gardens of Versailles,
Disneyland® Paris*

Experience
*The sumptuous estate of
Versailles or taking some air
in one of Paris's green lungs*

←

1 The interior of Notre-Dame

2 The Pont des Arts and Académie Française

3 Shakespeare and Company bookshop in the Latin Quarter

4 Jardin des Tuileries

Paris is a treasure trove of things to see and do, and its relatively compact size means that much exploring can be done on foot. These itineraries will inspire you to make the most of your visit.

5 HOURS

If you only have a few hours in Paris, a stroll along the River Seine is an ideal way to take in a plethora of sights. Begin in the Marais at the Hôtel de Ville (p95), the ornate city hall. Cross the river onto Île de la Cité, one of the oldest areas in Paris and home to major attractions such as Notre-Dame (p70). Pay a brief visit to the inside of the splendid cathedral before continuing your walk past the similarly impressive Sainte-Chapelle (p74). At the island's western tip, a statue of King Henri IV stands on the Pont Neuf (p78), the city's oldest bridge. Cross the bridge and head west towards the Louvre (p184), rising unmistakably just a few blocks away. Walk through its courtyard and admire the elegant wings and iconic pyramid, after stopping for coffee and a snack at Le Fumoir, located on Rue de l'Amiral de Coligny, behind the massive museum. There's no time to go inside to admire the art, but the beautifully manicured Jardin des Tuileries (p191) offers an inviting stroll through flower beds and leafy walkways lined with statues. Enter the gardens through the Arc de Triomphe du Carrousel (p192), one of two monumental arches built by Napoleon.

At the garden's far end, looking onto the Place de la Concorde (p224) and its Egyptian obelisk, sweeping views take in the Grand Palais (p225), the Arc de Triomphe (p218) and the Eiffel Tower (p200). Walk down to the square and cross the river towards the Romanesque National Assembly (p210), home to the lower house of the French Parliament. Follow the reclaimed riverbanks of the Berges de Seine (p210) east towards the Musée d'Orsay (p238), identifiable by its twin clock towers. Continue on Quai Voltaire towards the Pont des Arts bridge (p245), which affords great photo opportunities.

Proceed back along the Left Bank, browsing the stalls of the bouquinistes (used-book vendors), arriving at Place St-Michel (p256). Visit one of the many nearby bookshops, such as Shakespeare and Company (p258), before heading past Notre-Dame to intimate Île St-Louis. This little island sports no grand tourist attractions, but is the place to grab a cone of Berthillon ice cream (p77). End your stroll with a glass of wine and dinner at the Brasserie de l'Isle Saint-Louis on Quai de Bourbon, enjoying views of the Seine.

←

1 Pretty Canal St-Martin

2 The Colonne de Juillet in Place de la Bastille

3 Les Philosophes café

4 An exhibit in the Muséum National d'Histoire Naturelle

24 HOURS

Morning

Start with coffee and a pastry along the Canal St-Martin *(p118)*. Hipster coffee joints are in abundance here, and a take-away cappuccino pairs perfectly with a chocolate croissant from Du Pain et des Idées, the district's best bakery, on Rue Yves Toudic. Sit with your breakfast beside the canal, its green bridges arching gracefully over the water. Stroll the area and its shops on your way to the Upper Marais, just across nearby Place de la République, then live out noble fantasies while exploring the 17th-century mansion that houses the Musée Picasso *(p88)*. Browse the art and relax with a drink on the rooftop terrace before continuing.

Afternoon

Reach the heart of the Marais by foot, stopping for lunch in a café such as Les Philosophes on Rue Vieille du Temple, or queueing for the entirely worthwhile falafel at L'As du Fallafel *(p92)* on Rue des Rosiers. Indulge in some retail therapy before ducking down onto the Seine, along the Berges Rive Droite. This riverside pathway allows traffic-free strolling and features boats doubling as cafés. Cross a bridge onto Île St-Louis and make your way over to the Left Bank. Just to the east is the pristine Jardin des Plantes *(p268)*, an enclave for botany enthusiasts and a haven for anyone who appreciates natural beauty. It's also home to the Muséum National d'Histoire Naturelle *(p266)*, which is worth a quick look. At the far end of the garden, pause for some mint tea at the Grande Mosquée de Paris *(p268)*, just beyond the garden's gates.

Evening

Head back to the river and cross, walking along the stretch of canal that leads towards Place de la Bastille *(p104)*. Its July Column is visible from a distance. Plan on eating somewhere in the neighbourhood, such as Bistrot Paul Bert on Rue Paul Bert or Septime *(p107)* on Rue de Charonne, for a true Parisian dinner. Then hang around for drinks and cocktails in the vicinity of Rue de la Roquette *(p107)*, where the nightlife is sure to catch you up in its excitement.

←
1 The opulent Hall of Mirrors in the palace of Versailles

2 Cruising the Seine at sunset

3 A classic French breakfast

4 Art for sale in Place du Tertre in Montmartre

3 DAYS

Day 1

Morning Start the day in St-Germain-des-Prés with coffee and a croissant at any café, then take a leafy stroll through the nearby Jardin du Luxembourg (p286). Dip into St-Sulpice church (p243) to inspect the Delacroix paintings before going shopping along Boulevard St-Germain.

Afternoon Follow Rue de Seine towards the river, stopping for lunch at La Palette, a traditional café serving delicious *croque monsieur*. Stroll the Île St-Louis, popping into Notre-Dame (p70) before taking the Metro west to spend the rest of the afternoon exploring the Eiffel Tower (p200). Dare to walk the stairs if the elevator line is too long.

Evening Have dinner nearby at Café Christian Constant (p208), which serves classic French dishes. Follow this with a boat ride down the Seine as the sun sets.

Day 2

Morning Begin in hilly Montmartre, with a quick visit to the Sacré-Coeur basilica (p156). Browse the artists selling their wares in the open-air gallery of Place du Tertre (p158), then visit the Musée de Montmartre (p160) for a quick lesson on the 19th-century artists that made the district famous.

Afternoon Have lunch at Le Sancerre on Rue des Abbesses before heading down the hill towards Rue des Martyrs (p165), laden with pastry shops and boutiques. Consider a late afternoon jaunt through the Louvre (p184) to see the highlights, including *Mona Lisa* and the *Venus de Milo*. Soak up the views of the exterior with a coffee stop at the Café Marly, under the arcades of the Richelieu wing.

Evening Head to Les Halles for dinner at Champeaux (p189). Sip wine and people-watch for the rest of the evening along bustling Rue Montorgueil, or see what shows are playing at the nearby venues in the Opéra district, such as the historic Olympia music hall.

Day 3

Morning Travel less than an hour out of the city to Versailles (p296). Wander the world-famous gardens and 17th-century château, renowned for its opulent Hall of Mirrors.

Afternoon Splurge on lunch at Ore, an ornate little restaurant situated inside the château. Be sure to visit the outer estates, including the queen's fairy-tale hamlet with a working farm.

Evening Head back to Paris and share a bottle at an intimate venue like Willi's Wine Bar on Rue des Petits Champs, near the Louvre. If you've still got room after your lunch, have dinner in style at one of the city's iconic belle époque brasseries such as Bofinger (p107) or La Rotonde (p147).

PARIS FOR
ART LOVERS

Numerous figures have shaken up the art scene from the French capital, from Monet and the Impressionists to Dalí and the Surrealists. Countless masterpieces adorn Paris's greatest museums, while private galleries and even the streets offer a more personal look at contemporary art in the city.

World-Class Museums

Whatever your interest in art, one of Paris's museums has a collection for it. Highlights include the soaring gallery of the Musée d'Orsay (p238), a former train station famed for its Impressionist works, and the fascinating modern galleries of the Fondation Louis Vuitton (p292). Try to escape Mona Lisa's gaze while exploring the superlative collection at the Louvre (p184), before snaking up the panoramic escalator of the Pompidou Centre (p90) to marvel at Mondrian's deceptively simple squares. Smaller museums dedicated to Monet (p304) and Picasso (p88) will leave you swooning for these artistic icons.

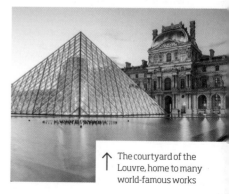

↑ The courtyard of the Louvre, home to many world-famous works

Create Your Own Collection

Paris is a nirvana for art collectors with any budget. High-end art galleries along the Left Bank sell some of Paris's most sought-after works, while at Place du Tertre in Montmartre *(p158)* you can mingle with local artists selling their canvases for a bargain. Visit the studios of little-known artists in Belleville *(p137)* – they might end up selling you something you didn't even know was for sale.

←

Place du Tertre in Montmartre, a hotspot for local artists exhibiting and selling their work

TOP 5 ART MUSEUMS

Musée du Louvre
The world's most visited museum and home of the *Mona Lisa (p184)*.

Musée d'Orsay
Dedicated to Western art between 1848 and 1914, its main draw is Impressionism *(p238)*.

Musée Picasso Paris
The greatest collection of the legendary artist's iconic works *(p88)*.

Pompidou Centre
An eye-catching modern building that houses an equally memorable art collection *(p90)*.

Palais de Toyko
A daring, and often overlooked, contemporary collection *(p231)*.

Striking Street Art

From the wily Space Invaders that dot the city to work of the iconic Miss.Tic, Paris is a haven for street art. Some of it appears clandestinely overnight while other murals, especially around the Canal St-Martin or even along Rue Denoyez in Belleville *(p133)*, are city initiatives to encourage street artists. Explore these ever-changing works by taking a wander around eastern Paris, or booking a tour with Street Art Tour Paris.

↑ An alley in the Marais decorated with some of the city's colourful street art

The "Sinking House"

The "sinking house" in Montmartre is a popular shot with travellers and locals alike. Walk up the stairs to the Sacré-Coeur (p156) and look to the right on the final flight, where you will see an orange apartment building peeking out behind the lawn. Tilt your camera to follow the angle of the grass for the full effect.

←

The illusory "sinking house" on a bright summer day

PARIS FOR
PHOTOGRAPHERS

A search for #paris on Instagram will supply a dizzying amount of results. Paris can't help being so photogenic – it's where photography was born in the 1800s with the daguerreotype, so the city has a history of smiling at the camera. Here's an insider's guide to finding Paris's most picturesque spots.

FAMOUS PHOTOGRAPHERS OF PARIS

Parisian painter Louis Daguerre was one of the fathers of modern photography and the inventor of the daguerreotype. It was here in the city, on Boulevard du Temple, that he used his innovative technology to take what became known as the first candid photo of a person: a man getting a shoeshine. Later photographers such as Henri Cartier-Bresson and Robert Doisneau helped turn photography into an art with their inventive shots of the city.

Rue Cremieux

Located by the Gare de Lyon (p108), Rue Cremieux and its colourful buildings are the stuff of Instagram lore. While the rest of the neighbourhood provides precious little beauty, these pastel façades shine on a sunny day.

→

Rue Cremieux, one of the prettiest streets in Paris

INSIDER TIP
Sunset Shot
Capture the golden hour in Paris on a bridge by Île de la Cité, looking west at the sunset.

The view from the top of Printemps at twilight
↓

Notre-Dame Gargoyles

You've seen the gargoyles overlooking the rooftops of Paris on a postcard, so now head up the bell towers of Notre-Dame *(p70)* to get your own shot. Arrive early in the morning before crowds line up at the cathedral, and snap away.

One of Notre-
Dame's photogenic
↓ gargoyles

Rooftop View

Shots of the the roofs of Paris are best taken from atop Printemps *(p177)*. Ride the escalator to the department store's roof for a postcard-perfect view. Looking northward in the early evening, the Sacré-Coeur glistens as Paris illuminates itself.

Eiffel Tower in a Puddle

It's as cliché as it comes, but who cares? Put a rainy day in Paris to creative use. The Champ-de-Mars *(p211)* is riddled with puddles after a shower, so score your own artful photo by taking a low-angled shot of the Eiffel Tower reflected in a pool of water.

→

A classic shot of the Eiffel Tower and its watery reflection

Go Wild at the Zoo

Paris has two zoos, and both will captivate small children and teens alike. Meet the world-famous primates at the Ménagerie in the Jardin des Plantes *(p268)*, Europe's second oldest zoo with enclosures dating back to the time of Napoleon. At the modern zoo in the Parc de Vincennes *(p294)*, visitors are immersed in animal habitats such as the grassy African savannah, where lanky giraffes and lazy lions await.

$\rightarrow$

Exotic birdlife at the Parc Zoologique de Paris in the Parc de Vincennes

PARIS FOR
FAMILIES

Paris is a playground for kids, with engaging parks and family-friendly events throughout the year. Children – and adults – will delight in riding the carousel in the Jardin des Plantes, watching a puppet show at the Jardin du Luxembourg or enjoying the beaches of the Paris Plages.

Take a Boat Trip

Boat cruises along the Seine or canal are a family favourite. Parents have the chance to relax while kids watch the city pass them by. Options along the Seine include Bateaux Mouches, Vedettes du Pont Neuf and Bateaux Parisiens, while the main company for the canal at La Villette is Canauxrama. The 19th century locks of the canal are especially curious, as is the cavernous tunnel that the tour takes you through.

A boat tour cruising along the Seine, past the Eiffel Tower $\uparrow$

Be a Chef for the Day

The kitchen is the heart of any family, so learn to cook together with a class at La Cuisine Paris *(p96)*. This well-appointed cooking school in the Marais offers English-language lessons in making a variety of traditional French dishes. Discover how to make buttery croissants or roll out your own baguettes before tasting the fruits, or rather pastries, of your labour. It's a sure-fire way to keep the whole family busy and smiling for a few hours, even if you'll end up covered in flour.

$\leftarrow$

Learning
the basics of
French baking
at a cooking school

TOP 5 RAINY DAY MUSEUMS

Muséum National d'Histoire Naturelle
Home to thousands of impressive animal specimens *(p266)*.

Musée de la Chasse et de la Nature
A collection of hunting trophies *(p96)*.

Aquarium de Paris - Cinéaqua
An underwater wonderland situated across from the Eiffel Tower *(p223)*.

Cité des Sciences et de l'Industrie
A huge science museum, packed with interactive exhibits *(p144)*.

Palais de la Découverte
Science for kids just off the Avenue des Champs-Élysées *(p228)*.

💬 INSIDER TIP
Eating Out

Parisians don't typically take their children to higher end restaurants, so choose somewhere more family oriented, such as the chain Hippopotamus or the budget-friendly Chez Gladines *(p255)*, where the food is still good but the atmosphere more relaxed.

Search for Hidden Treasure

Paris's museums are huge, but a treasure hunt provides an exciting new way of exploring them. A little rivalry, a bit of learning and a whole lot of fun await anyone who embarks on a hunt with THATMuse at the Louvre *(p184)* or Musée d'Orsay *(p238)*.

$\rightarrow$

Posing for a photograph
as part of a treasure
hunt at the Louvre

Daily Bread

Although French bread needs no introduction, there is, nevertheless, an art to choosing it. In Paris, all baguettes are not created equal. Ask for a *baguette à la tradition* to get the Parisian favourite, a regulated loaf that has nothing beyond the essentials inside. Crusty and handmade, these baguettes are tastier and delectably chewier than some regular crumbly baguettes. Try a *baguette bien cuite* if you like your bread well-baked and extra crispy.

$\rightarrow$

Fresh, crispy baguettes, available for sale at any neighbourhood boulangerie

PARIS FOR
FOODIES

Paris is legendary for its cuisine, so make sure you pack your appetite. Whether it's haute cuisine, rich, buttery pastries or rustic regional dishes, the city's delectable array of fresh, quality produce will delight your tastebuds – though perhaps not your waistline.

Flavourful fromage

Cheese is a way of life in France and punctuates any worthwhile meal. Cheesemongers dot Paris's streets and markets with hundreds of different pungent, subtle and salty varieties, their shops lined with huge, aged wheels and fresh, delicate discs. Try a bit of everything, following the vendor's suggestions. A mix of creamy, stinky but irresistible goat, cow and sheep's milk cheese is a perfect example of France's finest fromages.

$\leftarrow$

An array of cheeses at the annual Christmas market on Avenue des Champs-Élysées

TOP 4 ETHNIC CUISINES IN PARIS

With its multicultural population, the city also offers diners an amazing selection of world flavours – particularly those of France's former colonies.

North African
Couscous and tagine are popular dishes.

Vietnamese
Waves of immigration mean stellar *bo bun* and *bao mihn*.

Middle Eastern
Falafel in the Marais are unparalleled.

Japanese
Ramen around Rue Saint Anne is worth the wait.

→
Mouthwatering pastries for sale in one of the city's many pâtisseries, where delicate macarons *(above)* are a regular feature

MARKET STREETS

Shop like a Parisian on market streets, where stores focus on specific goods and outdoor stalls often pop up at weekends. Trendy Rue Montorgueil is a good stop for bread and cheese, while pastries are the draw on Rue Cler *(p209)*. Sample caramels and candies on Rue des Martyrs *(p165)* or shop for fresh produce along Rue Mouffetard *(p269)*.

Heavenly Pâtisserie

From the mighty macaron and spongy madeleines to creamy eclairs and tangy lemon tarts, Paris's pâtisseries are where taste buds go to be reawakened. Every corner bakery produces its own sweet, buttery or otherwise decadent versions of the classics. If there's a line at your chosen boutique, chances are you've made the right choice.

Opera and Ballet

The palatial Opéra Garnier (p172), home to the ballet, is a fairy-tale experience. Showing both opera and dance productions, it's a classic dose of Paris's musical heritage. The more modern Opéra Bastille (p106), a stunning glass venue, lacks the romance but delivers on acoustics. There's not a bad seat in the house to take in a production.

←

A ballet performance at the Opéra Garnier, the historic home of the ballet

PARIS FOR
LIVE MUSIC

From elegant symphonies to buskers in the Metro, Paris is a constant concert. World-class singers belt out centuries-old operas on stages that also welcome contemporary musical comedies or the latest pop artist. In the streets, the hum of accordions and funky jazz renditions infuse the air.

Paris Philharmonic

The glittering Philharmonie de Paris (p147) immerses spectators in the musical experience. You're never more than 32 m (105 ft) from the conductor, and cutting-edge acoustics mean you won't miss even the softest flute crescendo. Home to Paris's symphony, it's a daring space that will envelop you in sound.

↑ Chinese Pianist Lang Lang performing at the Philharmonie de Paris

Contemporary Music

Contemporary music flourishes in Paris, and local venues such as La Maroquinerie *(p134)* host up-and-coming artists. Familiar faces grace the stages of L'Olympia, where Edith Piaf famously sang, while smaller venues like La Cigalle offer a more intimate concert experience. Major pop and rock acts pass through the arena by Bercy *(p113)*, or even the Stade de France, for massive, bass-blowing concerts.

←

Major Lazer performing at L'Olympia

💬 INSIDER TIP
Music Festival

Celebrate the summer solstice with street buskers and concerts during June's all-night Fête de la Musique *(p36)*.

Musical Theatre

Paris has no Broadway or West End, but its growing musical theatre scene has French audiences applauding at the stage call. Experience classics such as *My Fair Lady* and *Singin' in the Rain* in English amid the splendour of the revamped 19th-century Théâtre du Châtelet. For French versions of modern musicals, from *Grease* to *Mamma Mia!*, head to the Théâtre Mogador *(p175)* in the Opéra district.

TOP 5 JAZZ VENUES

Sunset-Sunside
An intimate venue in Châtelet.

La Petite Halle
A newcomer on the scene in La Villette.

Duc des Lombards
In the Latin Quarter and practically a pilgrimage for musical artists.

New Morning
An obligatory stop for real jazz enthusiasts.

Chez Papa
An elegant jazz venue with restaurant.

↑ Homes of the musicals, the Théâtre du Châtelet and Théâtre Mogador *(inset)*

Idyllic Gardens

Flowers seem to bloom year-round in Paris's gardens. The hidden Jardin du Palais-Royal *(p188)* features fragrant roses, while the Jardin des Plantes *(p268)* grows exotic specimens from around the globe. The Luxembourg *(p286)* and Tuileries *(p191)* gardens are exquisite examples of royal property turned public.

←

An avenue of trees within the arcade-lined enclosure of the Jardin du Palais-Royal

PARIS FOR
GREEN SPACES

Perfectly manicured flower beds, sheared and shaped shrubbery, and spouting fountains decorate every corner of Paris. Former royal hunting grounds and private gardens are today lush green spaces where locals congregate to stroll or play a friendly game of *pétanque*.

TOP 4 LOCAL FAVOURITES

These lesser-known green spaces are popular spots where locals relax.

Parc des Buttes-Chaumont
Hilly, pristine and popular on weekends *(p146)*.

Parc Monceau
Well-heeled Parisians picnic here *(p228)*.

Parc de la Villette
Football matches and jogging are du jour here *(p140)*.

Place des Vosges
A tiny green space in a royal setting *(p92)*.

Innovative Reclaimed Space

Some of Paris's most successful modern green spaces have flourished out of former industrial expanses. Visit the Promenade Plantée (p106), an elevated train track that traded trains for tulips – the entire walkway is akin to a hanging garden sitting above the city. The Berges de Seine (p210), a pedestrianized roadway along the river, features barges doubling as floating gardens.

→

The Promenade Plantée, sitting above the city on a former railway track

INSIDER TIP
Flower Market

The Marché aux Fleurs Reine Elizabeth II (p77) is a gardener's playground. Flowers spill onto the street, while bulbs, seeds and tools fill the market stalls.

Relaxing Parks

In the 19th century, city planners built two green lungs – the Bois de Boulogne (p292) and Bois de Vincennes (p294) – on either side of Paris. Natural woodland, peaceful ponds and seemingly endless trails form this pair of bucolic havens. Each houses botanical gardens and various architectural features, as well as an array of surprises such as an open-air theatre. Beyond the gardens of Versailles (p296), the vast Parc de Versailles allows visitors to wander through pristine parkland.

↑ The verdant parkland of the Bois de Vincennes and Bois de Boulogne (inset)

On Stage and Screen

As the location of Molière's final performance (at the Palais Royal) and home of the world's oldest continuing theatre – the Comédie-Française, founded in 1680 – Paris has a rich pedigree when it comes to the stage. On the silver screen, the city has notably provided the backdrop to New Wave classics such as *Breathless* and *Jules et Jim*, and more recently to *Amélie*'s heartfelt quest for love in Montmartre – the Café des 2 Moulins, where she worked, can be visited on Rue Lepic.

←

Audrey Tatou as the title character in 2001's charming *Amélie*

INSIDER TIP
Famous Tombs

Visit icons such as Oscar Wilde and Edith Piaf at their final resting place in the Cimetière du Père Lachaise *(p130)*.

PARIS FOR
INSPIRATION

Paris has inspired countless thinkers and artists over the years. The centre of the Enlightenment, a fashion hub and a popular location for films since the Lumière brothers invented the cinema, the city is rich in cultural capital. Trace the steps of its icons to stimulate your own imagination.

Iconic Residents

From Chanel and Marie-Antoinette to Voltaire and Pasteur, Paris has hosted a long list of world-famous icons who have contributed to philosophy, art, science and culture. See Marie-Antoinette's bedchamber at Versailles *(p296)*, sip coffee in Les Deux Magots as Hemingway did *(p244)* and pay homage to Chanel at her first boutique on Rue Cambon.

↑ The legendary Chanel clothing boutique at 31 Rue Cambon

← Inside the opulent bedchamber of Marie-Antoinette at the Palace of Versailles

TOP 5 FOREIGN WRITERS WHO LIVED IN PARIS

Ernest Hemingway
The US author wrote *A Moveable Feast* about his time living in Paris from 1921 to 1926.

F Scott Fitzgerald
US writer Fitzgerald lived in Montparnasse in the 1920s.

George Orwell
The English novelist tells of his experiences living in poverty in *Down and Out in Paris and London* (1933).

James Joyce
Irish writer Joyce lived in Paris from 1920 to 1940. *Ulysses* was published here in 1922.

Anaïs Nin
US novelist Nin met her lover, fellow American Henry Miller, in Paris.

Literary Paris

The iconic Shakespeare and Company book shop *(p258)* is always bustling, a testament to the staying power of the written word. Paris has been the backdrop for countless epic novels, including *Notre Dame de Paris* and *Les Misérables*. Search for the phantom at the Opéra Garnier *(p172)*, stroll Rue Montorgueil like Florent in the *Belly of Paris* and keep an eye out for *Les Misérables'* Gavroche around the Bastille *(p104)* – or maybe in Victor Hugo's house *(p93)*, where he penned his most famous work.

← Shakespeare and Company, overflowing with literary treasures

Visitors walking through the beautifully landscaped Jardin des Tuileries ↑

PARIS ON A
SHOESTRING

Paris attracts droves of budget travellers with good reason. Free museums and green spaces keep visitors active during the day, while low-cost street food and happy hours make evenings a pleasure. And what beats a picnic along the Seine with a bargain bottle of wine, a baguette and some cheese?

Churches

Most churches in Paris are public property, open to visits for no fee. Avoid the tourist queues at Notre-Dame and the Sacré-Coeur, and instead head for the beautiful St-Sulpice *(p243)*, Paris's second largest church, which houses paintings by Delacroix. St-Étienne-du-Mont *(p257)*, next to the domed Panthéon, is often deserted, despite containing the tomb of St Geneviève – the patron saint of Paris. With stunning stained glass and countless artworks, these monuments are as awe-inspiring as they are budget-friendly.

→

The magnificent St-Étienne-du-Mont church

Parks and Gardens

From the top of Parc des Buttes-Chaumont (p146) to the furthest reaches of the Bois de Boulogne (p292) and the Bois de Vincennes (p294), greenery in Paris is, generally, free. Discover the ornate Médici Fountain in the Jardin du Luxembourg (p286) and view the obelisk at Place de la Concorde from the Jardin des Tuileries (p191). Have a pond-side picnic in Parc Monceau (p228) or join a game of *pétanque* in the Jardin du Palais-Royal (p188). It's astonishing that these pristine parks and gardens require no fee, but such is the magic of Paris.

← Locals playing a game of *pétanque* in the Jardin du Palais-Royal courtyard

Did You Know?

Many ticketed museums are free on the first Sunday of the month – check websites for details.

One of the lavishly decorated rooms in the Musée Carnavalet ↑

Municipal Museums

A selection of city-run institutions such as the Maison de Victor Hugo (p93) and the Musée Carnavalet (p97), dedicated to Parisian history, are free. While special exhibits are ticketed, the main collections are wide open to the public. Even contemporary art at the Musée d'Art Moderne de la Ville de Paris (p230) is accessible for a nod and a wave. The quaint Musée Cognacq-Jay (p92) fills a historical mansion, while the soaring Petit Palais (p225) is housed in an exhibit hall built for the 1900 Exposition Universelle.

High-End Shopping

The home of Chanel, Dior and Gaultier, Paris excels at high-end boutiques. The Avenue Montaigne (p228) is a sight in and of itself, with all of the designer names that most would recognize and few could afford. These aren't places to wander in casually in your trainers and shorts, they are the real deal – just ask the security guards who double as bouncers. Equally prestigious shops exist around Rue St-Honoré and in the St-Germain neighbourhood, while the Marais has recently become a centre for men's haute couture.

→

Rue St-Honoré and Avenue Montaigne (inset), two of the city's most pretigious shopping streets

PARIS FOR
SHOPPERS

Paris is synonymous with fashion, and for many people Parisian style is the ultimate in chic. In addition to clothing, the city is also a treasure trove of boutiques selling one-of-a-kind items that you can't get elsewhere. Whether it's a flea market find or a scarf from Hermès, the fun is in the hunt.

Department Stores

Paris brought department store shopping to life with Le Bon Marché (p243). Today there are several emporiums to choose from, but the formula is the same. Browse the designer outlets on the ground floors, amid masses of visitors queueing for the latest bag, before ascending the escalators through floor after floor of multi-brand bliss. When it all gets too much take a breather on the rooftop, at the scenic café atop Printemps (p177) or the deck at Galeries Lafayette (p175).

←

The stunning Art Nouveau interior of Galeries Lafayette

COCO CHANEL

Born into poverty and raised in an orphanage, the iconic Coco Chanel (1883–1971) opened her first shop in Paris in 1913. It sold hats and sportswear made from simple fabrics such as jersey, which proved popular with women seeking relief from restrictive corsets. The designer revolutionized fashion in the 1920s with the introduction of the little black dress and the launch of Chanel No.5, the first perfume to bear the name of a designer.

Did You Know?

The "Made in France" label signifies products that are authentic local items.

Shoppers browsing the ↑
wares at the Marché aux
Puces de St-Ouen

Flea Markets

Parisians frequently sell their belongings, and regular flea markets attract shoppers each weekend. The maze-like Marché aux Puces de St-Ouen at Porte de Clignancourt *(p305)* is the place to spend money on antique lamps, chairs and other homewares to create your own personal Versailles. Browse, feign interest and bargain when necessary – perhaps not on the €5 trinket box, but the €5,000 Louis XV chair may be negotiable.

World War II Scars

Hitler gave orders for Paris to be levelled at the end of the Nazi Occupation, but they were disobeyed by the general in charge of the city who instead surrendered. Relatively few physical scars remain from the Occupation of 1940–44, but marks on the front of the police office on Île de la Cité (p77) recall skirmishes between Resistance fighters and German forces.

←

The police office on Île de la Cité, the scene of fighting during World War II

PARIS FOR
HISTORY BUFFS

There are more than two millennia of history to visit in Paris. From Viking invasions and plagues to Revolution and Nazi Occupation, the past comes alive in the museums, streets and cafés – basically everywhere.

TOP 4 HISTORY MUSEUMS

Musée de l'Armée
Military history from medieval knights to Charles de Gaulle (p206).

Musée Carnavalet
An exploration of the history of Paris, located in a former mansion house (p97).

Pavillon de l'Arsenal
Houses an exhibition charting the evolution of architecture in Paris (p93).

Musée de Cluny
Specializes in medieval history, and also houses Gallo-Roman ruins (p254).

→

The Arc de Triomphe du Carrousel at the entrance to the Jardin des Tuileries

Napoleonic Memorials

The mark of 19th-century emperors Napoleon I and his nephew, Napoleon III, is visible throughout the city. If you see an "N" on a bridge or monument, as on the façade of the Louvre (p184), it's easy to date that particular work to one of those men. Napoleon I also commissioned several monuments in his own honour, including the Arc de Triomphe (p218), the smaller Arc de Triomphe du Carrousel (p192) and the bronze column at Place Vendôme (p193).

Roman Remains

Few are aware that Paris was once a bustling Roman town. Boulevard St-Michel is a former Roman road, and ruins of the baths there are still on display next to the Musée de Cluny (p254). The enormous Arènes de Lutèce (p268), which today hosts football matches and playdates, once was the staging ground for Roman theatre and combats.

→

The ruins of the Arènes de Lutèce, once a vast Roman arena

💬 INSIDER TIP
Historic Tales

Test your French by reading the 700 or so Histoire de Paris signs all over the city, which recount historic events at the location where they happened. The oar-shaped plaques were designed by Philippe Starck.

↑ Napoleon's commem- orative column in Place Vendôme

The Flame of Liberty

More recent history is commemorated by impromptu memorials such as the Flame of Liberty. A copy of the torch held by Lady Liberty in New York, it originally symbolized French-US relations. Today it informally honours Princess Diana, who tragically met her fate in 1997 after a car accident in the traffic tunnels below.

The golden Flame of Liberty, a tribute to Princess Diana ↓

PARIS
RAISE A GLASS

Parisians have always enjoyed their tipples. Wine, imported from all over France, remains a staple, while a new wave of cocktail bars have reinvented how the city enjoys spirits. Beer, once brewed in the belle époque brasseries, now gets the craft treatment in hip, upstart breweries.

Craft Beer

French beer has historically never been something to write home about. Today, however, bolshy breweries like Goutte d'Or and Paname Brewing Company *(p151)* are changing all of that. The brasseries of the 19th century have ceded their hops and barley to younger brewers bringing craft beer to Paris. Sample their wares at establishments like La Fine Mousse *(p108)*, which specializes in French and international craft beers.

→

The impressive beer selection at La Fine Mousse

Innovative Wine

Parisian wine tastes have moved far beyond the clichés of red with meat and white with fish. While there's no reason to stray from French wine in the city, prepare to experiment with pairings that you might not have considered. When in doubt, always trust your server, who can advise you which bottle will suit your needs. And if you're still unsure, sample the house wine – often a sure-fire monthly offering.

←

Red wine flowing at a dinner among friends, and for sale at one of the city's many wine shops *(below)*

WINE TASTING

Booking an official tasting is often the best way to engage more fully with French wine. At O Chateau *(p193)*, English-speaking specialists offer tastings, a Champagne cruise and even a dinner where you can discover multiple vintages. Classes at Le Foodist include a cheese pairing, doubling as lunch, with charcuterie, olives and various wine samplings. Events at Wine Tasting in Paris introduce participants to the various winemaking regions in France through different samplings.

Creative Cocktails

Bars like Candelaria and Prescription Cocktail Club have fully opened Parisian eyes to cocktails, a revolution that began over a century ago with the legendary Harry's Bar *(p175)*. A new wave of bartenders plays with a variety of ingredients and flavours, creating a host of inventive concoctions. Sit back and enjoy the show, and have your patience rewarded with an Instagram-worthy cocktail that also tickles the tastebuds.

↑ The attractive façade of the cocktail bar Candelaria

Above the Skyline

Paris rose to new heights in the modern era. At first declared an eyesore, the 19th-century Eiffel Tower *(p200)* became a symbol of the city with its brown iron lattices. Enjoy a bird's-eye perspective of Paris from its viewing gallery. Alternatively, ascend the 20th century Tour Montparnasse *(p284)* for panoramic views from a different angle. While not as elegant as the Iron Lady, its green makeover for the 2024 Olympic Games promises a change, joining shimmering contemporary structures like the Fondation Louis Vuitton *(p292)* and the Philharmonie de Paris *(p147)*.

→

The view from Tour Montparnasse, looking towards the Eiffel Tower

PARIS FOR
ARCHITECTURE

Planned and perfected, Paris showcases centuries of architectural styles. Jagged Gothic façades, soaring Neo-Classical domes and dazzling modern buildings dot the city. Admire Paris from a fresh perspective by tracing the city's architecture from its subterranean depths to the tip of the Eiffel Tower.

KEY ARCHITECTURAL STYLES

Gothic: this imposing style flourished in France, most famously at Notre-Dame *(p70)*.

Baroque: the lavish decoration of Versailles *(p296)* is typical of this style.

Neo-Classical: inspired by ancient Greece and Rome, this style is epitomized by the Panthéon *(p252)*.

Art Nouveau: incorporating curves and natural motifs, Art Nouveau details are still visible in the Metro station entrances.

Overhead

Most of Paris's architecture dates from the 19th century, when the city planner Baron Haussmann redesigned most of the city. His fashionable architectural innovations spread across France, and even to other countries. Amble along Haussmann's sweeping tree-lined boulevards and gaze up at the uniform façades that are a signature of his style. He was also known for the monumental intersections he created around lofty buildings, such as the cupcake-like Opéra Garnier *(p172)*.

Avenue de la Grande Armée, designed by Baron Haussmann ↑

Street Level

Medieval half-timbered houses and Renaissance palaces still dot the Marais, where history survived the ravages of conflict and city planning. See examples of both on Rue François Miron, or head over to the palatial Place des Vosges, lined with pretty pink brick façades, for a taste of French Renaissance architecture under Henri IV.

The courtyards of these mansions once welcomed the regal carriages of Parisian nobility.

← Hôtel de Soubise, one of the numerous historic mansions in the Marais

BARON HAUSSMANN

Lawyer by training and civil servant by profession, Georges-Eugène Haussmann worked under Emperor Napoleon III to redesign Paris. Working with the best architects and engineers of the day, he tore down old buildings and cut new boulevards across the city. His controversial plans angered many, but the result was, arguably, quite striking. During his time, modern sewers, green leafy parks and strict building regulations gave us the Paris that we adore today.

Below Ground

Underground, Paris is a world unto itself. Discover the 18th-century Catacombes (p285), a dark and twisted tangle of limestone quarries that house the bones of millions of Parisians, transferred from overflowing cemeteries. The 19th-century sewers (p209) are also open for visits, showcasing the potent and oftentimes rat-infested network to daring tourists.

↑ The macabre Catacombes de Paris, decorated with millions of bones

Walk the Canal Towards La Villette

Head to the Canal St-Martin *(p118)* to experience a local vibe. Few tour groups make it to the green bridges arching over the water, flanked by cute boutiques and coffee shops. Walk north along the canal to La Villette, a district worth the trek. The modern park *(p142)*, with its concert hall and science museum, draws Parisian families.

←

Canal St-Martin, a popular spot with locals for strolling and picnicking

PARIS OFF THE
BEATEN TRACK

It's easy to escape the crowds without going too far. Hidden courtyards and museums in the centre lure those who want something different, while the outer districts hold charming cafés, monumental churches and oddball galleries. Discover where the Parisians live and see the local side of the city.

Explore Multicultural Belleville

A bustling Vietnamese and Chinese district, Belleville is an enclave for Parisian artists and a new generation of hipsters. Take a rewarding excursion through the hilly Parc de Belleville *(p132)* for sweeping panoramas of the city, then be enticed by the smell of *pho* (Vietnamese soup) wafting along Rue de Belleville *(p132)*. Street art and quaint cafés decorate the district, which is especially lively during the market on Tuesday and Friday.

↑ Shoppers browsing a neighbourhood flea market in Belleville

Shop with Parisians at the Marché d'Aligre

Live like a Parisian for a day at the Marché d'Aligre (p106), one of Paris's most vibrant food markets. Barter for strawberries and have some mid-morning wine and oysters while filling your canvas bags with treats. The covered market, the Beauveau St-Antoine, is the best place to head for succulent sausages or tangy goat's cheese, while outside are fresh flowers, mountains of lettuce and stalls full of seasonal produce that will provide endless meal inspiration. The uncovered market also features stalls selling bric-a-brac and second-hand books.

←

Outdoor food stalls at the Marché d'Aligre, packed with an array of quality fresh produce

---

INSIDER TIP
Quiet Spots in the Louvre

You can even escape the crowds within the heart of the Louvre, the world's most visited museum. Head where tourist groups rarely go, upstairs to the Northern European painters or to the wings housing Islamic art or the Near Eastern antiquities.

Make an Excursion to Paris's Green Lungs

Rowing lazily across one of the lakes in the Bois de Vincennes (p294) or the Bois de Boulogne (p292), you'll wonder why all the tourists are still queuing for a boat ride along the Seine. These two large parks – lush green spaces situated on the outskirts of Paris – are often overlooked by visitors to the city. Stunning châteaux, exotic botanical gardens, a zoo, a mini amusement park and even the Fondation Louis Vuitton contemporary art gallery (p292) await those who make the trip across the Périphérique into these natural havens.

→

The Bois de Boulogne, home to the Fondation Louis Vuitton (above)

A YEAR IN
PARIS

JANUARY

△ **Fête des Rois** *(6 Jan)*. Feast on *galettes des rois* (a puff pastry cake) to celebrate the Epiphany.
Prix d'Amérique *(end Jan)*. World-famous trotting race, first held in 1920.

FEBRUARY

△ **Chinese New Year** *(5 Feb)*. Parades in Chinatown.
Retromobile *(early Feb)*. Retro car show.
Salon International d'Agriculture *(end Feb–early Mar)*. One of the world's largest farming fairs.

MAY

Shakespeare Garden Festival *(throughout until Oct)*. Plays performed in Bois du Boulogne.
Nuit Européenne des Musées *(mid-May)*. Museums open for one spring evening.
Taste of Paris *(mid-May)*. Four-day food festival at the Grand Palais.
△ **French Tennis Open** *(end May–early Jun)*. Major tennis tournament.
Le Printemps des Rues *(end May)*. Art and performance festival in east Paris.

JUNE

Fête de la Musique *(21 Jun)*. All-day celebration of music, with many free events across the city.
The International Paris Air Show *(17–23 Jun)*. One of the oldest and largest air shows in the world.
Les Grandes Eaux-Nocturnes *(mid-Jun–mid-Sep)*. Music and light show at Versailles gardens.
△ **Gay Pride** *(end Jun)*. Lively parade and festivities.
Fête du Cinema *(end Jun–early Jul)*. Four-day film festival with discounted tickets.
Paris Jazz Festival *(end-Jun–end Jul)*. A celebration of jazz music held in the Park Floral de Paris.

SEPTEMBER

Jazz à La Villette *(mid-Sep)*. Programme of jazz-related music, films and exhibitions.
Journées du Patrimoine *(mid-Sep)*. Historical buildings open their doors to the public.
△ **La Parisienne** *(mid-Sep)*. A running race just for women.
Techno Parade *(end Sep)*. Electronic music festival.

OCTOBER

Nuit Blanche *(1st Sat)*. All-night art installations.
△ **Prix de l'Arc de Triomphe** *(1st Sun)*. Renowned flat race at the Hippodrome de Longchamps.
Mondial de l'Automobile *(1st fortnight, alternate years)*. Commercial motor show.
Foire International d'Art Contemporain (FIAC) *(end Oct)*. Modern and contemporary art fair.
BNP Paribas Masters *(end Oct–early Nov)*. Prestigious indoor tennis tournament.

MARCH

Carnaval (3 Mar). Quirky costumed parades.
Printemps du Cinema (late Mar). Discounted tickets available for films shown citywide.
Festival des Arts Martiaux (late Mar). Martial arts fair.
△ **Foire du Trone** (Mar–May). Funfair held in Bois de Vincennes.

APRIL

△ **Paris Marathon** (14 Apr). A lengthy run through the streets of Paris.
Easter (19–22 Apr). Religious services plus chocolates galore.
Foire de Paris (27 Apr–8 May). Lifestyle, leisure, fashion and food at an enormous trade fair.

JULY

Festival du Cinéma en Pleine Air (mid-Jul–mid-Aug). Outdoor cinema in La Villette.
△ **Paris Plages** (Jul–Aug). The seaside comes to the Seine.
Paris Quartier d'Été (mid-Jul–early Aug). Citywide dance, music, theatre and ballet.
Bastille Day (14 Jul). Fireworks and festivities.
Tour de France (end Jul). The world's greatest cycle race arrives in Paris.

AUGUST

Festival Classique au Vert (mid-Aug–early Sep). Classical music in the Parc Floral.
△ **Rock en Seine** (end Aug). Major international rock music festival.

NOVEMBER

△ **Beaujolais Nouveau** (3rd Thu). Celebrations to mark the arrival of a new vintage wine on Parisian shelves.
Salon des Vins des Vignerons Indépendants (end Nov–early Dec). Independent festival for wine lovers and wine growers.

DECEMBER

Christmas illuminations (until Jan). Paris lights up to celebrate Christmas.
Nautic (early to mid-Dec). International boat show presenting the latest from the seas.
△ **New Year's Eve** (31 Dec). Light shows at the Arc de Triomphe bring in the new year.

A BRIEF
HISTORY

For over 2,000 years, Paris has survived endless invasions, wars and plagues that have tested the spirits of its citizens. The seat of power for world leaders such as Louis XIV and Napoleon, and the backdrop for events including revolution and Nazi invasion, Paris has endured, and with style.

From Roman Outpost to Capital City

The first permanent settlers, the Parisii, landed here around 2,500 years ago – though artifacts show that others were here before them. In 52 BC Rome conquered the Parisii, creating an outpost called Lutetia. By the fall of the Roman Empire in the 3rd century, Paris was on the rise. Clovis I, King of the Franks, made the city his kingdom's capital in AD 508 and, despite outbreaks of plague and English occupation hammering at the city's morale over the following centuries, art and culture flourished. Notre-Dame rose from Île de la Cité and the University of Paris became a centre for European education.

1 A medieval map of Paris ↑

2 The Sorbonne, seat of the University of Paris, in 1550

3 The Hundred Years' War between France and England

4 Revolutionaries storming the Bastille

Timeline of events

508

Clovis I, King of the Franks, establishes Paris as the capital of his kingdom, which becomes France

987

Hugh Capet, forbearer of all future kings of France, rules the Kingdom of Franks

1240

Church bells are regulated by clocks for the first time, facilitating the regulation of work hours in Paris

1429

Joan of Arc fails to retake Paris from English control and is burned at the stake one year later

A Cultural Centre

By the 1500s the Italian Renaissance had arrived in Paris by way of the de Médici family of Florence, and the city began to shine. Despite severe religious wars, exasperated by the Protestant faith of King Henri IV, culture thrived with new foods, fashions and even ballet. The Louvre became a royal palace and the nobility constructed mansions in the Marais. The French monarchs made Paris a world capital, epitomized by Louis XIV's opulent château and gardens at Versailles.

Revolution

In the 1700s the Enlightenment blossomed in Paris while the monarchy shrivelled. Famine and excessive spending at Versailles, as well as near-constant war, led to a call to arms. The French Revolution put a turbulent end to divine right as citizens stormed the Bastille prison on 14 July 1789. In 1793 Louis XVI and Marie-Antoinette both met their ends at Place de la Concorde, subjected to the guillotine. Parisians shook their city – and country – to the core, and a new government strove to regain order in a country divided by various ideologies.

FIRSTS IN PARIS

1348 Bubonic Plague first arrives
1660 Coffee first arrives from the East
1728 First street signs are erected
1827 First giraffe arrives in Paris, a gift from the ruler of Egypt
1907 First woman gets a taxi licence in Paris
1986 First Paris Marathon occurs
2014 Anne Hidalgo, first female mayor, is elected

1528

François I returns the monarchy to Paris after a century-long hiatus

1572

St Bartholomew's Day Massacre ends with some 2,000 Protestants dead in Paris, following the wedding of future king Henri IV and Marguerite de Valois

1671

Louis XIV moves the entire royal court to Versailles

1546

Work starts on the new Louvre palace and the first stone quay is built along the Seine

1789

French Revolution dethrones Louis XVI and Marie-Antoinette from Versailles

1

2

The Napoleonic Era

The rise to power of military leader Napoleon Bonaparte saw France's influence spread throughout its newly created Empire. The Bourbon kings briefly returned to power after Napoleon's downfall, before giving way to Louis-Napoleon Bonaparte, known as Napoleon III, who pursued France's Second Empire in his great-uncle's tradition. During the latter half of the 1800s, he charged administrator Baron Haussmann with modernizing Paris, creating the sweeping boulevards that define the city. By 1860 towns such as Montmartre and Belleville had been incorporated into Paris, establishing the present-day city limits.

The Belle Époque

The end of the brief and bloody Paris Commune of 1871, in which the citizens of Paris rose up against the French government, marked the emergence of the new Third Republic, which flourished during the belle époque (beautiful age) of the late 19th and early 20th century. The Eiffel Tower soared over Paris in 1889 and in 1900 the Metro opened. Paris truly was a glittering city at the cutting edge of art and technology.

↑ Louis-Napoleon Bonaparte, Emperor Napoleon III

Timeline continued

1804
Napoleon crowns himself Emperor of France

1853
Baron Haussmann's renovations of Paris begin

1871
The Bloody Week sees up to 10,000 French citizens killed at the hands of the army during the Paris Commune uprising

1941
The first Jewish Parisians are arrested by occupying forces

1944
Paris is liberated from Nazi occupation

Occupation and Recovery

In 1940, during World War II, the republic fell to Nazi Germany. Parisians survived the Occupation – albeit emerging beaten and subdued – and the city slowly recuperated. In 1968 student protests threatened to upturn the government, but the unrest quickly subsided. A series of ambitious architectural projects began around this time, and by the turn of the millennium Paris was a world-class city with modernization firmly in its sights The Vélib bike service changed the way Parisians travel, and cars were banned from the riverbanks, creating new green spaces.

Paris Today

Paris is a model city, attracting new businesses, embracing innovation and serving as an example for its European – and global – counterparts, while still retaining its traditional elements. The city was shaken again in 2015 by the Charlie Hebdo and Bataclan terrorist attacks, but it refuses to be cowed. Recently elected leaders, including future-facing mayors and a new president, have confirmed a commitment to Paris's status as a global city.

1 The Champ-de-Mars and Eiffel Tower during the Universal Exhibition of 1900

2 Students marching during the protests of 1968

3 The Vélib bike scheme, launched in 2007

4 A streetside memorial following the Charlie Hebdo attacks

1961–62
Often-deadly protests are held by Algerians in Paris over the French-Algerian War

1968
Student riots and worker strikes take place in the Latin Quarter

1977
Jacques Chirac is installed as the first elected mayor of Paris since 1871

1992
EuroDisney (now Disneyland® Paris) officially opens

2017
Emmanuel Macron, France's youngest president, moves into the Palais de l'Élysée

EXPERIENCE

A Notre-Dame gargoyle surveying the city

ÎLE DE LA CITÉ AND ÎLE ST-LOUIS

The history of Paris started on the Île de la Cité, an island formed by two meanders of the Seine. Inhabited by the Parisii Gauls from the 3rd century BC and taken over in 52 BC by Caesar's Romans, the Île de la Cité was the birthplace of river commerce, and in medieval times it became a centre of political and religious power. Some imposing evidence of this power can still be seen in the Conciergerie, a medieval palace-turned-prison, and in Notre-Dame, the island's world-famous Gothic cathedral. The huddles of tiny houses and narrow streets that once characterized the island were swept away by the spacious thoroughfares built in the 19th century, but there are still charming snippets of another time around the romantic Square du Vert-Galant and the venerable Place Dauphine.

At the island's eastern end, the St-Louis bridge connects it to the smaller Île St-Louis. This former swampy pastureland was transformed into an elegant 17th-century residential area, with picturesque tree-lined quays. More recently, rich artists, actresses and heiresses have lived here.

ÎLE DE LA CITÉ AND ÎLE ST-LOUIS

Must Sees
1. Notre-Dame
2. Sainte-Chapelle

Experience More
3. Mémorial des Martyrs de la Déportation
4. Conciergerie
5. Crypte Archéologique
6. Hôtel Dieu
7. Marché aux Fleurs Reine Elizabeth II
8. Palais de Justice
9. Place Dauphine
10. Pont Neuf
11. Square du Vert-Galant
12. St-Louis-en-l'Île

Eat
1. Berthillon

Stay
2. Paris Perfect Flat Place Dauphine
3. Saint-Louis en l'Isle
4. Hôtel du Jeu de Paume

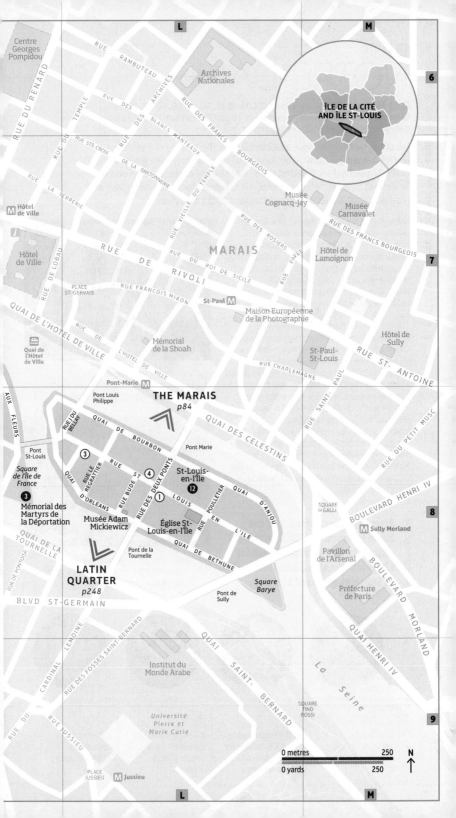

THE MARAIS
p84

LATIN
QUARTER
p248

Map Labels

Centre Georges Pompidou

RUE DU RENARD

RUE RAMBUTEAU

RUE DES ARCHIVES

Archives Nationales

RUE DU TEMPLE

RUE STE. CROIX

RUE DE LA BRETONNERIE

RUE VIEILLE DU TEMPLE

RUE DES FRANCS BOURGEOIS

Musée Cognacq-Jay

Musée Carnavalet

RUE DES FRANCS BOURGEOIS

Hôtel de Ville

Hôtel de Ville

RUE DE LA VERRERIE

RUE LA VERRERIE

MARAIS

RUE DE RIVOLI

RUE DU ROI DE SICILE

RUE DES ROSIERS

RUE PAVEE

Hôtel de Lamoignon

PLACE ST-GERVAIS

RUE FRANCOIS MIRON

St-Paul

Maison Européenne de la Photographie

Hôtel de Sully

RUE ST-ANTOINE

QUAI DE L'HOTEL DE VILLE

Quai de l'Hôtel de Ville

Mémorial de la Shoah

L'HOTEL DE VILLE

RUE CHARLEMAGNE

St-Paul-St-Louis

RUE SAINT PAUL

Pont-Marie

Pont Louis Philippe

RUE DU BELLAY

QUAI DE BOURBON

QUAI DES CELESTINS

RUE DU PETIT MUSC

AUX FLEURS

Pont St-Louis

Square de l'Île de France

Mémorial des Martyrs de la Déportation

QUAI D'ORLEANS

RUE LE REGRATTIER

RUE ST

RUE BUDE

RUE DES DEUX PONTS

Pont Marie

St-Louis-en-l'Île

LOUIS EN L'ILE

RUE POULLETIER

QUAI D'ANJOU

SQUARE H GALLI

BOULEVARD HENRI IV

Sully Morland

Musée Adam Mickiewicz

Église St-Louis-en-l'Île

QUAI DE BETHUNE

Pavillon de l'Arsenal

QUAI DE LA TOURNELLE

Pont de la Tournelle

Pont de Sully

Square Barye

Préfecture de Paris

RUE DE PONTOISE

BLVD ST-GERMAIN

BOULEVARD MORLAND

QUAI HENRI IV

RUE DU CARDINAL LEMOINE

RUE DES FOSSES SAINT BERNARD

Institut du Monde Arabe

QUAI SAINT-BERNARD

La Seine

SQUARE TINO ROSSI

RUE DE JUSSIEU

Université Pierre et Marie Curie

PLACE JUSSIEU

Jussieu

ÎLE DE LA CITÉ AND ÎLE ST-LOUIS

0 metres 250
0 yards 250

N

1 ⓐⓑ

NOTRE-DAME

📍 K8 🏛 Pl du Parvis Notre-Dame Ⓜ Cité 🚌 21, 38, 47, 58, 70, 72, 81, 82
🚇 Notre-Dame 🕐 8am–6:30pm Mon–Fri, 8am–7:15pm Sat & Sun 🚫 1 Jan,
1 May & 25 Dec 🌐 notredamedeparis.fr

No other building is more associated with the history of Paris than
Notre-Dame (Our Lady). The "heart" of the country, both geographically
and spiritually, the cathedral rises majestically at the eastern end of the
Île de la Cité. A Gothic masterpiece, it is famed for its stained glass and
rose windows, towers, flying buttresses and gargoyles.

Notre-Dame is built on the site of a Roman
temple. After Pope Alexander III laid the
first stone in 1163, an army of architects and
craftsmen toiled for 170 years to realize Bishop
Maurice de Sully's magnificent design. At
the time it was finished, in about 1334, it
was 130 m (430 ft) long and featured flying
buttresses, a large transept, a deep choir
and 69-m- (228-ft-) high towers.

Within the cathedral's hallowed walls,
kings and emperors were crowned and royal
Crusaders were blessed. But Notre-Dame was
also the scene of turmoil. Revolutionaries
ransacked it, banished religion, changed it into
a temple to the Cult of Reason, and then used
it as a wine store. Napoleon restored religion
in 1804 and architect Viollet-le-Duc later
restored the building, replacing missing
statues, as well as raising the spire and fixing
the gargoyles. Both the pointed arch and the
rose window were born elsewhere in Paris, but
Notre-Dame is the finest Gothic church in the
city, and the most impressive of the early
French cathedrals.

↑ Jean Ravy's spectacular flying
buttresses, with a span of 15 m (50 ft),
at the east end of the cathedral

↑ The cathedral's legendary gargoyles
(chimères), hiding behind a large upper
gallery between the towers

> **After Pope Alexander III laid the
> foundation stone in 1163, an army of
> architects and craftsmen toiled for
> 170 years to realize Bishop Maurice
> de Sully's magnificent design.**

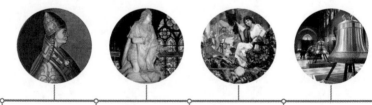

Timeline

1163
△ Foundation
stone laid by Pope
Alexander III

1708
△ Choir remodelled by
Louis XIV, fulfilling his
father's promise to
honour the Virgin

1793
△ Revolutionaries loot
the cathedral and
rename it Temple
of Reason

2013
△ The cathedral
celebrates its
850th anniversary

INSIDER TIP
Organ Recital

There are free organ recitals every Saturday at 8pm. The organ is one of the largest in France, with five keyboards and nearly 8,000 pipes.

↑ The West Front, featuring superb statuary, a central rose window and an openwork gallery

Inside Notre-Dame

Notre-Dame's interior grandeur is instantly apparent on seeing the high-vaulted central nave. This is bisected by a huge transept, at either end of which are medieval rose windows, 13 m (43 ft) in diameter. Works by major sculptors adorn the cathedral. Among them are Jean Ravy's old choir screen carvings, Nicolas Coustou's *Pietà* and Antoine Coysevox's Louis XIV statue.

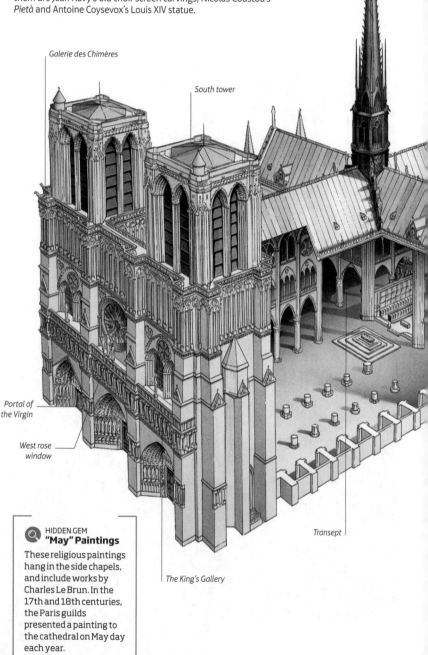

Spire

Galerie des Chimères

South tower

Portal of the Virgin

West rose window

Transept

The King's Gallery

387

steps up the north
tower lead to the
famous gargoyles.

Flying buttresses

South rose window

Treasury

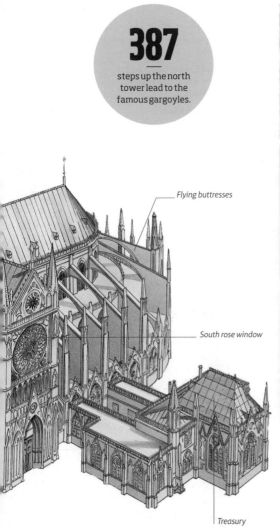

1. A 14th-century screen
enclosed the chancel, offering
canons at prayer peace from
noisy congregations.

2. Behind the high altar is
Nicolas Coustou's *Pietà*,
standing on a gilded base.

3. Only the north
window retains its 13th-
century stained glass.

A MEDIEVAL ROMANCE

The 12th-century romance
between the monk Pierre Abélard
and the young Héloïse began in the
cloisters of Notre-Dame. Abélard
was hired as a tutor to the 17-year-
old niece of a canon, and a love
affair soon developed between the
teacher and his pupil. In his wrath,
Héloïse's uncle had the scholar
castrated and Héloïse took refuge
in a convent.

2 ⊘ ⓜ 🛍

SAINTE-CHAPELLE

📍J7 ⌂ Blvd du Palais 75001 🚇 Cité 🚌 21, 27, 38, 85, 96 to Île de la Cité 🚆 St-Michel ◎ Notre-Dame ⏱ Apr-Sep: 9am-7pm daily; Oct-Mar: 9am-5pm daily 🚫 1 Jan, 1 May, 25 Dec 🌐 sainte-chapelle.fr

Ethereal and magical, Sainte-Chapelle has been hailed as one of the greatest architectural masterpieces of the Western world. In the Middle Ages, the devout likened this church to "a gateway to heaven". Today, no visitor can fail to be transported by the blaze of light created by the 15 magnificent stained-glass windows.

A Gothic Masterpiece

The chapel was built in 1248 by Louis IX to house Christ's purported Crown of Thorns (now housed in the Notre-Dame treasury). A Gothic masterpiece, its stunning stained-glass windows – the oldest extant in Paris – are separated by narrow columns that soar 15 m (50 ft) to the star-studded, vaulted roof. The windows portray over 1,000 biblical scenes, from Genesis right through to the Crucifixion, in a kaleidoscope of red, gold, green, blue and mauve. Servants and commoners worshipped in the Lower Chapel, while the Upper Chapel was reserved for the use of the king and the royal family.

Spire

Crown of Thorns decoration

Rose window

↑ The rose window, telling the story of the Apocalypse

Main portal

Lower Chapel

Did You Know?

The spire is 75m (245 ft) high. It was erected in 1853 after four previous spires burned down.

Angel

Upper Chapel

① The Lower Chapel is not as light and lofty as the Upper Chapel, but is still magnificent.

② The windows of the Upper Chapel contain 600 sq m (6,458 sq ft) of stained glass.

③ Carved stone statues of the Apostles adorn the 12 pillars of the Upper Chapel.

ST LOUIS' RELICS

Louis IX was extremely devout, and was canonized in 1297, not long after his death. In 1239, he acquired the Crown of Thorns from the Emperor of Constantinople and, in 1241, a fragment of Christ's Cross. He built this chapel as a shrine to house them. Louis paid nearly three times more for the relics than for the construction of Sainte-Chapelle. The Crown of Thorns is now kept at Notre-Dame.

EXPERIENCE MORE

3

Mémorial des Martyrs de la Déportation

◉ K8 ⌂ Sq de l'Île de France 75004 ☎ 01 46 33 87 56 Ⓜ St-Paul, Maubert Mutualité, Pont Marie ⓇⒺⓇ St-Michel ◷ 10am-5pm Tue-Sun (to 7pm Apr-Sep) ◷ 1 Jan, 1 May, 14 Jul, 15 Aug, 1 Nov & 25 Dec

The memorial to the 200,000 French men, women and children deported to Nazi concentration camps in World War II is covered with the names of the camps to which they were deported. Earth from these camps has been used to form tombs and the interior walls are decorated with poetry and thousands of glass crystals. At the far end is the tomb dedicated to the Unknown Deportee.

4

Conciergerie

◉ J7 ⌂ 2 Blvd du Palais 75001 Ⓜ Cité ◷ 9:30am-6pm daily ◷ 1 Jan, 1 May, 25 Dec Ⓦ paris-conciergerie.fr

The Conciergerie, part of the larger Palais de Justice (p78), was under the administration of the palace "concierge", the keeper of the king's mansion. When the monarch moved to the Marais (in 1417), the palace remained the seat of royal administration and law; the Conciergerie became a prison, with the "concierge" as its chief gaoler. Henry IV's assassin, Ravaillac, was imprisoned and tortured here.

During the French Revolution, the Conciergerie housed more than 4,000 prisoners, including Marie-Antoinette, who was held in a tiny cell,

and Charlotte Corday, who stabbed Revolutionary leader Marat as he lay in his bath. Ironically, the Revolutionary judges Robespierre and Danton also became "tenants" before being sent in turn to the guillotine.

The Conciergerie has a superb, four-aisled Gothic Salle des Gens d'Armes (Hall of the Men-at-Arms), the dining hall for the castle's 2,000 members of staff. The building, renovated in the

---

💬 INSIDER TIP
Ticket Savings

If you plan on visiting both the Conciergerie and Sainte-Chapelle on the same day, you can save money by buying a combined ticket.

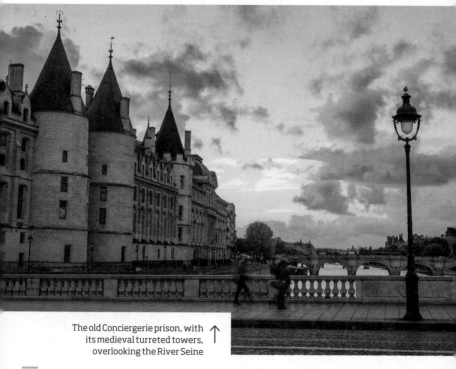

↑ The old Conciergerie prison, with its medieval turreted towers, overlooking the River Seine

↑ The Marché aux Fleurs, with its wonderful variety of seasonal and exotic flowers and plants

> **During the French Revolution, the Conciergerie housed more than 4,000 prisoners, including Marie-Antoinette, who was held in a tiny cell.**

19th century, retains the 14th-century clock on the Tour de l'Horloge (Clock Tower). It is the city's oldest public clock and is still operating.

Crypte Archéologique

📍 K8 📌 7 Pl du Parvis Notre-Dame 75004 Ⓜ Cité, St-Michel 🕐 10am–6pm Tue–Sun 🚫 1 Jan, 1 May, 8 May, 14 Jul, 15 Aug, 1 & 11 Nov, 25 Dec & religious hols 🌐 crypte.paris.fr

Situated on the main square (the *parvis*) in front of Notre-Dame and stretching 120 m (393 ft) underground, the Crypte Archéologique exhibits the remains of foundations and walls that predate the cathedral by several hundred years. The foundations of Paris's oldest rampart, dating from the 3rd century BC, are displayed, as are the medieval foundations of the Hôtel Dieu. Interactive touchscreens help to bring the exhibits to life. Within the crypt are also traces of a hypocaust, a sophisticated underground heating system used for heating ancient Roman thermal baths.

---

⑥ Hôtel Dieu

📍 K7 📌 1 Pl du Parvis Notre-Dame 75004 📞 01 42 34 82 34 Ⓜ Cité

On the north side of the Place du Parvis Notre-Dame is the Hôtel Dieu, the city's oldest hospital, dating back to the 12th century. The original building stretched across the island to both banks of the river, but was demolished to make way for one of Baron Haussmann's urban-planning schemes. It was rehoused on the site of an old orphanage in 1878. The building now faces an uncertain future, as its services are being wound down and transferred elsewhere. It was nearby, at the Préfecture de la Police, in 1944, that the Paris police courageously resisted the German army; the battle is commemorated by a monument on Cour du 19-Août, within the Préfecture.

EAT

Berthillon
Parisians flock to this ice-cream parlour for its unusual flavours.

📍 L8 📌 29–31 Rue St-Louis en l'Île 75004 🚫 Mon, Tue 🌐 berthillon.fr.

€ € €

⑦ Marché aux Fleurs Reine Elizabeth II

📍 K7 📌 Pl Louis-Lépine 75004 Ⓜ Cité 🕐 8am–7pm Mon–Sat

The year-round flower market adds colour and scent to an area otherwise dominated by administrative buildings. It is the most famous and, unfortunately, one of the last remaining flower markets in the city of Paris, its attractive iron pavilions harbouring both seasonal flowers and a wide range of specialist varieties such as orchids. Each Sunday, it makes way for the Marché aux Oiseaux, an animal and bird market, which is probably best avoided by sensitive animal-lovers.

8
Palais de Justice

J7 ⌂ 4-10 Blvd du Palais 75001 (main entrance by the Cour de Mai, 10 Blvd du Palais) Ⓜ Cité ⏱ 9am-6pm Mon-Fri 🖥 ca-paris.justice.fr

The monumental block of buildings stretching the entire width of the Île de la Cité was formerly the home of the central law courts, most of which have now moved into brand-new premises in the Clichy-Batignolles quarter in the 17th arrondissement. The site, occupied since Roman times, was the seat of royal power until Charles V moved the court to the Hôtel St-Paul in the Marais during the 14th century. In April 1793, the Revolutionary Tribunal began dispensing justice from the Première Chambre, but this court eventually degenerated during Robespierre's Reign of Terror. Plans are afoot to open up more of the site to the public.

9
Place Dauphine

J7 ⌂ 75001 (enter by Rue Henri-Robert) Ⓜ Pont Neuf, Cité

Southeast of Pont Neuf is this ancient square, laid out in 1607 by Henri IV and named after the Dauphin, the future Louis XIII. It is actually triangular in shape and lined with cafés, wine bars and restaurants. In the middle is a park with trees and benches. No. 14 is one of the few buildings to have avoided any subsequent restoration. This haven of 17th-century charm is popular with *pétanque* (boules) players.

→

The tranquil Square du Vert-Galant, at the extreme point of the Île de la Cité

10
Pont Neuf

J7 ⌂ Quai de la Mégisserie and Quai des Grands Augustins 75001 Ⓜ Pont Neuf, Cité

Despite its name (New Bridge), this is the oldest of the existing bridges in Paris and has been immortalized by major literary and artistic figures since it was built. The first stone was laid by Henri III in 1578, but it was Henri IV who inaugurated it and gave it its name in 1607. His statue stands in the central section.

The bridge, which was the widest of its kind in Paris, has 12 arches and spans 275 m (912 ft). The first stone bridge in the city to be built without houses and with pavements for pedestrians, it heralded a new era in the relationship between the Île de la Cité and the river.

From its very beginning, the Pont Neuf has had heavy traffic, and it has undergone many renovations and repairs over the centuries.

11
Square du Vert-Galant

J7 ⌂ Île de la Cité 75001 Ⓜ Pont Neuf, Cité

One of the most magical spots in Paris, this peaceful, tree-lined garden bears the nickname of Henri IV "*vert-galant*". This colourful monarch did much to beautify Paris in the early 17th century, and his popularity has lasted right up to this day. From here, there are splendid views of the Louvre and the Right Bank of the river, where Henri was assassinated in 1610. This is also the point from which the Vedettes du Pont Neuf pleasure boats depart.

Did You Know?

Henri IV's nickname, *vert-galant*, means "old flirt". The king was infamous for his womanizing.

→ The ornate interior of the Baroque church of St-Louis-en-l'Île

⑫

St-Louis-en-l'Île

📍L8 🏠19 Rue St-Louis-en-l'Île 75004 📞01 46 34 11 60 Ⓜ Pont Marie 🕐9:30am–1pm & 2–7:30pm daily (to 7pm Sun & public hols). Mass: 6:45pm Mon–Fri, 6:30pm Sat, 11am Sun

The construction of this church began in 1664 from plans by the royal architect Louis Le Vau, who lived on the island. It was completed and consecrated in 1726. Among its outstanding exterior features are the 1741 iron clock at the entrance and the pierced iron spire.

The interior, in the Baroque style, is richly decorated with gilding and marble. There is a statue of St Louis holding a Crusader's sword. A plaque in the north aisle bears the inscription "in grateful memory of St Louis in whose honour the City of St Louis, Missouri, USA is named". The church is also twinned with Carthage cathedral in Tunisia, where St Louis is buried.

Pont Neuf, straddling the Seine and the tip of the Île de la Cité

A SHORT WALK
ÎLE DE LA CITÉ

Distance 1.5 km (1 mile) **Nearest metro** Cité
Time 15 minutes

The origins of Paris are here on the Île de la Cité, the boat-shaped island on the Seine first inhabited over 2,000 years ago by Celtic tribes. There is no older place in Paris, and remains of the first buildings can still be seen today in the archaeological crypt under the square in front of Notre-Dame. A stroll of this part of the city takes you from one Parisian icon – the great medieval cathedral – to another: the Gothic masterpiece that is Sainte-Chapelle.

A grisly antechamber to the guillotine, the Conciergerie prison was much used in the Revolution (p76).

The colourful, lively Marché aux Fleurs Reine Elizabeth II is one of Paris's few remaining flower markets. Birds are sold at the Sunday market (p77).

The Cour du Mai is the impressive main courtyard of the Palais de Justice.

PONT AU CHANGE

QUAI D CORS

RUE DE LUTECE

BLVD DU PALAIS

START

QUAI DES ORFÈVRES

A jewel of Gothic architecture, Sainte-Chapelle is one of the most magical sights in Paris, noted for the magnificence of its stained glass (p74).

The Quai des Orfèvres owes its name to the goldsmiths (orfèvres) who frequented the area from medieval times onwards.

PONT ST-MICHEL

RUE DE LA CITÉ

QUAI DU MARCHE NEUF

PETIT PONT

With its ancient towers lining the quays, the Palais de Justice has a history that extends back over 16 centuries (p78).

The Préfecture de Police was the scene of intense battles during World War II.

Deep under the square, in the Crypte Archéologique, lie the remains of houses from 2,000 years ago (p77).

← A riverside view of the Conciergerie, a former prison

↑ Patrons sitting outside one of the delightful cafés on the quaint Rue Chanoinesse

Locator Map
For more detail see p68

Once an orphanage, the Hôtel Dieu is now a city hospital (p77).

Point Zéro is the point from which all distances are measured in France.

Notre-Dame cathedral is a superb example of French medieval architecture (p70).

Did You Know?

In ancient times the island was used as a river crossing between northern and southern Gaul.

The Rue Chanoinesse has many charming old restaurants, cafés and shops.

The quaint streets of the Ancien Cloître Quartier were once home to medieval clergymen and students.

The Square Jean XXIII is a peaceful square close to the river.

NOTRE-DAME

PONT D'ARCOLE

RUE D'ARCOLE

PLACE DU PARVIS NOTRE-DAME

RUE CHANOINESSE

RUE DU CLOÎTRE NOTRE-DAME

| 0 metres | 100 |
| 0 yards | 100 |

N ↑

PONT AU DOUBLE

FINISH

SQ. DU JEAN XXIII

The Statue of Charlemagne commemorates the King of the Franks, who was crowned emperor in 800. He united all the Christian peoples of the West. medieval architecture.

THE MARAIS

This district was little more than a muddy swamp until Henri IV built the Place Royale (now Place des Vosges) in 1605. But its position of prestige as a royal residence was soon swept away by the Revolution, which saw the Marais all but abandoned, before later descending into an architectural wasteland. Towards the end of the 19th century, a large number of Jewish settlers from Eastern Europe moved to the neighbourhood, establishing the Jewish Quarter around Rue des Rosiers. Beginning in the 1960s, sensitive restoration brought the Marais' historic buildings to life again; some of Paris's most popular museums are now housed in its elegant mansions, while the main streets and narrow passageways bustle with trendy restaurants, bars and chic boutiques. A hot spot for eclectic art galleries, the Marais is also the heart of the Parisian LGBT+ community.

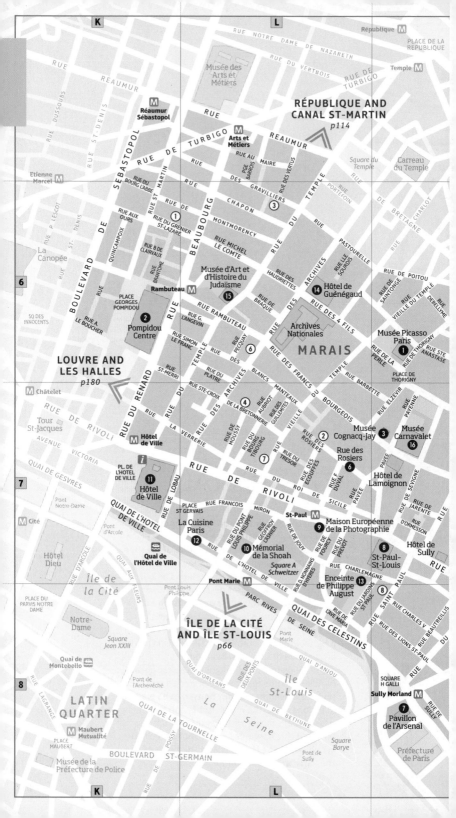

RÉPUBLIQUE AND CANAL ST-MARTIN
p114

LOUVRE AND LES HALLES
p180

MARAIS

ÎLE DE LA CITÉ AND ÎLE ST-LOUIS
p66

LATIN QUARTER

Métro stations: République, Temple, Réaumur Sébastopol, Arts et Métiers, Etienne Marcel, Rambuteau, Châtelet, Hôtel de Ville, Cité, St-Paul, Pont Marie, Sully Morland, Maubert Mutualité

Key locations: Musée des Arts et Métiers, Musée d'Art et d'Histoire du Judaïsme, Pompidou Centre, Rambuteau, Archives Nationales, Musée Picasso Paris, Musée Cognacq-Jay, Musée Carnavalet, Rue des Rosiers, Hôtel de Lamoignon, Hôtel de Sully, Hôtel de Ville, La Cuisine Paris, Maison Européenne de la Photographie, Mémorial de la Shoah, St-Paul-St-Louis, Enceinte de Philippe August, Pavillon de l'Arsenal, Hôtel de Guénégaud, Notre-Dame, Hôtel Dieu, Tour St-Jacques, La Canopée, Place Georges Pompidou

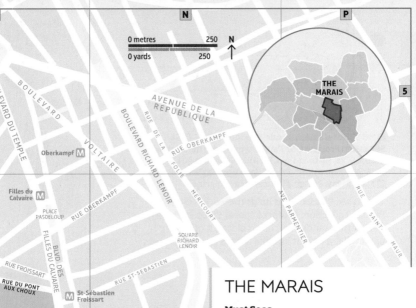

THE MARAIS

Must Sees
1 Musée Picasso Paris
2 Pompidou Centre

Experience More
3 Musée Cognacq-Jay
4 Place des Vosges
5 Maison de Victor Hugo
6 Rue des Rosiers
7 Pavillon de l'Arsenal
8 St-Paul-St-Louis
9 Maison Européenne
de la Photographie
10 Mémorial de la Shoah
11 Hôtel de Ville
12 La Cuisine Paris
13 Enceinte de Philippe August
14 Hôtel de Guénégaud
(Musée de la Chasse et de la Nature)
15 Musée d'Art et d'Histoire
du Judaïsme
16 Musée Carnavalet

Eat
1 L'Ambassade d'Auvergne
2 L'As du Fallafel

Stay
3 Hôtel Jules et Jim
4 Hôtel de la Bretonnerie
5 Le Pavillon de la Reine

Shop
6 Mazet de Montargis
7 Edwart Chocolatier
8 Village Saint-Paul

① 🖊️ 🎨 🖥️ 📷 🛍️

MUSÉE
PICASSO PARIS

📍 M6 🏠 Hôtel Salé, 5 Rue de Thorigny 75003 Ⓜ St-
Sébastien Froissart, St-Paul, Chemin Vert, Rambuteau
🚌 29, 69, 75, 96 to St-Paul, Bastille, Pl des Vosges
🕐 10:30am–6pm Tue–Fri; 9:30am–6pm Sat & Sun
🚫 1 Jan, 1 May, 25 Dec 🌐 museepicassoparis.fr

The Musée Picasso Paris holds the world's largest
Picasso collection. Comprising over 5,000 works and
tens of thousands of archived pieces, it offers an
unparalleled insight into the artist's creative process.

↑ *Head of a
Woman* (1931)

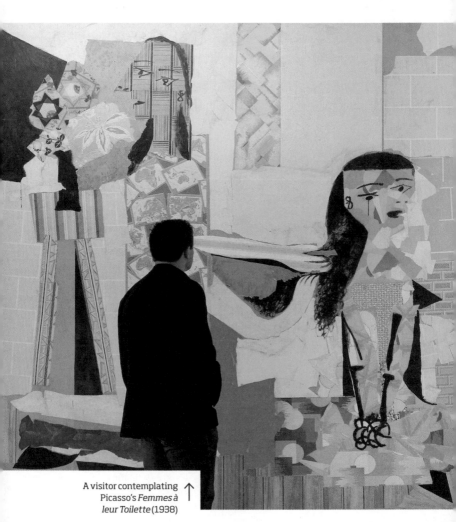

A visitor contemplating ↑
Picasso's *Femmes à
leur Toilette* (1938)

Spanish-born Pablo Picasso lived most of his life in France. Upon his death in 1973, the French state inherited many of his works in lieu of death duties. It used them to establish the Musée Picasso Paris, which opened in 1985. The museum is housed in a large 17th-century mansion, the Hôtel Salé, which was built in 1656 for Aubert de Fontenay, a salt-tax collector (*salé* means "salty"). The original character of the mansion has been preserved, and large sculptures adorn the garden and courtyard. Reopened in 2014 following a five-year renovation, the museum holds works spanning a full range of media – paintings, sculptures, ceramics, drawings and etchings – covering all of Picasso's creative periods. Be sure not to miss Picasso's own collection of paintings on the third floor.

↑ The Hôtel Salé, considered to be one of the most exquisite historic houses in the Marais

PICASSO IN FRANCE

Born in Malaga, Spain, Picasso first visited Paris in 1900. He moved to the city in 1904, before later settling in the south of France. After 1934, Picasso never returned to his homeland due to his rejection of Franco's regime. However, throughout his life in France he used Spanish themes in his art, such as the bull (often in the form of a minotaur) and the guitar, which he associated with his Andalusian childhood.

↑ *The Kiss* (1969), one of many works concerned with the theme of the couple painted by Picasso during his later years

2 🛹 🚲 🖥 👜 🍴

POMPIDOU CENTRE

📍 K6 🏠 Pl Georges Pompidou Ⓜ Rambuteau, Châtelet, Hôtel de Ville
🚌 21, 29, 38, 47, 58, 69, 70, 72, 74, 75, 76, 81, 85, 96 🕐 MNAM & temp
exhibitions: 11am–10pm Wed–Mon (to 11pm Thu); library: noon–10pm
Wed–Mon (from 11am Sat, Sun & pub hols); Atelier Brancusi:
2–6pm Wed–Mon 🌐 centrepompidou.fr

Home to the Musée National d'Art Moderne, with over 60,000 works of art
from over 5,000 artists, the Pompidou holds Europe's largest collection of
modern and contemporary art. Looking like a building turned inside out,
its exterior is as eye-catching as the works on display within.

Blue: air
conditioning

Did You Know?

The Pompidou Centre's
collection was originally
housed in the Palais
de Tokyo (p231).

← *With the Black Arc*
(1912) by Vassily
Kandinsky

← *Le Rhinocéros* (1999)
by Xavier Veilhan

Museum Guide

The "historical" collections bring together the great artistic movements of the first half of the 20th century, from Fauvism to Abstract Expressionism. The rich collection of Cubist sculptures is displayed, as well as examples of the great masters of the 20th century. Matisse, Picasso, Braque, Duchamp, Kandinsky, Léger, Miró, Giacometti and Dubuffet command large areas at the heart of the collection, which also shows the groups and the movements on which the history of modern art is based, or by which it has been affected, including Dada, Abstract Art and Informal.

The contemporary art section occupies the fourth floor. The collection starts with works by leading French artists of the second half of the 20th century: Louise Bourgeois, Pierre Soulages, Jean-Pierre Raynaud, François

↑ The escalator
overlooking the piazza

Morellet and Bertrand Lavier. The display is organized around a central aisle from which the rooms lead off. Certain areas have been designated to bring together different disciplines around a theme such as minimalist painting or conceptual art rather than a school or movement, while other rooms are artist-specific. Design and architecture are also covered, and there is a "global" room bringing together major pieces by African, Chinese, Japanese and American artists. A graphic arts exhibition room and a video area complete the collection.

———— Red: elevators
and escalators

———— Green: water

Yellow:
electricity

← The distinctive
exterior of the
Pompidou, with
service pipes that
are colour-coded
according to
their various
functions

BRANCUSI'S STUDIO

The Atelier Brancusi, on the piazza, is a reconstruction of the workshop of the Romanian-born artist Constantin Brancusi (1876–1957), who lived and worked in Paris from 1904. He bequeathed his entire collection of works to the French state on condition that his workshop be rebuilt as it was on the day he died.

EXPERIENCE MORE

③ Musée Cognacq-Jay

M7 **Hôtel Donon, 8 Rue Elzévir 75003**
St-Paul, Chemin Vert
10am–6pm Tue–Sun
Public hols **musee cognacqjay.paris.fr**

This small, fine collection of French 18th-century works of art and furniture was formed by Ernest Cognacq and his wife, Louise Jay, founder of the Art Deco La Samaritaine, on the Quai du Louvre, which was once Paris's largest department store. The collection was bequeathed to the city and is now housed here in the Hôtel Donon – an elegant building dating from 1575 with an 18th-century façade and wood-panelled rooms.

④ Place des Vosges

M7 **75003, 75004**
Bastille, St-Paul

This square is considered among the most beautiful in the world by Parisians and visitors alike. Its impressive symmetry – 36 houses, nine on each side, of brick and stone, with deep slate roofs and dormer windows over arcades – is still intact after 400 years. It has been the scene of many historic events over the centuries. A three-day tournament was held here to celebrate the marriage of Louis XIII to Anne of Austria in 1615. Cardinal Richelieu, pillar of the monarchy, stayed here in 1615; the famous literary hostess Madame de

Sévigné was born here in 1626; and the writer Victor Hugo lived here for 16 years. The arcades surrounding the square are full of art galleries and upmarket fashion boutiques and often ring out with the sound of buskers playing classical music or jazz, while at the centre of the *place* is a lovely formal garden with fountains and sandpits, popular with young families.

EAT

L'Ambassade d'Auvergne
Regional cooking with lots of cabbage and pork dishes. Shared tables are good for solo diners.

K6 **2 Rue du Grenier-Saint-Lazare 75003** **ambassade-auvergne.fr**

€€€

L'As du Fallafel
The best Middle Eastern food in Paris, if the queues at this bustling local favourite are any indication.

L7 **32 Rue des Rosiers 75004**
01 48 87 63 60

€€€

↑ A room decorated in Chinese style, in the Maison de Victor Hugo

⑤ Maison de Victor Hugo

📍 M7 🏠 6 Pl des Vosges 75004 Ⓜ Bastille, Chemin Vert, St-Paul ⏰ 10am-6pm Tue-Sun ⛔ Public hols 🌐 maisonvictorhugo. paris.fr

The French poet, dramatist and novelist lived on the second floor of the former Hôtel Rohan-Guéménée from 1832 to 1848. It was here that Victor Hugo wrote most of *Les Misérables* and completed many other famous works. On display are some reconstructions of the rooms in which he lived, his vivid pen-and-ink drawings and caricatures, and books and mementos from the crucially important periods in his life, from his childhood to his exile between 1852 and 1870. Temporary ticketed exhibitions on Hugo take place regularly.

⑥ 🍴 🖥 🏛 Rue des Rosiers

📍 L7 🏠 75004 Ⓜ St-Paul, Chemin Vert

The Jewish quarter in and around this street is one of the most colourful areas of Paris. The street's name refers to the rose bushes within the old city wall. A Jewish community first settled here in the 13th century, with a second wave of immigration occurring in the 19th century from Russia, Poland and Central Europe. Sephardic Jews arrived from North Africa in the 1950s and 1960s. Some 165 students were deported from the Jewish boys' school nearby at 10 Rue des Hospitalières-St-Gervais in World War II. *N'Oubliez pas* (Lest we forget) is engraved on the wall. Today, this area contains synagogues, bakeries and kosher restaurants.

⑦ 🏛 Pavillon de l'Arsenal

📍 M8 🏠 21 Blvd Morland 75004 Ⓜ Sully Morland, Bastille ⏰ 11am-7pm Tue-Sun ⛔ 1 Jan 🌐 pavillon-arsenal.com

The Pavillon de l'Arsenal houses a small but fascinating exhibition illustrating the architectural evolution of Paris. Using films, models and panoramic images, this permanent exhibition explores how Paris was built over the centuries, as well as looking at future plans for the city. The centrepiece of the exhibition is a large ground-level interactive screen showing Google Earth images of Paris and onto which are superimposed all the city's building projects planned for the next few years. Up to three temporary exhibitions are also programmed each year.

Paris's imposing town hall (Hôtel de Ville), with its elaborate façade ↑

8

St-Paul-St-Louis

📍M7 🏠99 Rue St-Antoine 75004 📞01 42 72 30 32 Ⓜ️St-Paul 🕐8am-8pm daily

A Jesuit church, St-Paul–St-Louis was an important symbol of the influence that the Jesuits held from 1627, when Louis XIII laid the first stone, to 1762, when they were expelled from France. The Gesù church in Rome served as the model for the nave, while the 60-m-(180-ft-) high dome was the forerunner of those of the Invalides (p204) and the Sorbonne (p255). Most of the church's treasures were removed during periods of turmoil, but Delacroix's masterpiece *Christ in the Garden of Olives* can still be seen. The church sometimes hosts concerts. It is on one of the main streets of the Marais, but can also be approached by the ancient Passage St-Paul.

9

Maison Européenne de la Photographie

📍L7 🏠5-7 Rue de Fourcy 75004 Ⓜ️St-Paul, Pont Marie 🕐11am-7:45pm Wed-Sun 🚫Public hols 🌐mep-fr.org

Located in the heart of the Marais, in the elegant 18th-century Hôtel Hénault de Cantobre, the Maison Européenne de la Photographie (MEP) hosts some of the best exhibitions of contemporary photography in Europe. It organizes cutting-edge shows alongside retrospectives on major photographers, and since opening its doors in 1996, it has hosted displays by such celebrated photographers as Elliott Erwitt, Don McCullin, Annie Leibovitz, Robert Doisneau and Henri Cartier-Bresson. The MEP's huge permanent collection on the history of photography is a must-see for anyone interested in exploring this medium.

THE MANSIONS OF THE MARAIS

In the 1500s, noble men and women began building sumptuous residences in the newly drained marshlands called the Marais. Many of these mansions, such as the Musée Carnavalet (p97) and Musée Cognacq-Jay (p92), have now been restored as museums.

DOOR DETAIL

Mazet de Montargis

This historical confectionery, dating back to 1903, makes nutty pralines and candies packaged in colourful containers.

📍L6 🏠37 Rue des Archives 75004 ⓦmazetconfiseur.com

Edwart Chocolatier

Gourmet chocolates with unusual flavours such as curry praline and Japanese whiskey are the star products at this sleek boutique.

📍L7 🏠17 Rue Vieille du Temple 75004 ⓦedwart.fr

Village Saint-Paul

These interlocking courtyards house all sorts of antique, interior-design, art and curiosity shops, as well as occasional flea markets.

📍M8 🏠Off Rue St-Paul 75004 ⓦlevillagesaintpaul.com

10

Mémorial de la Shoah

📍L7 🏠17 Rue Geoffroy-l'Asnier 75004 Ⓜ Pont Marie, St-Paul ⏰10am-6pm Sun-Fri (10am-10pm Thu); multimedia & reading rooms: 10am-5:30pm Sun-Fri (to 7:30pm Thu) 🔒Public & Jewish hols ⓦmemorialdelashoah.org

The eternal flame burning in the crypt here is the memorial to the unknown Jewish martyr of the Holocaust. Its striking feature is a large cylinder that bears the names of the concentration camps where Jewish victims of the Holocaust died. In 2005, a stone wall, engraved with the names of 76,000 Jews – 11,000 of them children – who were deported from France to the Nazi death camps, was put up here. Various drawings, letters and artifacts from the camps are also on display, as well as photos of deportees. Every other Sunday at 3pm guided tours take place in English.

11

Hôtel de Ville

📍K7 🏠Pl de l'Hôtel de Ville 75004 (visitor entrance 29 Rue de Rivoli, exhibitions entrance 5 Rue de Lobau) Ⓜ Hôtel de Ville ⏰Hours vary for temporary exhibitions 🔒Public hols, official functions ⓦparis.fr

Home of the city council, the town hall is a 19th-century reconstruction of the original building erected between 1533 and 1628, which was burned down in 1871. It is highly ornate, with elaborate stonework, turrets and statues overlooking a pedestrianized square whose fountains are lit up at night.

The square was once the main site for hangings, burnings and other executions. It was here that Ravaillac, Henri IV's assassin, was quartered alive, his body ripped to pieces by four strong horses.

Inside, a notable feature is the long Salle des Fêtes (ballroom), with adjoining salons devoted to science, literature and the arts. The impressive staircase, the decorated ceilings with their chandeliers, and the statues and caryatids all add to the air of ceremony and pomp. While these parts are mostly closed to the public (except during some of the Journées du Patrimoine and guided visits; email visites.hdv@paris.fr two months in advance), certain annexes are used for free, highly acclaimed temporary exhibitions on themes related to Paris.

Artworks on display in the Musée d'Art et d'Histoire du Judaïsme ↑

12 ⊘ ⓜ 🍴 ☕

La Cuisine Paris

📍L7 🏠80 Quai de l'Hôtel de Ville 75004 Ⓜ St-Paul
🌐lacuisineparis.com

With Paris having so many restaurants and bakeries, few visitors stop to think about learning to make their own French-inspired dishes. La Cuisine offers a variety of cooking classes run by real French cooks, who teach you how to make classic savoury dishes as well as sweet pastries in the slick kitchen boasting views over the Seine. English-speaking instructors demonstrate the techniques behind buttery croissants and crusty baguettes, and demystify many of France's most iconic dishes, such as fluffy soufflés and perfectly prepared crêpes. Some of the classes offered even combine a market visit with a cooking

class where you prepare a whole lunch. After rolling up their sleeves for a few hours, La Cuisine students walk away with either a full belly or a package of flaky, buttery, or otherwise decadent pastries. The school also offers culinary walking tours of the Marais and nearby neighbourhoods for visitors wanting to discover local shops and flavours. Classes and tours are open to all ages and levels of experience.

13

Enceinte de Philippe Auguste

📍L7 🏠13 Rue Charlemagne 75004 Ⓜ St-Paul, Sully Morland

Dating back to 1190, these fortifications are the remains of Paris's oldest wall. King Philippe Auguste built the wall around Paris to protect the

city from attacks while he was away fighting in the Crusades. A hallmark of the wall was a fortress where the Louvre now stands; its remnants are visible today in the museum's lower levels. The section here in the Marais, however, hides in plain sight. It is still possible to see the large tower, the Tour Montgomery, that formed part of the gates through which everyone had to pass in order to enter the city. The wall was an effective means of regulating trade, allowing the king to levy taxes on imports such as wine and furs, as well as many other goods.

---

14 ⊘ 🏛

Hôtel de Guénégaud (Musée de la Chasse et de la Nature)

📍L6 🏠62 Rue des Archives 75003 Ⓜ Hôtel de Ville
🕐11am-6pm Tue-Sun (to 10pm Wed) 🚫Public hols
🌐chassenature.org

The celebrated architect François Mansart built this superb mansion in the mid-17th century for Henri de Guénégaud des Brosses, who was Secretary of State and Keeper of the Seals. One wing

RIVERBANK WALK

After the success of the Left Bank renovation, Berges de Seine, Paris City Hall decided to tackle the Right Bank. In 2017, the Parc Rives de Seine opened, offering Parisians a place to stroll and jog along the waterfront. Citizens embraced the change, already acquainted with the car-free zone during the annual Paris Plages beach festival. Now, the festive atmosphere lasts all year long, with bars and cafés dotting the length of the promenade.

now contains the Musée de la Chasse et de la Nature (Hunting Museum), inaugurated by André Malraux in 1967. It holds the collections of industrialist François Sommer and his wife Jacqueline; exhibits include a fine collection of hunting weapons and stuffed animals. There are also drawings and paintings by Jean-Baptiste Oudry, Peter Paul Rubens (including *Diane and her Nymphs Preparing to Hunt*) and Rembrandt.

Musée d'Art et d'Histoire du Judaïsme

⑮ **📍L6** **🏛Hôtel de St-Aignan, 71 Rue du Temple 75003** **Ⓜ Rambuteau** **🕐11am–6pm Tue-Fri, 10am-6pm Sat & Sun** **🚫1 Jan, 1 May, Rosh Hashanah & Yom Kippur** **🌐mahj.org**

Housed in an elegant Marais mansion, the museum unites collections formerly scattered around the city, and commemorates the culture of French Jewry from medieval times to the present. There has been a sizeable Jewish community in France since Roman times, and some of the world's greatest Jewish scholars were French. Much exquisite craftsmanship is displayed, with elaborate silverware and Torah covers. There are also historical documents, photographs, paintings and cartoons.

---

⑯

Musée Carnavalet

📍M7 **🏛16 Rue des Francs-Bourgeois 75003** **Ⓜ St-Paul, Chemin Vert** **🌐carnavalet.paris.fr**

Currently closed for major building work, this fascinating museum, which charts the history of Paris, is scheduled to reopen in 2020 with completely refurbished displays of its vast collection. It occupies two adjoining mansions. The Hôtel Carnavalet, which was built as a town house in 1548, was transformed in the mid-17th century by architect François Mansart, while the neighbouring 17th-century Hôtel Le Peletier de St-Fargeau features superb early-20th-century interiors. In both, entire rooms are lavishly decorated with gilded wood panelling, furniture and objets d'art, including paintings and sculptures of prominent personalities, and engravings showing Paris being built. One of the most engaging parts of the museum is a section covering the French Revolution.

> After rolling up their sleeves for a few hours, La Cuisine students walk away with either a full belly or a package of flaky, buttery, or otherwise decadent pastries.

↑ The handsome Renaissance Musée Carnavalet

A SHORT WALK
THE MARAIS

Distance 1.5 km (1 mile) **Nearest metro**
Saint-Paul **Time** 20 minutes

Once an area of marshland as its name suggests (*marais* means swamp), the Marais grew steadily in importance from the 14th century, by virtue of its proximity to the Louvre, the preferred residence of Charles V. Its heyday was in the 17th century, when it became the fashionable area for the monied classes. They built many grand and sumptuous mansions (hôtels) that still dot the Marais today – some of these hôtels have been restored and turned into museums. Once again fashionable with the monied classes, designer boutiques, trendy restaurants, art galleries and cafés now line the streets.

START

The renovated Hôtel Salé is the setting for the Musée Picasso Paris. It boasts the largest collection of Picassos in the world, many of which came from Picasso's own collection after his death (p88).

RUE BARBETTE

RUE ELZEVIR

RUE PAYEN

RUE DES FRANCS

RUE DES HOSPITALIERES

ST GERVAIS

RUE DES ROSIERS

RUE PAVEE

RUE MALHER

The ancient street of Rue des Francs-Bourgeois is lined with intriguing buildings and trendy shops.

The smell of hot pastrami and borscht wafts from restaurants and shops on Rue des Rosiers, the heart of the Jewish area (p93).

Discover the exquisite collection of 18th-century paintings and furniture at the Musée Cognacq-Jay (p92).

Behind the ornate doorway of the fine Hôtel de Lamoignon is Paris's historical library.

←

Cycling down the shopping street of Rue des Francs-Bourgeois

↑ The façade of the Musée Carnavalet, housed in two adjoining mansions

Locator Map
For more detail see p86

THE MARAIS

The Hôtel Le Peletier de St-Fargeau adjoins the Hôtel Carnavalet to form the Musée Carnavalet (p97).

The statue of Louis XIV in Roman dress by Coysevox is in the courtyard of the Hôtel Carnavalet, home to the Musée Carnavalet.

Did You Know?

It took Victor Hugo nearly two decades to write *Les Misérables*.

PARC ROYAL

SEVIGNE

OURGEOIS

RUE DE

RUE DE TURENNE

RUE DE BEARN

| 0 metres | 100 |
| 0 yards | 100 |

N ↑

Once the site of jousting and tournaments, the historic Place des Vosges, in the very heart of the Marais, is a square of perfect symmetry (p92).

Author of Les Misérables, Victor Hugo lived at No. 6 Place des Vosges. The Maison de Victor Hugo is now a museum of his life and work (p93).

RUE DE BIRAGUE

FINISH ●

The Hôtel de Bethune-Sully was built for a notorious gambler.

BASTILLE AND OBERKAMPF

East of the Marais, Bastille and Oberkampf were once Parisian *faubourgs*, or suburbs, well outside the main city wall in the Middle Ages. Furniture-makers inhabited the area around Bastille, capitalizing on wood delivered at the nearby docks, while Oberkampf was a working-class neighbourhood filled with artisans, including leather-makers. Where the Opéra National de Paris Bastille stands today, Parisians once gaped at the mighty Bastille – an imposing medieval prison fortress and symbol of royal repression, which famously met its demise in 1789 during the French Revolution. Throughout the 19th century, this largely working-class neighbourhood grew into one of Paris's most densely populated districts. In 1840, the Colonne de Juillet rose in Place de la Bastille, joined some 150 years later by the modern Opéra. Many of the artisans disappeared during this time, but an energetic nightlife grew up in their wake, fuelled by the culturally diverse and generally younger populations living here.

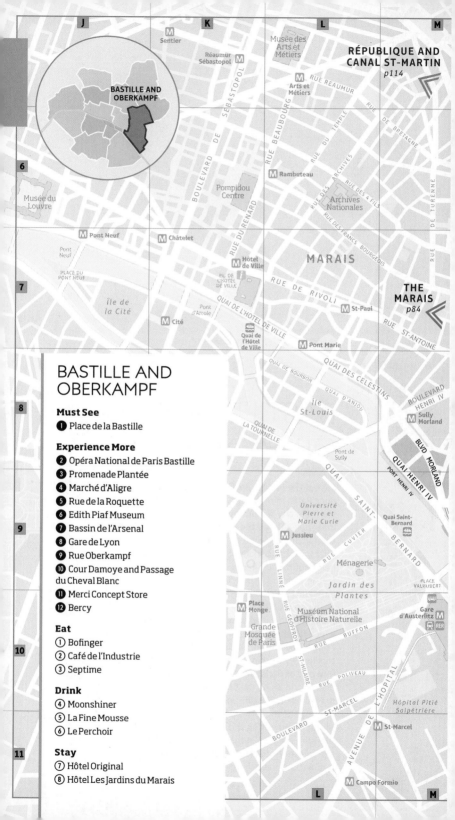

THE
MARAIS
p84

BASTILLE AND OBERKAMPF

Must See

1 Place de la Bastille

Experience More

2 Opéra National de Paris Bastille
3 Promenade Plantée
4 Marché d'Aligre
5 Rue de la Roquette
6 Edith Piaf Museum
7 Bassin de l'Arsenal
8 Gare de Lyon
9 Rue Oberkampf
10 Cour Damoye and Passage du Cheval Blanc
11 Merci Concept Store
12 Bercy

Eat

1 Bofinger
2 Café de l'Industrie
3 Septime

Drink

4 Moonshiner
5 La Fine Mousse
6 Le Perchoir

Stay

7 Hôtel Original
8 Hôtel Les Jardins du Marais

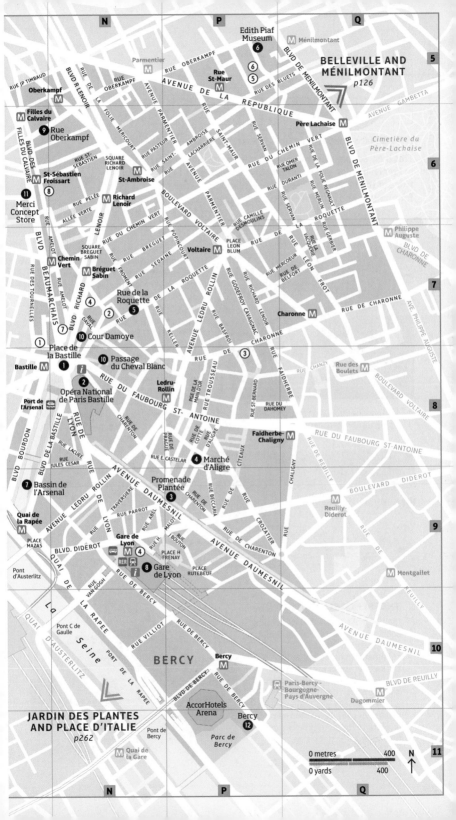

❶

PLACE DE LA BASTILLE

📍N8 **🏛Place de la Bastille 75004** **Ⓜ Bastille** **🚌20, 29, 65, 69, 76, 86, 87, 91**

This busy square was the scene of one of the most important events in French history – the storming of the Bastille on 14 July 1789. Little trace of the infamous prison remains, and today the square is a hub for nightlife and cultural events such as concerts.

↑ The Marché Bastille on nearby Boulevard Richard Lenoir

← The Opéra National de Paris Bastille *(p106)*, designed by Carlos Ott

At the centre of the large square that marks the site of the prison is the Colonne de Juillet. Topped by the elegant, gilded statue of the winged "genius of liberty", this column of hollow bronze reaches 50.5 m (166 ft) into the sky. It is a memorial to those who died in the street battles of July 1830 that led to the overthrow of the monarch. The crypt contains the remains of 504 victims of the violent fighting and others who died in the 1848 revolution.

Place de la Bastille was once the border between central Paris and the eastern working-class areas *(faubourgs)*. Gentrification, however, is well under way. Just east of the Opéra Bastille is the starting point of the Promenade Plantée *(p106)*, an elevated walking trail built on a disused railway line, while work to pedestrianize half of the square and connect it to the Bassin de l'Arsenal marina *(p108)* is currently in progress. The first phase is scheduled to be complete by the summer of 2019.

THE FRENCH REVOLUTION

In 1789, most Parisians were living in squalor and poverty. Rising inflation and opposition to Louis XVI culminated in the storming of the Bastille, the king's prison; the Republic was founded three years later. However, the Terror soon followed, when those suspected of betraying the Revolution were executed without trial: more than 60,000 people lost their lives.

INSIDER TIP
Chocolate Treat

Chocaholics should head to Alain Ducasse's La Manufacture du Chocolat on Rue de la Roquette. It sells a decadent array of ganaches, pralines and truffles in an assortment of flavours.

The Colonne de Juillet, ↑
commemorating the 1830 revolution
that saw the fall of King Charles X

EXPERIENCE MORE

Opéra National de Paris Bastille

📍N8 🏠120 Rue de Lyon 75012 Ⓜ Bastille 🌐 operadeparis.fr

The controversial "people's opera" was officially opened on 14 July 1989 to coincide with the bicentennial celebrations of the storming of the Bastille. Carlos Ott's imposing building is a notable break with 19th-century opera-house design, epitomized by Charles Garnier's opulent Opéra in the heart of the city (p172). The Bastille opera house is a massive, modern, curved, glass building. The main auditorium seats an audience of 2,700; its design is functional and modern, the black upholstered seats contrasting with the granite of the walls and the impressive glass ceiling. With its five moveable stages, this opera house is certainly a masterpiece of technological wizardry and it's well worth seeing a performance here; the website has full details of what's on and also has information about guided tours (in French).

3 Promenade Plantée

📍P9 🏠1 Coulée Verte René-Dumont 75012 Ⓜ Bastille 🕐8am-7.30pm (to 6pm in winter)

This former elevated railway hosts Paris's most exclusive verdant walkway. Rising up to 10 m (33 ft) above the streets, the promenade, planted with many varieties of flowers and trees, stretches for about 5 km (3 miles) between the Opéra Bastille and the Périphérique city boundary to the east. The original railway closed in 1969 but the city preserved the structure and opened the Promenade Plantée (also known as the Coulée Verte René-Dumont) in 1993, serving as a model for urban renewal that has been replicated around the world. The topography varies from planted gardens and larger parks to narrow walkways snaking between apartment buildings. A stroll or jog along the Promenade Plantée is a delightful traffic-free experience, with epic views of the city. Underneath the red-brick railway arches by the opera house, the Viaduc des Arts houses artisan and craft shops and fashion boutiques. All along the promenade, staircases lead down to street level, where cafés and bakeries are rarely far away for a quick pick-me-up while exploring Paris's eastern extremities in bucolic bliss.

> **A stroll or jog along the Promenade Plantée is a delightful traffic-free experience, with epic views of the city.**

Did You Know?

Remnants of the moat of the Bastille prison can be seen in the Bastille Metro.

4 Marché d'Aligre

📍P8 🏠Place d'Aligre 75012 Ⓜ Ledru-Rollin 🕐7:30am-1pm Tue-Sun (indoor market 9am-1:30pm & 4-7:30pm Tue-Sat, 9am-1:30pm Sun)

On Sunday mornings, this lively and good-value market offers one of the most colourful sights in Paris. French, Arab and African traders hawk fruit, vegetables, flowers, clothing, bric-a-brac and second-hand books on the

The tree-lined Promenade Plantée, an elevated walkway ↑

Busy Rue de la Roquette with its lively cafés and restaurants ↑

streets, while the adjoining covered market, the Beauveau St-Antoine, offers fruit, vegetables, a great selection of cheese, charcuterie and olive oils, plus many intriguing international delicacies.

The Marché d'Aligre is where old and new Paris meet. Here, the established community of this old artisan quarter coexists with a more recently established group of hip urban professionals, lured here by the transformation of the nearby Bastille area. Some parts of the indoor market have been renovated following a fire in 2015.

5 🍴 🖥 🏛

Rue de la Roquette

📍 N7 Ⓜ Bastille, Voltaire

This bustling street, lined with bars, cafés and restaurants, stretches from the Opéra Bastille towards Père Lachaise Cemetery (p130). At No. 17 stands the house of Symbolist poet Paul Verlaine, a 19th-century regular in the neighbourhood. At No. 70, a 19th-century fountain once brought water from the canal into the densely populated district. The five stone slabs in the road where the street meets Rue de la Croix Faubin are an eerie reminder of a much darker history. They are the foundations of the guillotine where inmates of the Prison de la Roquette met their fate, usually in front of a crowd of onlookers. Around 200 executions were carried out between 1851 and 1899, while some 4,000 women, members of the French Resistance, were incarcerated in the prison in 1944. The former entrance can still be seen across the street, on Square de la Roquette. Rue de la Roquette and the surrounding area, particularly cobbled Rue de Lappe, with its numerous bars, gets pretty animated at night.

EAT

Bofinger
This classic 19th-century brasserie serves up Alsatian fare in a glitzy setting.

📍 M7 🏠 5 Rue de la Bastille 75004
Ⓦ bofingerparis.com

€€€

Café de l'Industrie
Simple food and a funky setting make this a neighbourhood favourite.

📍 N7 🏠 16 Rue Saint-Sabin 75011
Ⓦ cafedelindustrie paris.fr

€€€

Septime
Innovative cuisine and a relaxed atmosphere combine for perfect Michelin-star dining.

📍 P8 🏠 80 Rue de Charonne 75011
📅 Sat & Sun Ⓦ septime-charonne.fr

€€€

→

Memorabilia, paintings and artifacts in the small Edith Piaf Museum

6

Edith Piaf Museum

📍P5 🏠5 Rue Crespin du Gast 75011 📞01 43 55 52 72 Ⓜ Ménilmontant ⏰By appt 1–6pm Mon–Wed, 10–noon Thu

Legend has it that singer Edith Piaf was born in the street in nearby Belleville (p132). Historians debate that story, but she did actually live in this tiny apartment, now a museum dedicated to the singer's legacy. It is privately owned by a fan who has curated a collection of memorabilia and personal artifacts that belonged to the chanteuse. Just 1.42 m (4 ft 8 inches) tall and known as the "Little Sparrow", her voice was anything but small, echoing across concert halls worldwide. Buried in nearby Père Lachaise Cemetery (p130), Piaf is today best known for songs such as "La Vie en Rose". An engaging collection of souvenirs, prints and Piaf's signature black dresses are on display. The museum, unlike most in Paris, requires visitors to call and book in advance. A charming, intimate experience, it should appeal to both die-hard fans and visitors with just a casual interest.

7

Bassin de l'Arsenal

📍M9 🏠5 Quai de la Rapée Ⓜ Bastille

Between Place de la Bastille and the Seine, this pleasure-boat arena hides below street level. A lock joins it to the River Seine. The location of a weapons storehouse since the 16th century, the arsenal eventually fell into disuse as revolutionaries removed the Bastille fortress, stone by stone. Nowadays, the tiny marina hosts private watercraft and is also the starting point for tour cruises along the Canal St-Martin (p118). There is a café, Le Grand Bleu, at the north end, though on warm evenings most Parisians picnic along the traffic-free waterfront. Two bridges crossing the water offer picture-postcard views of the July Column in the Place de la Bastille.

8 🍴 🍺

Gare de Lyon

📍N9 🏠Place Louis-Armand 75012 Ⓜ Gare de Lyon. Le Train Bleu: 🌐le-train-bleu.com

Built for the 1900 Universal Exhibition, this station is the third busiest in France,

DRINK

Moonshiner
This 1920s-inspired speakeasy hides behind a pizzeria. It can be crowded, but serves great cocktails.

📍N7 🏠5 Rue Sedaine 75011 📞09 50 73 12 99

La Fine Mousse
It's all about craft beer here, with up-and-coming local brews on tap. They also offer tasting workshops.

📍P5 🏠6 Ave Jean Aicard 75011 🌐lafinemousse.fr

Le Perchoir
Clink glasses and feast on light fare from this rooftop bar with a 360-degree view of the city.

📍P5 🏠14 Rue Crespin du Gast 75011 ⏰Sun & Mon 🌐leperchoir.tv

With high-end restaurants, gourmet coffee shops, craft beer and spicy Mexican fare, Rue Oberkampf caters to all sorts of flavours and fancies.

INSIDER TIP
Chambelland

Chambelland, at 14 Rue Ternaux, is one of the few gluten-free bakeries in Paris, serving a delicious array of bread, biscuits and pastries.

with about 90 million annual passengers. It welcomes trains from throughout France, as well as Italy, Switzerland and other international destinations. In the summer months you'll notice many sun-kissed travellers returning from the Côte d'Azur, as this station serves Nice and other southern French destinations. On the exterior of the station looms the iconic clock tower, reminiscent of the UK Parliament's Big Ben tower. Inside the Gare de Lyon is the illustrious restaurant Le Train Bleu, a glitzy dining experience that has been in operation for over a century. The ornate dining rooms are decorated with gilded carvings, mouldings and chandeliers, as well as 41 paintings representing French cities or regions by prominent French artists including François Flameng and Henri Gervex. Even if you're not catching a train to some sun-soaked destination, it's worth a visit to the station to sip a glass of wine amid the restaurant's sumptuous décor.

Rue Oberkampf

⑨ M6 Ⓜ Oberkampf, Parmentier

Rue Oberkampf stretches from the Upper Marais all the way to Ménilmontant, with most of the action happening around Metros Parmentier and Oberkampf. Dating back to the 1500s, the street gained its name in the 19th century from the German-born industrialist Christophe-Philippe Oberkampf, who contributed to the manufacturing of painted French cloth *(toile)*. Today, the area is anything but old-fashioned. With high-end restaurants, gourmet coffee shops, craft beer and spicy Mexican fare, Rue Oberkampf caters to all sorts of flavours and fancies in its many bars and eateries. The street becomes especially lively at night, with younger Parisians congregating at watering holes like Café Charbon or Le Quartier Général and crowds gathering under clouds of smoke at the live-music venues that dot the street. There are few, if any, tourist attractions here. It's all about local colour. Plan on spending an evening or afternoon hopping from venue to venue in search of the perfect fit.

The opulent interior of Le Train Bleu restaurant, inside the Gare de Lyon

The Bassin de l'Arsenal, a pleasure boat arena

⑩ Cour Damoye and Passage du Cheval Blanc

◐ N7 Ⓜ Bastille, Voltaire, Brégnet Sabin

Amid the bustle of Place de la Bastille, there are tiny enclaves of calm hidden in two historic passages, the Cour Damoye and the Passage du Cheval Blanc. Most people walk right by their entrances without daring to enter, but they are public walkways. This area has been a centre of carpentry and French furniture design since the time of the Middle Ages. Its location near a port on the Seine that dealt with wood and timber made it popular with craftsmen, and many high-end artisans producing fine furnishings can still be found in the district. The late-18th-century Cour Damoye is today largely residential, with a few small businesses still functioning,

FURNITURE-MAKING DISTRICT

Close to the former docks at Quai de la Rapée, this district east of the Place de la Bastille served to stock lumber, leading to its renown as a centre for furniture- and cabinet-making and their related trades. The craftsmen even caught the eye of Louis XIV, and his Minister of Finances, Colbert, established the royal mirror factory here. Today, there are still antique sellers, cabinet-makers and craftsmen dotted around Rue du Faubourg Saint-Antoine, especially on Le Passage du Chantier.

but remnants of its former artisan workshops are visible in the façades. The Passage du Cheval Blanc, just off Rue de la Roquette, is named after the sign of a horse that once adorned the entrance. Offering a peaceful respite from the busy Faubourg Saint-Antoine, its small labyrinth of cobbled courtyards, named after the months of the year (Cour de Janvier etc), hide architecture companies and apartments, with wooden beams still visible in some buildings. The Cité Parchappe spills you back out onto the main road.

⑪ Merci Concept Store

◐ M6 ⌂ 111 Boulevard Beaumarchais 75003 Ⓜ St-Sébastien Froissart ⏰ 10am–7:30pm ✖ Sun 🌐 merci-merci.com

Paris has grand department stores and luxury boutiques aplenty, but around Bastille, Merci is the place for retail therapy. A concept store housed in an old wallpaper factory, it opened in 2009 and curates the best in fashion and design. Homewares, clothing and kitchen products are housed under a glass atrium, spread across multiple floors. It has none of the glitz or brand names of big-brother department stores like Printemps or Le Bon Marché.

↓ The bold new architecture of Bercy, a former wine-trading district

Instead, it reflects the neighbourhood's character, featuring up-and-coming designers and local brands. If you're not interested in swiping your cards on trendy accessories, you could join the locals at Merci's popular restaurant and two cafés. The Used Book Café, set among towering shelves of literature, is especially appealing for afternoon tea or coffee. Fresh salads, egg dishes and *tartines* are all on the menu. The shop also houses temporary exhibitions and pop-up events that manage to keep it feeling fresh and exciting for locals and visitors alike.

12

Bercy

P11 **75012** **M Bercy, Cour St-Émilion**

This former wine-trading quarter east of the city centre, with its once-grim warehouses, pavilions and slum housing, has been transformed into a modern district. An automatic Metro line (Line 14) links it to the heart of the city. The centrepiece is the AccorHotels Arena, whose vast pyramidal structure has become a contemporary landmark. Many sports events are held here, as well as operas and rock concerts.

Other architecturally adventurous buildings dominate Bercy, notably Chemetov's gigantic building for the Ministry of Finance, and Frank Gehry's American Center. This houses the Cinémathèque Française, a wonderful cinema museum that hosts frequent retrospectives of famous directors.

At the foot of these structures, the imaginatively designed 70-ha (173-acre) Parc de Bercy provides a welcome green space for this part of the city.

Former wine stores and cellars along Cours St-Émilion have been restored as bars, restaurants and shops, and one of the warehouses now contains the Musée des Arts Forains (Fairground Museum), open for private tours only.

↑ The contemporary landscape design of the attractive Parc de Bercy

RÉPUBLIQUE AND CANAL ST-MARTIN

Lying beyond central Paris, this area was once farmland. The Knights Templar established their European headquarters here during the medieval period, at which time it was also home to a community of lepers. In the 17th century, King Henri IV built a hospital for plague victims, while the 18th century saw a new wall envelop these districts within the city limits. Following industrialization of the area in the 19th century, thanks to Napoleon's canal, the neighbourhood became largely working class. It suffered from dereliction in the 20th century, although strong African communities grew up here, especially around Chateau d'Eau. In the 1990s, a class of bohemian-bourgeois Parisians – known as *bobos* – began to gentrify the district. Place de la République, totally redesigned in 2013, now welcomes street fairs and public demonstrations. Even Gare du Nord, hub for the London-bound Eurostar, has cleaned up in recent years.

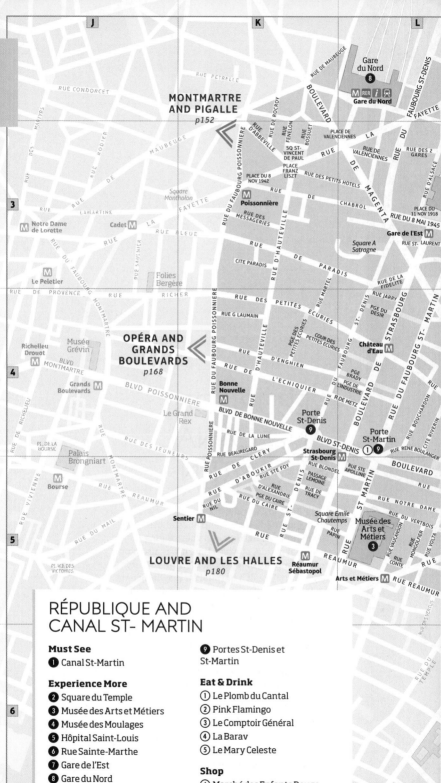

J **K** **L**

RUE CONDORCET

RUE PETRELIE

MONTMARTRE
AND PIGALLE
p152

Gare
du Nord
8

M RER *i* 🚆
Gare du Nord

RUE DE MAUBEUGE

BOULEVARD

LA

RUE DU

FAUBOURG ST-DENIS

FAYETTE

RUE DES 2
GARES

RUE D'ALSACE

RUE D'ABBEVILLE

RUE DE ROCROY

RUE FÉNELON

RUE BOSSUET

PLACE DE
VALENCIENNES

SQ ST-
VINCENT
DE PAUL

PLACE
FRANZ
LISZT

RUE DE
VALENCIENNES

RUE DE

MAGENTA

PLACE DU 8
NOV 1942

RUE DES PETITS HOTELS

Poissonnière

RUE DES
MESSAGERIES

FAYETTE

RUE DU FAUBOURG POISSONNIERE

RUE D'HAUTEVILLE

CHABROL

RUE DU 8 MAI 1918

PLACE DU
11 NOV 1918

Gare de l'Est M

RUE ST-LAURENT

3

RUE

LAMARTINE

M Notre Dame
de Lorette

RUE BLEUE

Cadet M

LA

Square
Montholon

RUE

RUE SAULNIER

DE PARADIS

Square A
Satragne

RUE DE LA
FIDELITE

CITE PARADIS

RUE DES

PETITES ECURIES

RUE MARTEL

RUE JARRY

ST-DENIS

DE

STRASBOURG

RUE DU FAUBOURG ST-MARTIN

M
Le Peletier

Folies
Bergère

RUE DE PROVENCE

RUE DE LA FAUBOURG POISSONNIERE

RICHER

RUE G LAUMAIN

RUE D'HAUTEVILLE

PGE DES
PETITES ECURIES

COUR DES
PETITES ECURIES

PGE DU
DESIR

**Château
d'Eau** M

Richelieu
Drouot

Musée
Grévin

BLVD
MONTMARTRE

M Grands
Boulevards

**OPÉRA AND
GRANDS
BOULEVARDS**
p168

RUE

D'ENGHIEN

L'ECHIQUIER

RUE DE METZ

PGE
BRADY

PGE DE
L'INDUSTRIE

DE

BOULEVARD

RUE DU FAUBOURG ST-MARTIN

RUE BOUCHARDON

RUE

4

M

RUE DE RICHELIEU

RUE

MONTMARTRE

BLVD POISSONNIERE

**Bonne
Nouvelle**

RUE DE
RUE DE

L'INDUSTRIE

Porte
St-Denis
9

RUE RENE BOULANGER

CITE RIVERIN

Le Grand
Rex

BLVD DE BONNE NOUVELLE

RUE DE LA LUNE

BLVD ST-DENIS

Porte
St-Martin
① **9**

PL. DE LA
BOURSE

Palais
Brongniart

RUE DES JEUNEURS

RUE DE CLERY

RUE BEAUREGARD

**Strasbourg
St-Denis** M

RUE BLONDEL

RUE STE
APOLLINE

ST-MARTIN

BOULEVARD

RUE

5

M
Bourse

RUE VIVIENNE

RUE

MONTMARTRE

RUE

REAUMUR

RUE

D'ABOUKIR

RUE STE FOY

PGE DU CAIRE

RUE DU NIL

RUE DE CLERY

ST-DENIS

PASSAGE
LEMOINE

RUE
D'ALEXANDRIE

RUE DE TRACY

RUE DU VERTBOIS

RUE NOTRE DAME

RUE VAUCANSON

RUE MONGOLFIER

RUE VOLTA

Square Émile
Chautemps

**Musée des
Arts et
Métiers**
3

RUE DU MAIL

Sentier M

RUE

RUE

RUE PAPIN

LOUVRE AND LES HALLES
p180

M
**Réaumur
Sébastopol**

REAUMUR

RUE CONTE

RUE

PLACE DES
VICTOIRES

Arts et Métiers M RUE REAUMUR

RUE DU TEMPLE

RÉPUBLIQUE AND
CANAL ST- MARTIN

Must See

① Canal St-Martin

Experience More

② Square du Temple
③ Musée des Arts et Métiers
④ Musée des Moulages
⑤ Hôpital Saint-Louis
⑥ Rue Sainte-Marthe
⑦ Gare de l'Est
⑧ Gare du Nord

⑨ Portes St-Denis et
St-Martin

Eat & Drink

① Le Plomb du Cantal
② Pink Flamingo
③ Le Comptoir Général
④ La Barav
⑤ Le Mary Celeste

Shop

⑥ Marché des Enfants Rouge

L

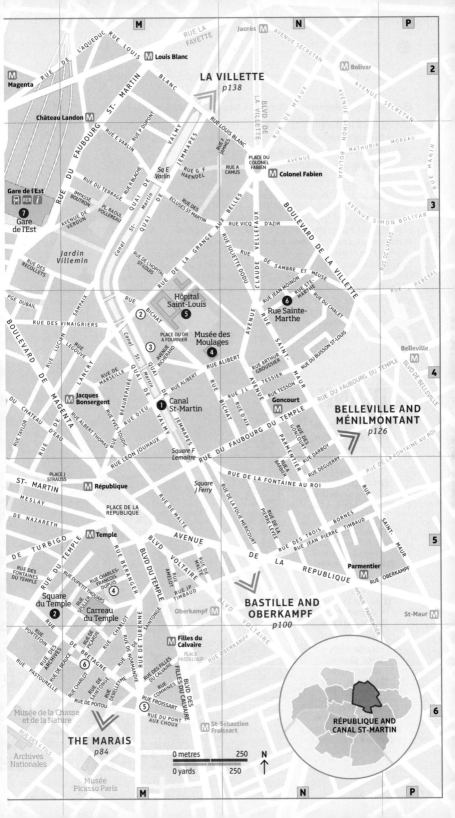

①

CANAL ST-MARTIN

⚲ M4   Ⓜ Jacques Bonsergent, Goncourt, République   🚌 26, 46, 75

Dating back to the time of Napoleon, this 4.5-km (2¾-mile) waterway flows through one of Paris's trendiest districts. Colourful shops and cafés line its banks, where locals spend weekends picnicking or cycling along the waterfront.

Stretching between the Seine in the south and the Bassin de la Villette in the north, the Canal St-Martin opened in 1825 as a means of bringing fresh water to Paris's polluted city centre. However, in the late 19th century part of the canal was covered to make way for new roadways, and within a few decades the canal and the boats that worked upon it had become obsolete. City officials almost drained and filled the entire waterway in the 1970s, but by the turn of the millennium it had became a popular location for wealthy young Parisians to buy and renovate properties. This once-derelict district is now one of the Right Bank's most desirable areas, a culturally mixed neighbourhood where Paris's hipsters mingle among families and international arrivals.

> 💬 INSIDER TIP
> ### Canalside Pizza Delivery
>
> Order a pizza from Pink Flamingo *(p125)*, grab a bright pink balloon, then find a comfortable spot along the canal and wait for the restaurant to deliver it to you.

DRINK

Here are the best coffee shops along the canal:

Ten Belles
⚲ M4   🏠 10 Rue de la Grange aux Belles 75010   🌐 tenbelles.com

HolyBelly
⚲ L4   🏠 5 Rue Lucien Sampaix 75010
🌐 holybellycafe.com

Craft
⚲ M4   🏠 24 Rue des Vinaigriers 75010
🌐 cafe-craft.com

Radiodays
⚲ M4   🏠 15 Rue Alibert 75010
🌐 radiodays.cafe

DonAntónia
⚲ M4   🏠 8 Rue de la Grange aux Belles 75010
🌐 donantonia.paris

1 Cafés and restaurants populate the neighbourhood around the canal.

2 A selection of tasty treats at the Bakery du Pain et des Idées on Rue Yves Toudic.

3 The Canal St-Martin is punctuated by romantic bridges, including two swing ones.

2km

of the canal passes through an underground tunnel.

↑ Strolling along the canal reveals Paris at its most picturesque

EXPERIENCE MORE

② Square du Temple

📍 L5 📮 75003
Ⓜ Temple

A quiet and pleasant square today, this was once a fortified centre of the medieval Knights Templar. A state within a state, the area contained a palace, a church and shops behind high walls and a drawbridge, making it a haven for those who were seeking to escape from royal jurisdiction. Louis XVI and Marie-Antoinette were held in the Temple fortress after their arrest in 1792. The king set out from here for his execution by guillotine.

Did You Know?
—
The Square du Temple contains 70 species of trees, including an 18-m- (59-ft-) tall Turkish hazel.

③ Musée des Arts et Métiers

📍 L5 📮 60 Rue Réaumur 75003 Ⓜ Arts et Métiers
🕙 10am–6pm Tue–Sun (to 9:30pm Thu) 🚫 1 May & 25 Dec 🌐 arts-et-metiers.net

Housed within the old Abbey of St-Martin-des-Champs, the Arts and Crafts Museum was founded in 1794. After major renovations in the 1990s it reopened in 2000 as an excellent museum of science and industry displaying 5,000 items (it has 75,000 additional artifacts in storage that are available to academics and researchers). The museum's theme is man's ingenuity and the worlds of invention and manufacturing, covering such topics as textiles, photography and machines. Among the most entertaining displays are those of musical clocks, mechanical musical instruments and automata (mechanical figures). One of these figures, the "Joueuse de Tympanon", is said to represent Marie-Antoinette.

④ Musée des Moulages

📍 M4 📮 1 Ave Claude Vellefaux 75010
📞 01 42 49 99 15
Ⓜ Goncourt, Colonel Fabien
🕙 9am–4.30pm Mon–Fri

Housed inside the Hôpital Saint-Louis, this museum boasts 4,807 wax moulds of horrific skin diseases of the 1800s. Dr Lallier of the Hôpital Saint-Louis hired Jules Baretta, a wax-fruit maker, to create models of real diseases to teach students about

↑ The pretty Square du Temple garden with its bandstand and pond

↑ A plane on display at the Museé des Arts et Métiers, housed in a former church

SHOP

Marché des Enfants Rouges

This historical market on shop-laden Rue de Bretagne is full of food stalls and international cuisine, and is usually packed at lunchtime.

🅟 M6 🅐 39 Rue de Bretagne 75003
🅒 Mon

---

things such as syphilis and elephantiasis. Baretta would spend time with patients in the hospital, carefully using plaster of Paris to create his moulds. He would then paint them in great detail, even adding hair to keep them realistic. While many of the faces and body parts are unsettling in their realism, they are true works of art. Cyclopoid babies, various stages of then-fatal syphilis, and all sorts of abnormal skin growths are as fascinating as they are gruesome. The collection is an enlightening look into how far medicine has come in the past 150 years, to a time before the discovery of antibiotics that could cure

many of these diseases. Today, few students visit the antiquated learning tools, so the museum is often empty. Call ahead to arrange an appointment, and purchase tickets within the modern hospital's register adjacent to the original structure.

5
Hôpital Saint-Louis

🅟 M4 🅐 1 Ave Claude Vellefaux 75010
Ⓜ Goncourt, Colonel Fabien

Built by order of King Henri IV in 1607 and completed after his death, this hospital originally served the growing number of plague victims at the time. Patients crowded into the rooms surrounding the square courtyard, reminiscent of Place des Vosges in the Marais *(p92)*, and constructed by the same architect. Most would never see the sky again except for a rare stroll through that grassy courtyard. Conditions in the hospital worsened over time, but eventually

→

A statue at the Musée des Arts et Metiers

the plague passed. The building later served as a dermatology hospital and a prison for nuns during the French Revolution. Today, modern facilities next to the 17th-century buildings still function as a hospital. A small adjacent chapel – built for local farmers and not for plague victims – was used for King Henri IV's funeral in 1610. The main courtyard is open to the public and is an almost hauntingly calm respite in the heart of Paris. One of its wings is home to the Musée des Moulages, a museum dedicated to skin diseases.

The Gare de l'Est, lit up at night

6 🍴 🖥 🛍
Rue Sainte-Marthe

📍 N4 🏠 75010
Ⓜ Goncourt, Belleville

Just north of the Hôpital Saint-Louis, this tiny little street feels more like a walk through some southern provincial French town than central Paris. Colourful doors and façades contrast with the often grey Parisian skies. Each one opens up to an artist's studio, a workshop, a quirky restaurant, or some oddball boutique. There is little historical significance in these former workers' quarters, but the area is a unique slice of Parisian life. Look for olives in the independent grocery, try some Chilean food, or spend an evening with a glass of wine and charcuterie at any of the local bars here. Tourists rarely make it this far, stopping instead at the Canal St-Martin. A walk along Rue Sainte-Marthe, however, is a very Parisian experience.

---

7 🍴 🖥 🛍
Gare de l'Est

📍 L3 🏠 Place du 11 Novembre 1918 75010
Ⓜ Gare du Nord

Whether travelling to Germany or just passing through the neighbourhood, visitors should take a moment to marvel at one of Paris's oldest train stations. Opened in 1849, it had doubled in size by 1931 after several renovations. Statues atop the façades represent Strasbourg and Verdun, two of the original destinations served by the station. In 1883, the very first Orient Express departed from Gare de l'Est for Istanbul. Inside the main hall, a massive painting by American artist Albert Herter depicts French troops leaving the station for the Front during World War I in 1914. German forces transformed an underground air-raid shelter into a wartime bunker during World War II, which is still preserved under the station, though it is not open to visitors.

🔍 HIDDEN GEM
Marché Saint-Quentin

The 19th-century covered market Marché Saint-Quentin on Boulevard de Magenta makes a handy stop for last-minute cheese and wine before you board a train from the Gare de l'Est or Gare du Nord.

← Statues adorning the huge façade of the Gare du Nord station

8 Gare du Nord

⊙ L2 🏠 18 Rue de Dunkerque 75010
Ⓜ Gare du Nord

Opened in 1864, this train station is best known today as the hub for the Eurostar to London, as well as services to Brussels and Amsterdam. This massive station is Europe's busiest, with over 200 million passengers per year. The imposing façade is dotted with sculptures representing other European capitals, including Berlin and London. The soaring iron structure inside creates a romantic departure hall, and has been used as a film location for several movies. Inside the station, a new wave of cafés and restaurants is reinventing the travelling experience, as well as the surrounding neighbourhood. The station is undergoing further refurbishments in preparation for the 2024 Olympic Games.

9 Portes St-Denis et St-Martin

⊙ K4, L4 🏠 Blvds St-Denis & St-Martin 75010
Ⓜ Strasbourg-St-Denis

These imposing gates give access to the two ancient and important thoroughfares whose names they bear, running across Paris in a north–south direction. They once marked the entrance to the city. The Porte St-Denis is 23 m (76 ft) high and was built in 1672 by François Blondel. It is decorated with figures by Louis XIV's sculptor, François Girardon. The gates commemorate the victories of the king's armies in Flanders and the Rhine that year. Porte St-Martin is 17 m (56 ft) tall and was built in 1674 by Pierre Bullet, a student of Blondel. It celebrates the capture of Besançon and the defeat of the Triple Alliance of Spain, Holland and Germany.

EAT & DRINK

Le Plomb du Cantal
A local establishment serving well-prepared, no-frills, traditional French food.

⊙ L4 🏠 4 Bvld St-Denis 75010 🕐 Tue
🖥 leplombducantal.com

€€€

Pink Flamingo
Unique, delicious pizzas with eclectic ingredients such as figs, chutney and duck.

⊙ M4 🏠 67 Rue Bichat 75010
🖥 pinkflamingo pizza.com

€€€

Le Comptoir Général
This quirky venue hosts events and has a bar popular during the evenings and on Sunday afternoons.

⊙ M4 🏠 80 Quai de Jemmapes 75010
🖥 lecomtoirgeneral.com

La Barav
This popular wine bar fills up with locals sharing bottles and cheese plates.

⊙ N5 🏠 6 Rue Charles-François Dupuis 75003
🖥 lebarav.fr

Le Mary Celeste
Go for cocktails, stay for the small plates, and then have more cocktails.

⊙ M6 🏠 1 Rue Commines 75003
🖥 lemaryceleste.com

↓ The impressive interior of Gare de l'Est

One of Belleville's colourful street-art-lined thoroughfares

BELLEVILLE AND MÉNILMONTANT

Belleville and Ménilmontant are two of the newest districts to have been incorporated into the city. Various religious orders called the area home in the Middle Ages, and the land was cultivated by monks. Belleville was famous as a wine-growing suburb of Paris, with vineyards covering the hilly district. Both districts were beyond the tax reaches of the city, and in the 18th century Ménilmontant became popular with the working classes, who would drink cheaply at watering holes called *guinguettes*. After city planners removed the wall circling Paris in 1860, the two areas were absorbed into the 20 arrondissements, and much of the farmland and vineyards gave way to new homes. The districts became militant hotbeds during the 1871 Paris Commune, when clashes with the army erupted in the streets. Throughout the 20th century, the area attracted immigrants fleeing persecution, including Jewish people from Europe and inhabitants of former French colonies in North Africa. A bustling Chinese community added to the multicultural fabric of the districts, where cheap rent continues to attract many artists and migrants today.

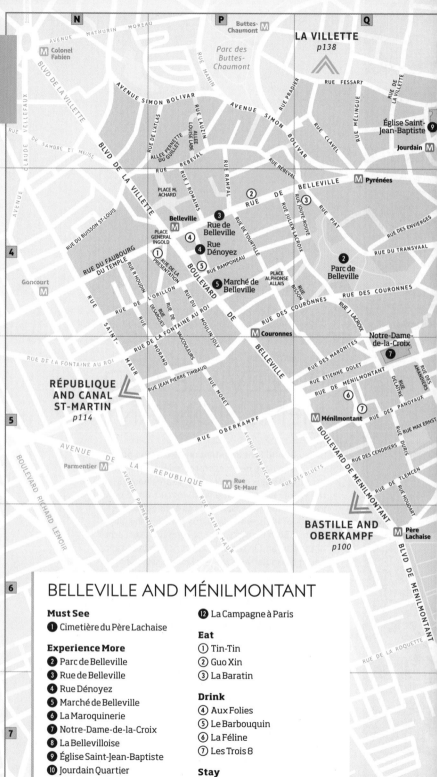

BELLEVILLE AND MÉNILMONTANT

Must See
1 Cimetière du Père Lachaise

Experience More
2 Parc de Belleville
3 Rue de Belleville
4 Rue Dénoyez
5 Marché de Belleville
6 La Maroquinerie
7 Notre-Dame-de-la-Croix
8 La Bellevilloise
9 Église Saint-Jean-Baptiste
10 Jourdain Quartier
11 Regard Saint-Martin
12 La Campagne à Paris

Eat
① Tin-Tin
② Guo Xin
③ La Baratin

Drink
④ Aux Folies
⑤ Le Barbouquin
⑥ La Féline
⑦ Les Trois 8

Stay
⑧ Mama Shelter

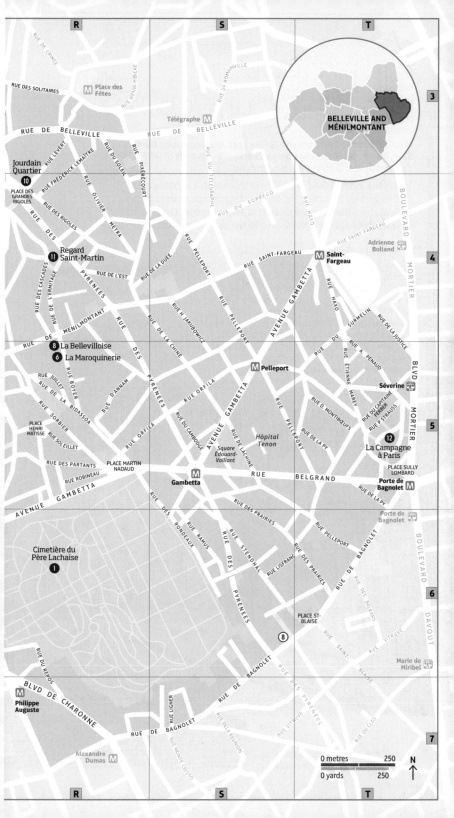

R

S

T

RUE DE CRIMÉE

RUE DES SOLITAIRES

Place des
Fêtes

RUE HENRY KIBELKE

RUE DE ROMAINVILLE

3

BELLEVILLE AND
MÉNILMONTANT

Télégraphe M

RUE DE BELLEVILLE

RUE DE BELLEVILLE

RUE DE BELLEVILLE

RUE LEVERT

RUE FRÉDÉRICK LEMAÎTRE

RUE DU SOLEIL

RUE PIXÉRÉCOURT

RUE DU TÉLÉGRAPHE

Jourdain
Quartier
10

PLACE DES
GRANDES
RIGOLES

RUE OLIVIER

RUE DES RIGOLES

METRA

RUE DE LA DUÉE

RUE DU BORREGO

BOULEVARD MORTIER

RUE PELLEPORT

RUE NAXO

4

Regard
Saint-Martin
11

RUE DE L'EST

RUE DES CASCADES

RUE DE L'ERMITAGE

PYRENEES

RUE SAINT-FARGEAU

Saint-
Fargeau

Adrienne
Bolland

M Saint-
Fargeau

RUE SAINT-FARGEAU

RUE DE MÉNILMONTANT

RUE DE LA CHINE

RUE H. JAKUBOWICZ

RUE PELLEPORT

AVENUE GAMBETTA

RUE HAXO

RUE DU SURMELIN

RUE DE LA JUSTICE

8 La Bellevilloise

6 La Maroquinerie

RUE DES

RUE JUILLET

RUE BOYER

RUE DE LA BIDASSOA

RUE D'ANNAM

RUE ORFILA

PYRENEES

RUE DU CAMBODGE

M Pelleport

RUE A. PENAUD

RUE ÉTIENNE MAREY

RUE D. MONTIBŒUFS

RUE DU CAPITAINE FERBER

RUE P STRAUSS

Séverine

BLVD MORTIER

5

RUE SORBIER

PLACE
HENRI
MATISSE

RUE SOLEILLET

RUE ORFILA

AVENUE GAMBETTA

RUE DE LACHINE

Square
Édouard-
Vaillant

Hôpital
Tenon

RUE PELLEPORT

RUE DE LA PY

12

La Campagne
à Paris

RUE DES PARTANTS

RUE ROBINEAU

PLACE MARTIN
NADAUD

M
Gambetta

RUE

BELGRAND

PLACE SULLY
LOMBARD

Porte de
Bagnolet M

RUE DE LA PY

AVENUE GAMBETTA

RUE DES RONDEAUX

RUE DES PRAIRIES

Porte de
Bagnolet

6

RUE RAMUS

RUE STENDHAL

RUE DES

RUE LISFRANC

RUE DES PRAIRIES

RUE PELLEPORT

RUE DE BAGNOLET

BOULEVARD

DAVOUT

Cimetière du
Père Lachaise
1

PYRENEES

PLACE ST-
BLAISE

RUE DES BALKANS

RUE SAINT-

RUE VITRUVE

Marie de
Miribel

8

RUE DU REPOS

BLVD DE CHARONNE

RUE LIGNER

RUE DE BAGNOLET

RUE DE LA RÉUNION

RUE DE BAGNOLET

RUE MONTE-CRISTO

RUE DES PYRENEES

RUE VITRUVE

RUE DU CLOS

RUE SAINT- BLAISE

M
Philippe
Auguste

RUE DE BAGNOLET

7

Alexandre
Dumas M

0 metres   250

0 yards   250

N

R

S

T

CIMETIÈRE DU PÈRE LACHAISE

R6 Blvd de Ménilmontant Père Lachaise, Alexandre Dumas
60, 61, 64, 69, 26 to Pl Gambetta 8am–5:30pm daily (from 8:30am Sat, 9am Sun; mid-Mar–early Nov: to 6pm)

This is the most visited cemetery in the world. It contains over 70,000 graves, including the tombs of numerous famous figures, such as the writer Honoré de Balzac, the composer Frédéric Chopin, the singer Jim Morrison and the actor Yves Montand.

Paris's most prestigious cemetery is set on a wooded hill overlooking the city. The land was once owned by Père de la Chaise, Louis XIV's confessor, but it was bought in 1803 by order of Napoleon to create a new cemetery. Père Lachaise, the first cemetery in France with a crematorium, became so popular that it was expanded six times during the 19th century.

Today the cemetery is a place of pilgrimage for rock fans, who come from around the world to see the grave of Jim Morrison of The Doors. With its moss-grown tombs and ancient trees, as well as striking funerary sculpture, Père Lachaise is an atmospheric and rather romantic place for a stroll.

Did You Know?

The remains of Molière were transferred here in 1817 to add historic glamour to the new cemetery.

→ A visitor exploring the funerary art among the lanes of Père Lachaise

← Théodore Géricault's tomb, with a depiction of *The Raft of the Medusa*

MUR DES FÉDÉRÉS

Following France's defeat in the Franco-Prussian War in 1871, a left-wing group revolted, setting up the Paris Commune. After 72 days, government troops marched on the city and in a week of brutal street fighting, much of the city was burned and thousands were killed. Mur des Fédérés in Père Lachaise is where the last Communard rebels were shot by government forces.

Notable Residents

Allan Kardec

▶ Kardec was the founder of a 19th-century spiritual cult, which still has a strong following. His tomb is perpetually covered in pilgrims' flowers.

George Rodenbach

The monument to this 19th-century poet depicts him rising out of his tomb with a rose in the hand of his outstretched arm.

Oscar Wilde

◀ The Irish dramatist, aesthete and great wit was exiled from virtuous Britain to die of drink and dissipation in Paris in 1900. American-British artist Jacob Epstein sculpted his tomb.

Marcel Proust

The French novelist brilliantly chronicled the belle époque in *Remembrance of Things Past*.

Sarah Bernhardt

▶ The great French tragedienne, who died in 1923 aged 78, was once the most famous actress in the world.

Edith Piaf

Known as the "Little Sparrow because of her size, Piaf was the 20th century's greatest French popular singer. In her tragic voice, she sang of the sorrows and woes of the Paris working class.

Jim Morrison

▶ The Doors' lead singer died in Paris in 1971. The circumstances of his death are still a mystery.

EXPERIENCE MORE

2

Parc de Belleville

Q4 | 47 Rue des Couronnes 75020
Couronnes, Belleville
8am-9.30pm (to 7pm in winter)

It has less of the manicured appeal of some of Paris's other parks, but the Parc de Belleville has views that no other green space can boast. This steep garden offers unparalleled panoramas of Paris, including the Eiffel Tower and Notre-Dame. The hill was originally settled by religious orders, who purch-ased parcels of land and planted vines. *Guinguettes* popped up in the Middle Ages, the outdoor pubs or beer gardens of their day. It was here that Parisians drank "*piquette*", a young wine from the area, which today is also French slang for bad wine. Eventually windmills domin-ated the landscape, owing to the park's altitude.

The park is a welcome green space in densely populated east Paris. Between the patches of exquisitely maintained flowerbeds are stairs and pathways crisscrossed by waterways and trestles. There is even a waterfall that trickles 100 m (328 ft) from the top of the grounds to the bottom. In a throwback to Belleville's wine-making past, 140 grapevines grow on the slopes, and the grapes are harvested each year.

3

Rue de Belleville

P4 | 75020
Belleville, Pyrénées, Jourdain

The main street of the former Belleville village, the Rue de Belleville cuts through the district from Belleville Metro station. The street used to be the location of the old wall that separated Paris from its suburbs. Belleville gets its name from a deformation of the French words *belle vue*, or "beautiful view" – the reason for which becomes apparent when you look downhill from the street towards where the Eiffel Tower rises up in the distance. The stretch between the Metro stations Belleville and Pyrénées is the most interesting. At No. 72, a plaque commemorates the birth in 1915 of Edith Piaf, who, according to popular legend, was born here on the steps. Over the past decades, many ethnic restaurants and East Asian shops have sprung up along the street as immig-rants have moved into the area, and all sorts of exotic and inexpensive food items can be found here. Restaurants serve a variety of dumplings, pork-filled *bao* and *banh mi* sandwiches that are worth the hike up the hilly street. Cafés are far from fussy affairs, serving inexpensive wine and beer in the old working-class Belleville tradition.

> ### Did You Know?
> At 108 m (354 ft), Parc de Belleville is the highest park in Paris.

→ The streets of Belleville, with stalls selling fresh produce *(above)*

The "open-air art gallery" of Belleville's Rue Dénoyez

 4

Rue Dénoyez

P4　75020
Belleville

Throughout Paris, street artists take advantage of any surface they can. In Rue Dénoyez, however, it seems as if the city actively encourages it. This narrow street, tucked away off Rue de Belleville and formerly rather run down, is essentially an outdoor contemporary art gallery where street artists constantly leave their mark. It is named after a local family who ran a popular dance hall in the 1830s, but today it is all about street art, reflecting the lively, bohemian spirit of the neighbourhood. On any given day, someone will be out there, spray-painting their newest mural on one of the walls. The buildings are mostly artists' studios – some will let you in if you are lucky – but the real draw is the colourful and daring works on the walls. In recent years, some of the studios have been replaced by more modern social housing, but the artistic spirit of Rue Dénoyez remains. Parisians still gather at the end of the street at Aux Folies, a bar known for its cheap drinks and a sea of plastic chairs spilling onto the sidewalk, while at the other end of the street Le Barbouquin is a great place to relax with a drink and a book from one of its groaning shelves.

DRINK

Aux Folies
Plastic chairs all over the terrace give this a homey feel, reinforced by cheap drinks and loud locals.

P4　8 Rue de Belleville 75020
aux-folies-belleville.fr

Le Barbouquin
This cosy café – part coffee shop, part bar and part bookshop/library – is an ideal chill-out spot. It also hosts regular music nights.

P4　1 Rue Dénoyez 75020　09 84 32 13 21

La Féline
An edgy dive bar decorated with 1950s posters, home to regular rock shows and a local crowd.

Q5　6 Rue Victor Letalle 75020　lafelinebar.com

Les Trois 8
A wide range of artisan and international beer is the main draw at this trendy local watering hole.

Q5　11 Rue Victor Letalle 75002
lestrois8.fr

The ever-popular
La Maroquinerie rock, pop
and world music venue ↑

5 🏛

Marché de Belleville

📍P4 🅰Blvd de Belleville
75020 Ⓜ Belleville
🕐Tues & Fri 7am-2:30pm

Every Tuesday and Friday morning, the Belleville outdoor market comes alive, stretching from the Belleville Metro station to Couronnes. It dates back to the 19th century, when it was just a little market for the independent commune outside of Paris's wall, and is still a popular and inexpensive source of fresh produce for eastern Parisians. The stalls follow the seasons, with clementines in the winter, strawberries in the spring, and the best tomatoes in late summer. Some stalls sell odds and ends such as wine openers, French candy bars

and bags of olives – it's the place to stock up on anything and everything. Vendors yell out prices, pushing the foods that need to go. By the end of the market, they start selling large piles of produce for a euro, so there are true bargains to be had. The locals pile into the crowded market rain or shine, so be prepared to manoeuvre around caddies and Parisians arguing about bruised apples.

6

La Maroquinerie

📍R5 🅰23 Rue Boyer
75020 Ⓜ Ménilmontant,
Gambetta 🌐lamaro
quinerie.fr

True music fans will want to visit this former leather workshop turned concert

Did You Know?

The first ever telegraph was communicated from Ménilmontant in 1793.

venue. It's intimate, with a capacity of about 500, and has hosted some big names before they hit success. Bruno Mars and Mumford & Sons are just some of the acts who have played here. The bohemian-chic venue also has a restaurant with a constantly changing menu of French classics, and a terrace bar for drinking the night away. Book in advance for a wide range of musical productions, from pop to world music.

7

Notre-Dame-de-la-Croix

📍Q5 🅰3 Place
de Ménilmontant
75020 Ⓜ Ménilmontant,
Couronnes 🕐8am-7pm
🌐notredamedelacroix.com

Consecrated in 1863 under the reign of Napoleon III, this stunning church looms over Ménilmontant, built as the

NIGHTLIFE HOTSPOT

Both Belleville and Ménilmontant have historically been popular drinking locations with a reputation for being cheap and rowdy - labels that locals would defend proudly. Their former position just outside the tax wall meant that drinks were cheaper, so Parisians flocked to the *guinguettes* (taverns) that made these districts popular. Today the area is still known as inexpensive, whether it's for cheap Vietnamese food or drinks at Les Trois 8. Nightlife has evolved from *guinguettes* as well, and popular hotspots such as La Bellevilloise and La Maroquinerie keep the neighbourhood lively at night.

population of the area boomed. Its architecture is an odd mix of Romanesque and Gothic elements, with an enormous tower reaching 78 m (256 ft) high. In terms of size, it's actually the third-largest church in Paris after Notre-Dame and Saint-Sulpice.

This district was particularly caught up by the Paris Commune of 1871 when Parisians rose up against the government, which had been exiled to Versailles by Prussian forces. During this turbulent time the Communards, as the rebels were known, held meetings in Notre-Dame-de-la-Croix. It was here that they decided to execute the Archbishop, Georges Darboy, who had been taken hostage by the Communards, on 24 May at the prison on Rue de la Roquette (p107).

The church does not stir up much of this stormy history, but instead offers a splendid visit devoid of the tourists crushed into other monuments. Look out for the organ, constructed in two separate parts in order to avoid obstructing the rose window overhead. The church also has two significant artworks: *Christ in Limbo* (1819) by Pierre Delorme and *Christ Curing the Sick* (1827) by Jean-Pierre Granger.

EAT

Tin-Tin
A hole-in-the-wall Vietnamese eatery that never fails to produce great pho and bo bun.

📍 P4 🏠 17 Rue Louis Bonnet 75011 📞 01 43 55 50 13 🕒 Wed

€€€

Guo Xin
It's all about the dumplings here – cheap and delicious. Eat at tables packed together.

📍 Q5 🏠 47 Rue de Belleville 75019 📞 01 42 38 17 53

€€€

La Baratin
An institution; go to experience quintessentially meaty French fare.

📍 Q4 🏠 3 Rue Jouye-Rouve 75020 📞 01 43 49 39 70 🕒 Sun, Mon

€€€

---

8 ♿ 🍴

La Bellevilloise

📍 R5 🏠 19 Rue Boyer 75020 Ⓜ Ménilmontant, Gambetta 🌐 labelle villoise.com

Set up in 1877, this community art centre's original aim was to bring cultural education to less affluent Parisians. This spirit lives on in its numerous events, which include concerts – often jazz or Latin – and art exhibits, as well as freelancer fairs, vintage markets and the occasional jazz brunch. A standout feature is the Halle aux Olives, a glass atrium performance area with tables surrounded by an urban jungle of sorts.

→

The Neo-Romanesque façade of Notre-Dame-de-la-Croix

The soaring Neo-Gothic interior of Église Saint-Jean-Baptiste ↑

⑨

Église Saint-Jean-Baptiste

🏛 Q3 🏠 139 Rue de Belleville 75019 Ⓜ Jourdain ⏰ 8:15am-7:45pm daily (Mon 9:30am-8:30pm, Fri to 8:30pm) 🌐 sjbb.fr

As far as churches go, the Neo-Gothic Saint-Jean-Baptiste de Belleville flies under the radar of most people in Paris. Set high above the city in a vibrant district full of shops, it's an exciting find for architecture enthusiasts. Built to replace the original church dating back to the 1600s, the current structure was erected between 1854 and 1859. The architect, Jean-Baptiste Antoine Lassus, was a specialist in medieval architecture. He is largely responsible for bringing back Gothic themes in modern structures and participated heavily in the restorations of Notre-Dame and other monuments. Though a master in his craft, Lassus is often overlooked for the more famous Viollet-le-Duc, who lauded this structure after Lassus' death. It was, in fact, Lassus' final project. This church, with its twin bell towers and vaulted ceilings, evokes the grandeur and traditions of churches such as the Sainte-Chapelle (p74).

Stone carvings, Église Saint-Jean-Baptiste ↑

⑩ 🍴 📺 🏠

Jourdain Quartier

🏛 R4 🏠 75020 Ⓜ Jourdain

If you are looking to get away from the crowds but still get a taste of Parisian life, an afternoon wandering the Jourdain quarter is a perfect start. Sprawling out from the Neo-Gothic Saint-Jean-Baptiste church, the area has really come into its own. The central square, full of cafés and quintessentially Parisian shops – cheese here, meat there, pastries everywhere – is little visited by tourists; this is one of the rare districts of Paris that still retains a village feel. It might be towards the edge of the city, but it is a quick and easy trip on line 11 of the Metro from Hôtel de Ville in the centre. The nearby Parc des Buttes-Chaumont (p146) pairs nicely with a visit to Jourdain, as does a detour to Le Plateau on Rue des Alouettes, an industrial-white exhibition space run by Frac (the Fonds régional d'art contemporain, or regional collection of contemporary art). It displays modern art – including paintings, photography and everything in between – from its 1,600-piece collection. There's also occasional performance art.

⑪ Regard Saint-Martin

🔲 R4 🅰️ 42 Rue des Cascades 75020 Ⓜ️ Jourdain, Pyrénées

This curious little stone building on Rue des Cascades was once vital to ensuring medieval Parisians had clean drinking water. Known as a *regard* – or, essentially, a manhole – it was part of a system to collect rainwater from the hilly area of Belleville and channel it to the fountains of Paris below. The water of the Seine was infamously dirty, polluted by the mix of sewage and chemicals from tanners flowing into it. These stone structures provided fresh water before the 19th-century canals were constructed. Renovated in the 17th century (as a plaque in Latin on the building testifies), but dating from the 12th century, the Regard Saint-Martin still functions, except that nowadays the water makes it no further than the sewers.

⑫ La Campagne à Paris

🔲 T5 🅰️ Rue du Père-Prosper-Enfantin, Rue Irénée Blanc, Rue Mondonville, Rue Jules Siegfried 75020 Ⓜ️ Porte de Bagnolet

This former housing estate is one of the most picturesque parts of Paris, with stone-fronted houses lining the cobbled streets. La Campagne, literally "the countryside", feels exactly like that. A pastor, Sully Lombard, conceived of the development in 1907 for lower-income Parisians. Built on top of an old gypsum quarry and completed well after World War I, the 90-odd houses stood out from the rest of Paris's architecture. Brick façades, creeping ivy and wisteria, and tiny gated gardens full of roses and clematis adorn the two-storey houses. These provincial-looking cobbled streets offer some splendid photo opportunities and are a wonderful oasis of calm away from the bustle of urban Paris.

One of the pretty village-like streets that make up La Campagne à Paris →

The Philharmonie de Paris, designed by Jean Nouvel

LA VILLETTE

A Gallo-Roman town once stood in this area, which subsequently became home to religious workers at a nearby leper colony. It remained an agricultural hamlet beyond the city wall for many years, but gained attention when Napoleon began his canal project here. The district formally joined Paris in 1859. La Villette is best known for its large 19th-century slaughterhouses, constructed under Napoleon III. The giant halls replaced those in five other locations in Paris, centralizing the city's meat industry. By the 1970s, the slaughterhouses had ceased operations and the mayor decided to revive the area with a new park. Designed in the 1980s, Paris's third-largest green space evokes post-modern and deconstructive concepts, with standout cultural centres like Europe's largest science museum and the Philharmonie de Paris, designed by Jean Nouvel. Outside the park there are theatres and art centres to explore, as well as another of Paris's most iconic green spaces, the Buttes Chaumont.

LA VILLETTE

Must Sees
1. Parc de la Villette
2. Cité des Sciences et de l'Industrie

Experience More
3. Parc des Buttes-Chaumont
4. Cinéma Quai de la Loire and Quai de Seine
5. Philharmonie de Paris
6. Cabaret Sauvage
7. La Grande Halle de la Villette
8. Le 104

Eat
1. La Rotonde
2. Le 25 Degrés Est
3. Chez Mezig

Drink
4. Pont Éphémère
5. Paname Brewing Company
6. Le Pavillon Puebla

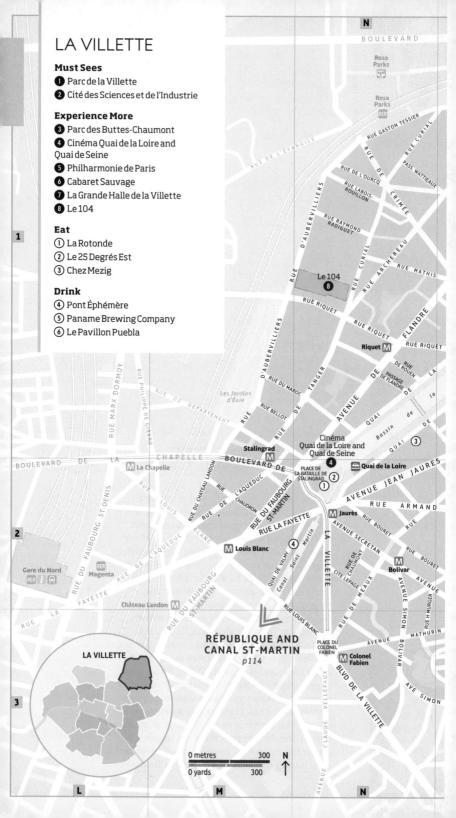

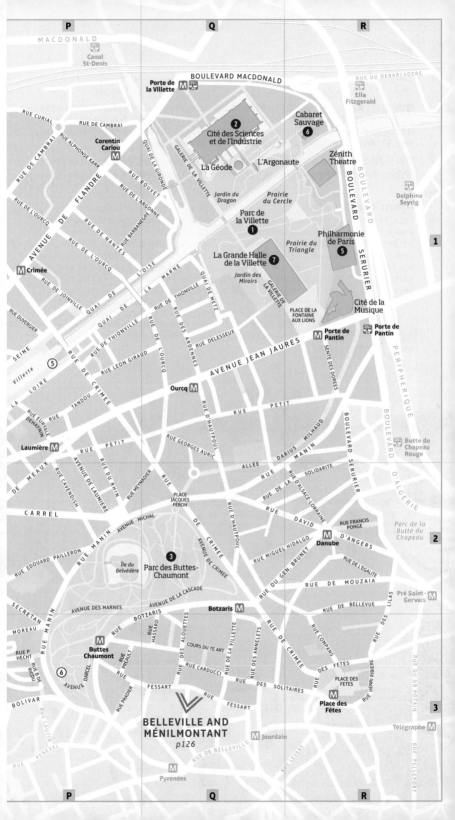

❶ 🖥

PARC DE LA VILLETTE

📍Q1 🏠211 Ave Jean Jaurès 75019 Ⓜ Porte de Pantin, Porte de la Villette 🚌75, 139, 150, 152, 375 🚊T3b 🕐Public spaces: 24 hrs daily; gardens: May-Sep: 3-7pm Sat & Sun (Oct-Mar: by reservation only); Jardin des Vents et des Dunes: 10am-8pm daily (Nov-Mar: only Wed, Sat & Sun, plus public and school holidays) 🌐lavillette.com

This inventive urban park offers an appealing combination of nature and modern architecture, containing gardens, playgrounds and a variety of cultural spaces.

Urban Regeneration

Once home to slaughterhouses and a livestock market, this former industrial area has been transformed into a vibrant urban park. Designed by Bernard Tschumi, its vast facilities cover 55 ha (136 acres) of a previously run-down part of the city. The plan was to revive the tradition of parks for meetings and activities, and to stimulate interest in the arts and sciences. Work began in 1984, and the park has grown to include the Cité des Sciences et de l'Industrie – a high-tech hands-on science museum (p144) – a cutting-edge concert hall, an exhibition pavilion, a spherical cinema, a circus and a music centre. Linking them all is the park itself, Paris's third largest, with its follies, walkways, gardens and playgrounds. In the summer, the park holds several festivals, including an open-air film one.

10 million
people visit Parc de la Villette every year.

OPEN-AIR FILM FESTIVAL

Each summer the park hosts the free Festival de Cinéma en Plein Air *(p59)*, screening a mix of French and international films in the open air every evening for a month. Deckchairs and blankets are available for hire, and many people bring their own picnic to make an evening of it.

↑ Taking time out in the sunshine in front of the park's striking red café

The view from the rooftop
↓ of the Philharmonie de Paris concert hall *(p147)*

Le grand récit d

CITÉ DES SCIENCES ET DE L'INDUSTRIE

Q1 **30 Ave Corentin Cariou 75019** **Porte de la Villette**
75, 139, 150, 152, 375 **T3b** **10am–6pm Tue–Sat, 10am–7pm Sun**
1 Jan, 1 May, 25 Dec **cite-sciences.fr**

Located within the Parc de la Villette, the Cité des Sciences et de l'Industrie is an interactive science and technology museum that is hugely popular with families.

The museum occupies the largest of the old Villette slaughterhouses. Architect Adrien Fainsilber has created an imaginative interplay of light, vegetation and water in the high-tech, five-storey building, which soars 40 m (133 ft) high, stretching over 3 ha (7 acres). At the museum's heart is the Explora exhibit, a fascinating guide to the worlds of science and technology. Visitors can take part in computerized games on space, the earth, transport, energy, design and sound. On other levels, there is a children's science city with machines to play and experiment with, a planetarium, a library and shops.

3

greenhouses on the front
of the museum link the
building to the park.

Quelles loi
pour l'Univ

Univers – entrée

↑ The Story of the Universe, taking
visitors back 13.7 billion years to
the creation of the first atom

↑ The museum building, encircled by a moat
and joined to the park via raised walkways

← Youngsters
observing
plants and
insects in the
garden of
the children's
science city

LA GÉODE

Fittingly for a building
that looks as if its
from the set of a sci-fi
movie, this Adrien
Fainsilber-designed
sphere houses a cinema
showing IMAX and 3D
films. The enormous
1,000 sq m (11,000 sq ft)
screen provides a truly
immersive experience.

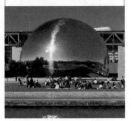

EXPERIENCE MORE

3 🍴

Parc des Buttes-Chaumont

📍 Q2 🚪 Rue Manin 75019 (main access from Rue Armand Carrel) Ⓜ Botzaris, Buttes-Chaumont ⏰ 7am–8pm daily (open 24 hrs in summer)

For many, this is the most pleasant and unexpected park in the city. The panoramic hilly site was formerly a gallows for the execution of criminals, a lime

---

🔍 **HIDDEN GEM**
Rosa Bonheur

Named after a 19th-century artist, Rosa Bonheur is a popular *guinguette* in the Parc des Buttes-Chaumont. It's a bucolic spot for a glass of wine and tapas, and on Sunday nights it's a popular LGBT venue.

---

quarry and a rubbish dump. It was converted in the mid-1860s, one of Napoleon III's many projects to renovate the city. Baron Haussmann worked with the landscape architect/designer Adolphe Alphand, who organized a vast programme to furnish the new pavement-lined avenues with benches and lampposts. Others involved in the creation of this large park were the engineer Darcel and the landscape gardener Barillet-Deschamps. They created a lake, made an island with real and artificial rocks, gave it a Roman-style classical temple (the Temple de la Sibylle, modelled after the Temple of Sybil in Tivoli, Italy) and also added a waterfall, streams, and two footbridges to connect the island to the park. Today, visitors will also find boating facilities.

→ The romantic Parc des Buttes-Chaumont

4 🛹 🍴 🖥 🛍

Cinéma Quai de la Loire and Quai de Seine

📍 N2 🚪 7 Quai de la Loire & 14 Quai de la Seine 75019 Ⓜ Stalingrad, Jaurès 🌐 mk2.com

These two cinemas on opposite banks of the canal basin are popular hangouts during the evenings. Neighbouring cafés and bars fill with cinephiles who are waiting to see the latest release. The cinemas screen a large selection of French and international movies that cater to both art-house and blockbuster crowds, sometimes showing

↑ Views from the Temple in Parc des Buttes-Chaumont

The state-of-the-art interior of the new Paris Philharmonic concert hall ↑

Hollywood pictures before their US release. When buying a ticket, note which cinema your film is in; if it's on the opposite bank, a water shuttle will carry you across the canal. Bear in mind that international films are shown in VO *(version originale)* or VF *(version française)*. If you don't want to watch a film dubbed into French buy tickets for the VO version. Afterwards, you could join a game of *pétanque* along the canal, just next to the cinema, where Parisians while away their evenings.

Philharmonie de Paris

R1 **221 Ave Jean Jaurès 75019** **Porte de Pantin** **noon-6pm (from 10am Sat & Sun)** **Mon** **philharmoniedeparis.fr**

Built in 2015, the futuristic Philharmonie, designed by French architect Jean Nouvel, rises above Parc de la Villette like a silver spaceship. The main concert hall seats up to 3,650 people, depending on the configuration and the placement of floating balconies. The idea is that spectators are never further than 32 m (105 ft) from the conductor, creating a more immersive, intimate experience. The building went well over budget – more than double the expected €170 million – causing quite a scandal. Still, the hall's inaugural concert, held in honour of the victims of that year's *Charlie Hebdo* attacks was well attended, with patrons including then-president François Hollande.

The Philharmonie caters mostly to symphonic concerts, but also hosts jazz and world music performances. It houses cultural centres and exhibition halls, as well as smaller concert halls. Visitors can book a concert or just pop into one of its two restaurants for a meal with views over the park. The Philharmonie offers guided tours, with bookings available through their website. Smaller-scale concerts are also held at the neighbouring Cité de la Musique, designed in 1995 by Christian de Portzamparc and now rechristened Philharmonie 2.

> **Built in 2015, the futuristic Philharmonie, designed by French architect Jean Nouvel, rises above Parc de la Villette like a silver spaceship.**

EAT

La Rotonde
Part of Paris's last great peripherary wall, this lovely classical-style rotonda is now a great stop for afternoon or evening drinks.

N2 **6-8 Place de la Bataille de Stalingrad 75019** **grandmarche stalingrad.com**

€€€

Le 25 Degrés Est
With a terrace overlooking the canal, this laid-back bar-restaurant attracts sun-seekers in the summer.

N2 **10 Place de la Bataille de Stalingrad 75019** **25est.com**

€€€

Chez Mezig
Located on the canal, this local joint, with adorably mismatched furniture, serves up reliable, standard fare.

N1 **44 bis Quai de la Loire 75019** **09 81 42 98 14**

€€€

The rooftop of Jean Nouvel's Philharmonie de Paris

↑ The Fontaine aux Lions in front of La Grande Halle de la Villette

 6

Cabaret Sauvage

📍R1 🏠59 Blvd Macdonald 75019 Ⓜ Porte de la Villette ⓦ cabaret sauvage.com

On the bank of the canal, just before leaving Paris's city limits, a curious venue stands all by itself in the Parc de la Villette. Opened in 1997, the Cabaret Sauvage is an entertainment venue unlike any other in Paris. Algerian-born Méziane Azaïche created the space, which welcomes all sorts of up-and-coming and little-known artists. Concerts and shows range from contemporary acrobatic and circus displays to dance and West African musical performances, and international artists such as Redman, Mos Def and Noel Gallagher have played here over the years. The structure itself is entirely unassuming on the outside. Once inside the red velour draping, however, spectators cannot help but be drawn into the Cabaret Sauvage's unqiue circus-ring atmosphere. Tickets are available in advance for all the different shows, with 600 seated places and 1,200 spots for events where audiences stand. A night out at the Cabaret Sauvage is sure to be as memorable as it is individual.

7

La Grande Halle de la Villette

📍Q1 🏠211 Ave Jean Jaurès 75019 Ⓜ Porte de Pantin ⓦ lavillette.com

A former slaughterhouse, this massive hall is one of three that were once in this part of La Villette. In the 19th century, Haussmann decided it would be easier to concentrate all of the meat industry in one spot. Eventually, and perhaps unsurprisingly, the area gained the nickname "City of Blood". In the 1980s the veal hall was destroyed while the sheep hall was

---

BASSIN DE LA VILLETTE

The Bassin de la Villette hosts activities all year. Join Parisians, both young and old, in a game of *pétanque* on the banks, or try your hand at Mölkky, a Finnish game with wooden pins. The canal is popular with locals for rowing, but visitors can also hit the water by renting a motorboat from the Marin d'Eau Douce. A Paris Plage (beach) is set up here in July and August, and includes swimming and boating. The most popular activity, however, is picnicking. Head here early, especially in the summer, to secure a space along the waterfront.

> **Once inside the red velour draping, however, spectators cannot help but be drawn into the Cabaret Sauvage's unqiue circus-ring atmosphere.**

deconstructed in hopes of rebuilding it elsewhere. President Mitterrand preserved this iron beauty, used for slaughtering cows for beef, and today it houses an event space. Concerts, plays, exhibitions and other events take place regularly. Drop into the café/restaurant for a coffee or meal; it has an inviting garden area for when the weather is fair.

Le 104

📍 **N1** 🏠 **5 Rue Curial 75019** Ⓜ **Riquet, Stalingrad** 🕐 **Noon-7pm** 🚫 **Mon** 🌐 **104.fr.**

It might not be obvious upon entering, but this art centre was originally built by the Parisian Archbishop in 1874 for funeral services. It housed a coffin warehouse, stables for horses and shops where individuals could purchase decorations for tombs. Eventually the hearses of the 20th century disappeared when the public sector lost its monopoly on conducting funeral services. The space, however, underwent a renaissance. The vast hall, with iron beams and a glass roof, was slowly transformed into Le 104 (or Le Centquatre), an artists' residence and exhibition space. The centre is an excellent example of urban renewal in a city skilled at repurposing its historic structures. The mayor inaugurated the space in 2008, and the city still funds the majority of its costs. Today there are performances, concerts and art shows year-round, open to the public. Visitors can see artists at work experimenting with different media. Le Centquatre is quickly becoming a major player on the art scene among local and international artists: it has hosted exhibitions dedicated to well-known contemporary artists such as Keith Haring and Krijn de Koning.

DRINK

Point Éphémère
Part concert hall, part drinking venue. There are often special nights with food trucks or other pop-ups.

📍 **N2** 🏠 **200 Quai de Valmy 75010** 🌐 **pointephemere.org.**

Paname Brewing Company
Perched on the canal in an old warehouse; local craft beers are the favourite here.

📍 **P1** 🏠 **41 bis Quai de la Loire 75019** 🌐 **panamebrewing company.com.**

Le Pavillon Puebla
Nestled in the greenery of Parc des Buttes-Chaumont, this is a peaceful oasis with a mix of Moroccan and modern touches.

📍 **P3** 🏠 **39 Avenue Simon Bolivar 75019** 🌐 **leperchoir.tv**

A cobbled street leading to Montmartre's Sacré-Coeur

MONTMARTRE AND PIGALLE

Once a separate village outside Paris, Montmartre was formerly a rural district dotted with windmills and vineyards. Following its incorporation into the city limits in 1860, it swiftly transformed into an urban neighbourhood that was popular with the working classes for its low-cost housing. By the end of the 19th century, this bohemian area had a reputation for decadence and free living, which turned it into a magnet for artists, writers and intellectuals. The still-standing Bateau-Lavoir was a shared studio and home to artists like Matisse, Picasso and Modigliani. Montmartre's reputation for depravity stemmed in large part from its numerous dance halls, among them the infamous Moulin Rouge, said to have been the birthplace of the cancan dance. Although some of the entertainment has taken on a seedier character, Montmartre and Pigalle are still popular nightlife destinations, with numerous lively bars and restaurants.

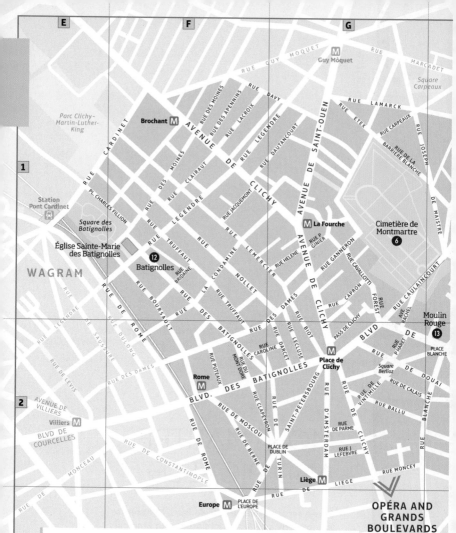

MONTMARTRE AND PIGALLE

Must See
1 Sacré-Coeur

Experience More
2 St-Pierre de Montmartre
3 Place du Tertre
4 St-Jean l'Evangéliste de Montmartre
5 Place des Abbesses
6 Cimetière de Montmartre
7 Espace Dalí Montmartre
8 Musée de Montmartre
9 Moulin de la Galette
10 Au Lapin Agile
11 Halle Saint-Pierre
12 Batignolles
13 Moulin Rouge
14 Musée de la Vie Romantique
15 Rue des Martyrs

Eat
1 Un Zèbre à Montmartre
2 Le Pantruche
3 Restaurant Caillebotte

Stay
4 Hôtel Amour
5 Le Pigalle
6 Hôtel Particulier Montmartre

Shop
7 Maison Arnaud Demontel
8 Mesdemoiselles Madeleine
9 Poppelini
10 Henri Le Roux

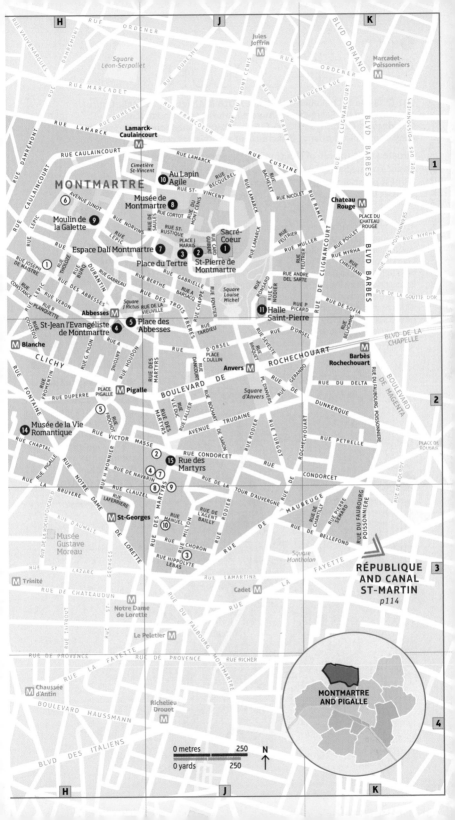

① ⊗ ⑪

SACRÉ-COEUR

⑨ J1 **⌂** 33 Rue du Chevalier-de-la-Barre 75018 **Ⓜ** Abbesses (then take funicular to the steps of the Sacré-Coeur), Anvers, Barbès-Rochechouart, Lamarck-Caulaincourt **🚌** 30, 31, 54, 80, 85 **⊘** 6am–10:30pm daily; dome: 9:30–5pm daily (May-Sep: 9am-8pm daily) **🖥** sacre-coeur-montmartre.com

Situated atop the hill of Montmartre, the spectacular white basilica of the Sacré-Coeur watches over Paris from the city's highest point. It stands as a memorial to the 58,000 French soldiers killed during the Franco-Prussian War.

At the outbreak of the Franco-Prussian War in 1870, two Catholic businessmen made a private religious vow to build a church dedicated to the Sacred Heart of Christ, should France be spared the impending Prussian onslaught. The two men, Alexandre Legentil and Hubert Rohault de Fleury, lived to see Paris saved from invasion despite the war and a lengthy siege – and were able to witness the start of work on the Sacré-Coeur basilica. The project was taken up by Archbishop Guibert of Paris and construction began in 1875 to Paul Abadie's designs, which were inspired by the Romano-Byzantine church of St-Front in Périgueux. The basilica was completed in 1914, but its consecration was forestalled by World War I until 1919, when France was victorious.

THE SIEGE OF PARIS

Prussia invaded France in 1870. During the four-month siege of Paris, instigated by the Prusso-German statesman Otto von Bismarck, hungry Parisians were forced to eat the city's horses and other animals.

Spiral staircase

Ovoid dome

Bell tower

Statue of Christ

Equestrian statues

Main entrance

↑ The 83-m- (272-ft-) high basilica

Crypt vaults

PICTURE PERFECT
The Basilica and the City

The best view of the Sacré-Coeur is from the gardens below, but for a 360-degree panorama of the city, climb the 300 steps to the top of the basilica dome.

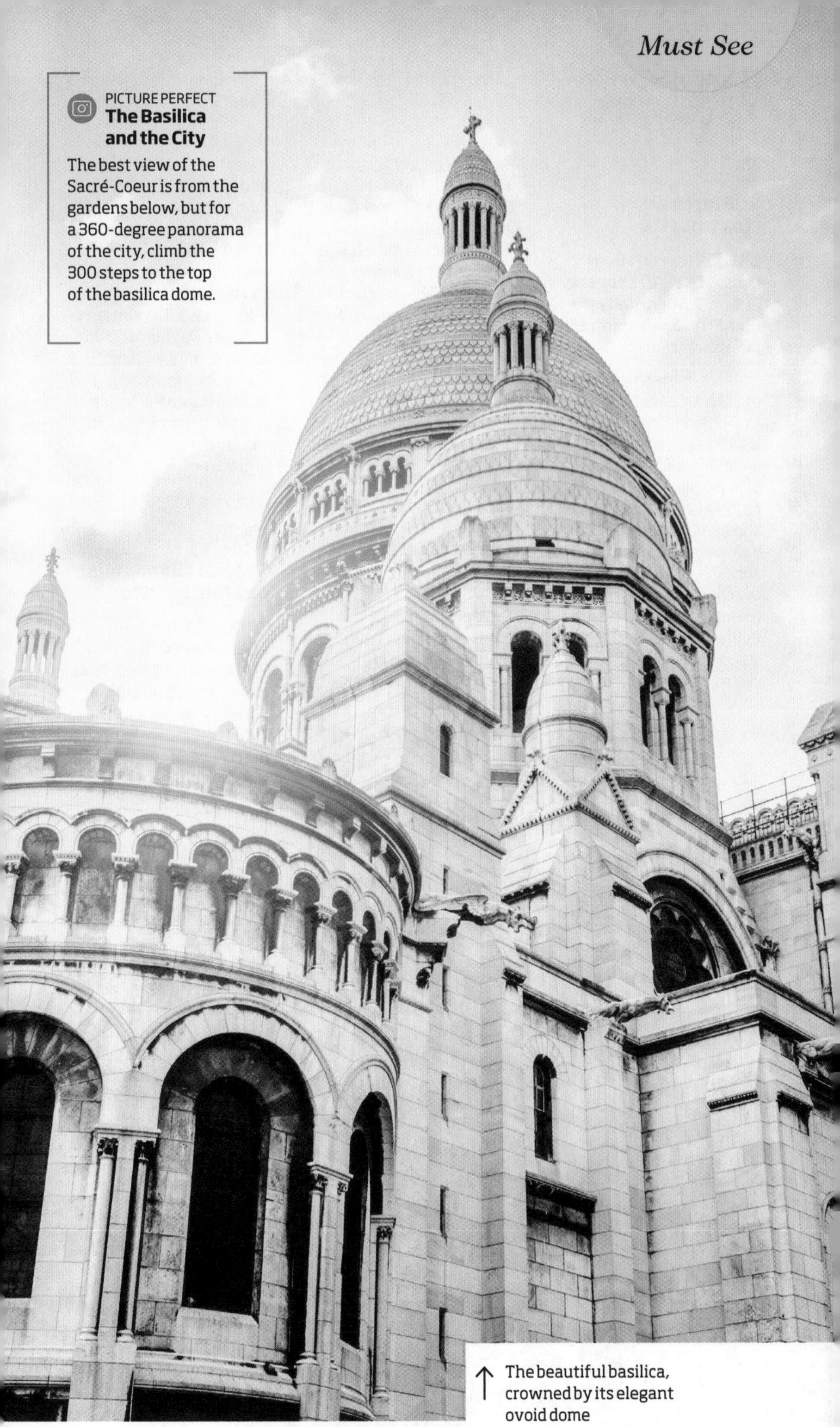

↑ The beautiful basilica, crowned by its elegant ovoid dome

EXPERIENCE MORE

② St-Pierre de Montmartre

📍J1 🏠2 Rue du Mont-Cenis 75018 Ⓜ Abbesses 🕐9am–7:30pm daily (to 6pm Fri) 🌐saintpierrede montmartre.net

Situated in the shadow of the Sacré-Coeur basilica, St-Pierre de Montmartre is all that remains of the great Benedictine Abbey of Montmartre, which was founded in 1133 by Louis VI and his wife, Adelaide of Savoy, who – as its first abbess – is buried here. Inside the church are four marble columns supposedly from a Roman temple which once stood on the site. The vaulted choir dates from the 12th century, the nave was remodelled in the 15th century and the west front in the 18th. During the Revolution, the abbess was executed by guillotine, and the church fell into disuse. St-Pierre was reconsecrated in 1908. Gothic-style stained-glass windows replace those destroyed by a bomb in World War II. The tiny cemetery opens to the public only once a year, on 1 November.

---

③ Place du Tertre

📍J1 🏠75018 Ⓜ Abbesses

Tertre means "hillock", or mound, and this picturesque square is the highest point in Paris at 130 m (430 ft).

The church of St-Pierre de Montmartre

It was once the site of the abbey gallows but is associated with artists, who began exhibiting paintings here in the 19th century. It is lined with colourful restaurants – La Mère Catherine dates back to 1793. The house at No. 21 was formerly the home of the irreverent "Free Commune", founded in 1920 to perpetuate the bohemian spirit of the area. The Old Montmartre information office is now here.

---

④ St-Jean l'Évangéliste de Montmartre

📍H2 🏠19 Rue des Abbesses 75018 Ⓜ Abbesses 🕐9am–7pm Mon–Sat; 9:30am–6pm Sun (to 7pm summer) 🌐saintjeandemont martre.com

Designed by Anatole de Baudot and completed in 1904, this church was, controversially, the first to be built from reinforced concrete. The flower motifs on the interior are typical of the Art Nouveau style, while its interlocking arches suggest Islamic architecture. The red-brick facing has earned it the nickname St-Jean-des-Briques.

---

⑤ Place des Abbesses

📍H2 🏠75018 Ⓜ Abbesses

This is one of Paris's most picturesque squares. It is sandwiched between the rather dubious attractions of Place Pigalle, with its strip clubs, and Place du Tertre, which is mobbed by hundreds of tourists. Be sure not to miss the Abbesses Metro station with its unusual green wrought-iron arches and

→ The lively Place du Tertre with its many restaurants

amber lights. Designed by the architect Hector Guimard, it is one of the few surviving original Art Nouveau stations.

6

Cimetière de Montmartre

📍 G1 🏠 20 Ave Rachel 75018 📞 01 53 42 36 30 Ⓜ️ Place de Clichy, Blanche 🕐 8am–6pm Mon–Fri, 8:30am–6pm Sat, 9am–6pm Sun; to 5:30pm in winter

This has been the resting place for many artistic luminaries since the beginning of the 19th century. The composers Hector Berlioz and Jacques Offenbach (who wrote the famous cancan tune) are buried here, alongside many other celebrities, such as La Goulue (stage name of Louise Weber, the cancan's first star performer and Toulouse-Lautrec's model), the painter Edgar Degas, writer Alexandre Dumas, German poet Heinrich Heine,

Russian dancer Vaslav Nijinsky and film director François Truffaut. Cimetière de Montmartre is an evocative, atmospheric place, conveying some of the heated energy and artistic creativity of the area a century ago.

Nearby, close to Square Roland Dorgelès, is the often overlooked **Cimetière St-Vincent**. Here lie more of the great artistic names of the district, including Swiss composer Arthur Honegger and writer Marcel Aymé. Most notable of all is the grave of the great French painter Maurice Utrillo, one of the few famous Montmartre artists actually born in the area and many of whose works afford some of the most enduring, evocative images of the district.

Cimetière St-Vincent

🏠 6 Rue Lucien-Gaulard 75018 📞 01 46 06 29 78 Ⓜ️ Lamarck-Caulaincourt 🕐 8am–6pm Mon–Fri, 8:30am–6pm Sat, 9am–6pm Sun; to 5:30pm in winter

---

> **Cimetière de Montmartre is an evocative, atmospheric place, conveying some of the heated energy and artistic creativity of the area a century ago.**

EAT

Un Zèbre à Montmartre

This is a great go-to for a lunchtime *croque monsieur* or an evening salmon tartare.

📍 H1 🏠 38 Rue Lepic 75018 Ⓦ zebreamontmartre.fr

€€€

Le Pantruche

A hand-written menu is always a good sign; here they serve French classics with fun twists.

📍 J2 🏠 3 Rue Victor Massé 75009 📞 01 48 78 55 60

€€€

Restaurant Caillebotte

Lunchtime specials are a steal at this little modern bistro, owned by the team behind *Le Pantruche* (above).

📍 J3 🏠 8 Rue Hippolyte Lebas 75009 📞 01 53 20 88 70 🚫 Sat, Sun

€€€

→

The Moulin de la Galette, one of two windmills that can still be seen in Montmartre

STAY

Hôtel Amour

Lively and contemporary, but always with a romantic undertone.

📍 J2 🏠 8 Rue de Navarin 75009
🌐 hotelamourparis.fr

€€€

Le Pigalle

Rooms are decorated with a tasteful play on the former Red Light district surroundings. Great breakfast and restaurant downstairs.

📍 H2 🏠 9 Rue Frochot 75009 🌐 lepigalle.paris

€€€

Hôtel Particulier Montmartre

Suites in this 19th-century mansion are ideally located for exploring the Montmartre and Pigalle districts.

📍 H1 🏠 23 Ave Junot 75018
🌐 hotel-particulier-montmartre.com

€€€

---

7 ⬦ 🛍️

Espace Dalí Montmartre

📍 J1 🏠 11 Rue Poulbot 75018 Ⓜ Abbesses
🕐 10am-6pm daily (to 8pm Jul-Aug) 🌐 daliparis.com

A permanent exhibition of 330 works by the prolific painter and sculptor Salvador Dalí is displayed here in the heart of Montmartre. Inside, the vast, dark setting reflects the dramatic character of this 20th-century genius, as moving lights grace first one, then another, of his Surrealist works to a soundtrack of Dalí's recorded voice. This fascinating museum also houses a commercial art gallery, a library and a shop selling books, prints and postcards.

---

8 ⬦ 🍽️ 🖥️ 🛍️

Musée de Montmartre

📍 J1 🏠 12 Rue Cortot 75018 Ⓜ Abbesses, Anvers 🕐 10am-6pm daily (to 7pm Apr-Sep) 🌐 museedemontmartre.fr

During the 17th century, this charming home belonged to the actor Rose de Rosimond (Claude de la Rose), a member of Molière's theatre company. From 1875, the big white house, undoubtedly the finest in Montmartre, provided living and studio space for artists, including Maurice Utrillo and

his mother Suzanne Valadon, a former acrobat and model who became a talented painter, as well as Raoul Dufy and Auguste Renoir.

The museum recounts the history of Montmartre through artifacts, drawings and photographs. It is particularly rich in memorabilia of bohemian life, and has a reconstruction of the Café de l'Abreuvoir, Utrillo's favourite watering hole. Valdon's studio-apartment was renovated and opened to the public in 2014, as was the Hôtel Demarne, which stages temporary exhibitions on Montmartre themes.

9

Moulin de la Galette

📍 H1 🏠 T-junction at Rue Tholozé and Rue Lepic 75018 Ⓜ Lamarck-Caulaincourt, Abbesses

Once, some 14 windmills dotted the Montmartre skyline and were used for grinding wheat and pressing grapes. Today, only two remain, both on Rue Lepic: the Radet, now above a restaurant confusingly named Moulin de la Galette, and the reconstructed Moulin de la Galette, originally built in 1622 and formerly known as the Blute-fin. One of its mill owners, Debray, was supposedly crucified on one of the windmill's sails during the 1814 Siege of Paris. He had been trying to repulse the invading Cossacks. At the end of the 19th century, both mills became famous dance halls providing inspiration for many artists, notably Pierre-Auguste Renoir and Vincent van Gogh.

The steep Rue Lepic is a busy shopping area. The Impressionist painter Armand Guillaumin once lived on the first floor of No. 54. Van Gogh inhabited its third floor, and painted the view from there.

10

Au Lapin Agile

📍 2 F5 🏠 22 Rue des Saules 75018 Ⓜ Lamarck-Caulaincourt 🕐 9pm–1am Tue–Sun 🌐 au-lapin-agile.com

The former Cabaret des Assassins derived its current name from a sign painted by the humorist André Gill. His picture of a rabbit escaping from a cooking pot *(Le Lapin à Gill)* is a pun on his own name. The club enjoyed popularity with intellectuals and artists at the start of the 20th century. Here in 1911,

the novelist Roland Dorgelès and a group of other regulars staged one of the modern art world's most celebrated hoaxes, with the help of the café owner's donkey, Lolo. A paintbrush was tied to Lolo's tail, and the resulting daub was shown to critical acclaim at the Salon des Indépendants, under the enlightening title *Sunset over the Adriatic*, before the joke was revealed.

In 1903, the premises were bought by the cabaret entrepreneur Aristide Bruand (painted in a series of posters by Toulouse-Lautrec). Years later, the cabaret venue manages to retain much of its original atmosphere.

11

Halle Saint-Pierre

📍 J1 🏠 2 Rue Ronsard 75018 Ⓜ Anvers 🕐 10am–6pm Mon–Fri, 11am–7pm Sat, noon–6pm Sun 🚫 1 Jan, 1 May, 14 July, Aug, 25 Dec 🌐 hallesaintpierre.org

In 1945, the French painter Jean Dubuffet developed the concept of *Art Brut* (Outsider

or Marginal Art) to describe works created outside the boundaries of "official" culture, often by psychiatric patients, prisoners and children. The Halle Saint-Pierre, at the foot of the Butte, is a museum and gallery devoted to these "raw" art forms. It also hosts avant-garde theatre and musical productions, holds regular literary evenings and debates and runs children's workshops. In addition to temporary exhibitions, the permanent collection includes more than 500 works of Naïve art collected by the publisher Max Fourny in the 1970s. There is also a specialist bookshop and café.

↑ Suzanne Valadon's studio-apartment at the Musée de Montmartre

The stunning view from the Sacré-Coeur in Montmartre

⑫ Batignolles

🚩F1 🚇75007 Ⓜ Place de Clichy, Rome, Brochant

Formerly used as a royal hunting ground, this neighbourhood in the 17th arrondissement of northwestern Paris later grew into a small hamlet. Although it officially became part of the city in the second half of the 19th century, it still feels like a small French village inside cosmopolitan Paris. In the 19th century, the area had a lively cultural vibe and counted among its residents the painter Edouard Manet and his fellow artists (who became known as the Groupe des Batignolles), the writer Émile Zola and, later, the Belgian singer Jacques Brel.

The lovely church of Sainte-Marie des Batignolles sits in the heart of the neighbourhood. While Batignolles has a calm, community feel, it also has a slightly urban atmosphere, with a good mix of well-frequented bars, stylish boutiques and restaurants. It was one of the first areas in Paris to label its up-and-coming class of residents *bobos*, a short-hand term for "bourgeois bohemians".

Two markets are held in the area: the organic Marché Biologique des Batignolles on Boulevard des Batignolles and the covered market on Rue Lemercier, which dates back to 1846. At weekends, families converge on the area's several parks, the two largest being the Square des Batignolles

Did You Know?

The Pigalle district was dubbed "Pig Alley" by Allied troops after WWII because of its bawdy nightlife.

and the Parc Clichy – Martin-Luther-King, which features playgrounds, duck ponds, a skate park and running trails. The district has undergone substantial development in recent years, and there are modern flats, shops and office buildings, including the new Paris law courts.

⑬ Moulin Rouge

🚩H2 🏠82 Blvd de Clichy 75018 Ⓜ Blanche ⏰Dinner: 7pm; shows: 9pm and 11pm daily 🌐moulinrouge.fr

Built in 1885, the Moulin Rouge was turned into a dance hall as early as 1900. The cancan originated in Montparnasse, in the polka gardens of the Rue de la Grande-Chaumière, but it will always be associated with the Moulin Rouge, where the wild and colourful dance shows were immortalized in the posters and drawings of Henri de Toulouse-Lautrec. The high-kicking routines of famous "Doriss girls" such as Yvette Guilbert and Jane Avril continue

↑ The Moulin Rouge, an iconic symbol of Parisian nightlife

today in a glittering, Las Vegas-style revue that includes sophisticated light shows and displays of magic.

⑭ Musée de la Vie Romantique

🚩H2 🏠16 Rue Chaptal 75009 Ⓜ Blanche, Pigalle ⏰9am–5pm Tue–Sun 🌐museevieromantique. paris.fr

This quaint, tiny 19th-century house was once home to Ary Scheffer, the portrait painter of the monarch during the Bourbon Restoration. Here, the artist welcomed great cultural icons of the mid-1800s, including Eugène Delacroix and Charles Dickens. Now a museum, the house displays 19th-century paintings, and artifacts that

---

MONTMARTRE'S WINDMILLS

Windmills were common in Montmartre in the late 19th century, when the area was still essentially a village. As the city began to consume the local farmland, proprietors turned their nearly defunct windmills into entertainment venues such as the Moulin de la Galette *(p160)*. The most famous windmill, the Moulin Rouge, pays homage to these parties, though it was never actually a functional windmill itself.

SHOP

Maison Arnaud Demontel

Come for exquisite bread and pastries from this award-winning bakery.

📍 J2 🏠 39 Rue des Martyrs 🌐 arnaud-demontel.com

Mesdemoiselles Madeleine

It's all about multiple varieties of the madeleines here.

📍 J3 🏠 37 Rue des Martyrs 🌐 mllesmadeleines.com

Poppelini

Cream-filled choux and nothing else – well, what else is there?

📍 J3 🏠 44 Rue des Martyrs 🌐 popelini.com

Henri Le Roux

Salted-butter caramels and chocolate fill this boutique.

📍 J3 🏠 24 Rue des Martyrs 🌐 chocolatleroux.com

belonged to celebrated author George Sand, as well as her lover Frédéric Chopin. Sand was a prolific writer and critic of the populist uprising known as the Commune. She also famously wore men's clothes in public and smoked tobacco, unlike most women of the time. The museum has a lovely garden café.

destinations adored by Parisians and visitors alike: pastry shops, restaurants, cafés, and even a boutique dedicated to salted butter caramel. A few recognizable brands pop up here and there, but overall the street is one of the most individual and fashionable in Paris.

15 🍴 🥤 🛍️

Rue des Martyrs

📍 J2 🏠 75009
Ⓜ Pigalle

This quintessentially Parisian street owes its name to Saint Denis, who was martyred nearby. Rue des Martyrs retains much of the local, market-street vibe that has been lost in many similar locations in Paris. The street is full of tried-and-tested

The pretty garden café at the Musée de la Vie Romantique ↑

A SHORT WALK
MONTMARTRE

Distance 1.5 km (1 mile) **Nearest metro** Abbesses
Time 20 minutes

The steep hill of Montmartre has proved a draw for Parisians and visitors for centuries. Artists Théodore Géricault and Camille Corot came here at the start of the 19th century, and in the 20th century Maurice Utrillo immortalized the streets in his works. Today, this picturesque district, which in places still preserves the atmosphere of pre-war Paris, is a perfect place to wander. A stop at the Place du Tertre is recommended: admire the works of street artists and relax with a coffee and pastry before heading back down the hill.

Au Lapin Agile, a rustic café and cabaret, was a popular meeting point for artists including Picasso (p161).

Musée de Montmartre features the work of artists who lived in the area. Look out for the Portrait of a Woman (1918), by the Italian painter and sculptor Amedeo Modigliani (p160).

Clos Montmartre is one of the last surviving vineyards in Paris. The grape harvest is celebrated on the first Saturday in October.

Metro Lamarck Caulaincourt

RUE ST-VINCENT

RUE DE L'ABREUVOIR

RUE DES SAULES

RUE CORTOT

RUE ST-RUSTIQUE

RUE LEPIC

PL J B CLEMENT

RUE NORVINS

RUE POULBOT

RUE DE LA MIRE

RUE RAVIGNAN

RUE GABRIELLE

RUE DREVET

RUE BERTHE

RUE DES TROIS FRERES

The Espace Dalí Montmartre is France's only permanent collection of the Surrealist master's sculptures, paintings and graphic works (p160).

The bustling Place du Tertre is the tourist centre of Montmartre and is full of portraitists and other easel artists (p158). Cafés and bars surround the square.

↑ Admiring the works of street artists in the lively Place du Tertre

| 0 metres | | 100 |
| 0 yards | | 100 |

N ↑

A La Mère Catherine was a favourite eating place of Russian Cossacks in 1814. They would bang on the table and shout "Bistro!" (Russian for "quick") – hence the Paris bistro was born.

St-Pierre de Montmartre became the Temple of Reason during the Revolution (p158).

MONTMARTRE AND PIGALLE

Locator Map
For more detail see p154

↑ The beautiful Sacré-Coeur, illuminated at sunrise

The Romano-Byzantine Sacré-Coeur, started in the 1870s and completed in 1914, is a highlight of the area (p156).

RUE DU CHEVALIER

RUE DU MONT CENIS

RUE DU CARDINAL GUIBERT

RUE LAMARCK

RUE PAUL ALBERT

PL DU PARVIS DU SACRÉ-COEUR

RUE AZAIS

RUE ST-ELEUTHÈRE

RUE DU CARDINAL DUBOIS

Halle Saint-Pierre hosts exhibitions of Art Brut and Naïve Art (p161).

SQ WILLETTE

RUE CH NODIER

Did You Know?

Montmartre's name is ascribed to local martyrs tortured in around AD 250: *mons martyrium.*

RUE CHAPPE

START

RUE TARDIEU

PL ST-PIERRE

FINISH

RUE DE STEINKERQUE

The funiculaire, or cable railway, at the end of Rue Foyatier takes you to the foot of the basilica of Sacré-Coeur. Metro tickets are valid on it.

Square Willette lies below the parvis (forecourt) of Sacré-Coeur. It is laid out on the side of the hill in a series of descending terraces with lawns, shrubs, trees and flowerbeds.

OPÉRA AND GRANDS BOULEVARDS

Known for its elegant avenues and the Opéra Garnier, this area was an important focus of Baron Haussmann's renovation of Paris in the 19th century. The crowded streets of the medieval city were demolished to make way for a series of Grands Boulevards – Madeleine, Capucines, Italiens and Montmartre – wide avenues flanked by imposing stone buildings with intricate wrought-iron balconies. Many glass-roofed shopping arcades were also constructed around this time, followed by the Printemps and Galeries Lafayette department stores, which firmly established the area's reputation as a major shopping destination. It also became a popular entertainment district, with venues including the dazzling Opéra National de Paris Garnier, and in 1895 the Lumière brothers held the world's first public film show at the Grand Café on Boulevard de Capucines. Today the area is more of a business hub, but night-time revellers will still find a host of clubs and theatres to enjoy.

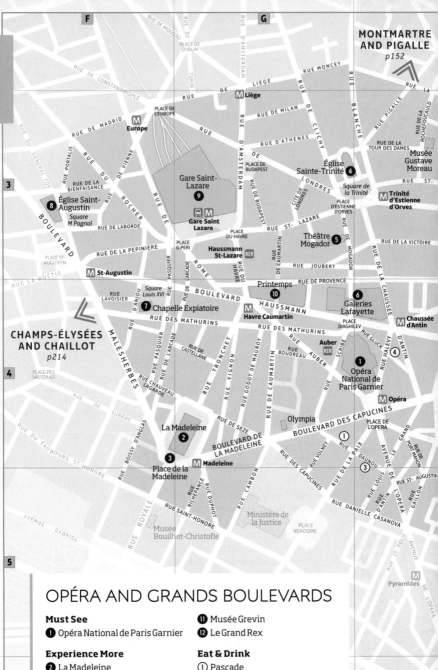

OPÉRA AND GRANDS BOULEVARDS

Must See

1. Opéra National de Paris Garnier

Experience More

2. La Madeleine
3. Place de la Madeleine
4. Église Sainte-Trinité
5. Théâtre Mogador
6. Galeries Lafayette
7. Chapelle Expiatoire
8. Église Saint-Augustin
9. Gare Saint-Lazare
10. Printemps
11. Musée Grevin
12. Le Grand Rex

Eat & Drink

1. Pascade
2. Chartier
3. Harry's Bar

Stay

4. W Hôtel
5. Hôtel Chopin
6. Hôtel Parister

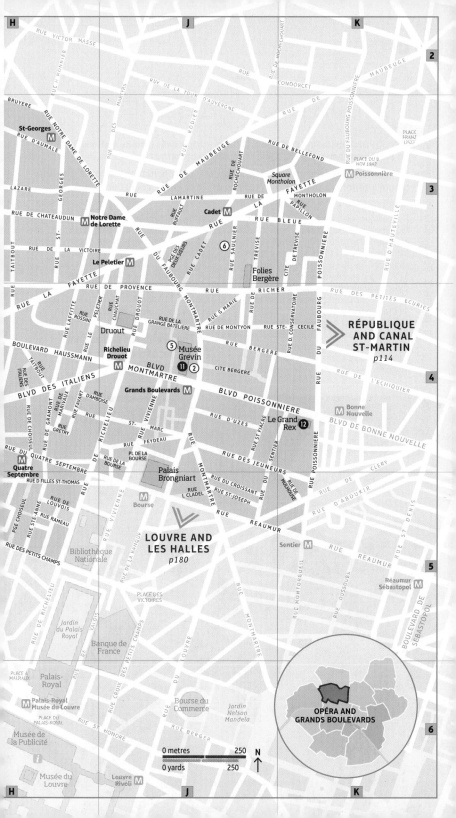

1 🏛️ 🎭 🛍️ 🍽️

OPÉRA NATIONAL DE PARIS GARNIER

📍 H4 🏠 Pl de l'Opéra 75009 Ⓜ Opéra 🕐 10am–4:30pm daily (1pm on matinée days); mid-Jul–late Aug: 10am–5:30pm 🚫 1 Jan, 1 May 🌐 operadeparis.fr

Sometimes compared to a giant wedding cake, this palatial opera house with its ornate interior is a sumptuous setting in which to enjoy a ballet or opera.

The building was designed by Charles Garnier for Napoleon III; construction started in 1862 and finished in 1875 after interruptions from the Prussian War and 1871 uprising. Its unique appearance is due to a mixture of materials (including stone, marble and bronze) and styles, ranging from classical to Baroque, with a number of columns, friezes and sculptures on the exterior.

Behind the flat-topped foyer, the cupola sits above the auditorium, while the triangular pediment that rises up behind the cupola marks the front of the stage. Don't miss the magnificent Grand Staircase, made of white marble with a balustrade of red and green marble, and the Grand Foyer, its domed ceiling covered with mosaics. The five-tiered auditorium is a riot of red velvet, plaster cherubs and gold leaf. The false ceiling was painted by Marc Chagall in 1964.

Operas are performed both here and at the Opéra National de Paris Bastille *(p106),* but the ballet predominantly remains here.

> **The five-tiered auditorium is a riot of red velvet, plaster cherubs and gold leaf.**

EXPERIENCE Opéra and Grands Boulevards

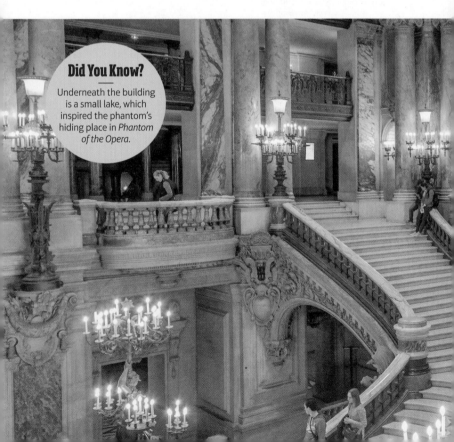

Did You Know?

Underneath the building is a small lake, which inspired the phantom's hiding place in *Phantom of the Opera.*

1 With nearly 480,000 visitors each year, the Opéra is one of Paris's most-visited sights.

2 The auditorium, which can accommodate 2,054 spectators, was designed so that the audience can see and be seen.

3 The ceiling of the Grand Foyer is decorated with paintings by Paul Baudry.

↑ The Grand Staircase, an awe-inspiring welcome to the building

EXPERIENCE MORE

② La Madeleine

📍 G4 🏛 Pl de la Madeleine 75008 Ⓜ Madeleine
🕐 9:30am–7pm daily
🌐 eglise-lamadeleine.com

This church, dedicated to Mary Magdalene, is one of the best-known buildings in Paris because of its prominent location and great size. It stands facing south to Place de la Concorde and is the architectural counterpoint of the Palais-Bourbon (home of the Assemblée Nationale, the French parliament) across the river. It was started in 1764 but construction halted with the onset of the Revolution in 1789 and there were proposals to convert it into a parliament, a stock exchange or the city's first train station. After the battle of Jena (Iéna) in 1806, Napoleon decided to build a temple dedicated to military glory and he commissioned Pierre Vignon to design it. The church was consecrated in 1845.

A colonnade of Corinthian columns encircles the building and supports a sculptured frieze. The bas-reliefs on the bronze doors by Henri de Triqueti show the Ten Commandments. The interior is decorated with marble and gilt, and has some fine sculpture, notably François Rude's *Baptism of Christ*. The church has a rich musical tradition; Gabriel Fauré and Camille Saint-Saëns were both organists here. Concerts, especially choral and organ recitals, take place regularly.

> **Did You Know?**
>
> The flower market at Place de la Madeleine has sold colourful bouquets since the early 1800s.

③ Place de la Madeleine

📍 F4 🏛 75008 Ⓜ Madeleine
🌸 Flower market: 8am–7.30pm Mon–Sat

The Place de la Madeleine was created at the same time as the Madeleine church. It is a food lover's paradise, with many shops specializing in truffles,

> Inside the Église Sainte-Trinité, each chapel reveals rich paintings and decorations celebrating saints.

champagne, caviar and handmade chocolates. Fauchon, the luxury super-market, is situated at No. 26. The large house at No. 9 is where Marcel Proust spent his childhood. To the east of La Madeleine are a small flower market and some excellently preserved 19th-century Art Nouveau public toilets.

④ Église Sainte-Trinité

📍 G3 🏛 Place d'Estienne d'Orves 75009 Ⓜ Trinité-d'Estienne d'Orves ⏰ 8am–7pm

Inspired by Renaissance-era Italian churches, this 19th-century masterpiece was consecrated in 1913. The church, often referred to simply as La Trinité, is the monumental centrepiece of the busy Place d'Estienne d'Orves intersection, created by Baron Haussmann and named after a French resistance fighter. Haussmann moved the church a few hundred metres from its original location as part of his grand project to redesign Paris. Decorated with a large belfry dominating the façade, the church actually cost very little to build. Inside the Église Sainte-Trinité, each chapel reveals rich paintings and decorations celebrating saints such as local favourites Geneviève and Vincent de Paul.

⑤ Théâtre Mogador

📍 G3 🏛 25 Rue de Mogador 75009 📞 01 53 32 32 32 Ⓜ Trinité-d'Estienne d'Orves

The Théâtre Mogador was built by London theatre mogul Alfred Butt. It was inaugurated in 1919 by future American president Franklin Delano Roosevelt. Numerous politicians were in town to negotiate the Treaty of Versailles after World War I, so taking in a show must have seemed like a good idea. It once hosted operettas and Sergei Diaghilev's Ballets Russes, but has also featured classic musicals such as *Hello, Dolly!* and *Les Misérables*. Now, this majestic three-tier theatre produces mostly big-budget Broadway shows in French, such as *Phantom of the Opera* and *Grease*.

⑥ Galeries Lafayette

📍 H4 🏛 40 Blvd Haussmann 75009 Ⓜ Chaussée d'Antin-Lafayette ⏰ 9:30am–8:30pm daily (Sun 11am–7pm) 🌐 haussmann.galerieslafayette.com

Dating back to 1893, this store is a Parisian icon and an essential stop on any visit to the city. The massive complex includes men's and women's fashion, a homewares department and a gourmet food hall. At Christmas, a massive tree fills the Art Nouveau cupola, while the windows tell whimsical holiday stories popular with kids. Anyone can take the escalator to the rooftop terrace, where spectacular views of the city await. The store can become a madhouse during the biannual sales, the *soldes*, but it's all part of the Galeries Lafayette experience.

EAT & DRINK

Pascade
The chef offers an innovative take on a sort of crêpe-like dish filled with gourmet ingredients.

📍 G4 🏛 14 Rue Daunou 75002 🚫 Sun, Mon 🌐 pascade.fr

€€€

Chartier
This old workers' canteen is still a budget favourite for French classics.

📍 J4 🏛 7 Rue du Faubourg Montmartre 75009 🌐 bouillon-chartier.com.

€€€

Harry's New York Bar
Birthplace of the Bloody Mary – and other cocktails – it's tradition to make a stop here.

📍 H4 🏛 5 Rue Daunou 75002 🌐 harrysbar.fr

← The ornate high altar of the Église de la Madeleine

THE VICTIMS OF THE GUILLOTINE

Along with Louis XVI and Marie-Antoinette, numerous other famous figures were buried where the Chapelle Expiatoire now stands. Among them were Murat's murderer Charlotte Corday, writer and feminist Olympe de Gouges, Louis XV's mistress Jeanne du Barry and Madame Roland.

7

Chapelle Expiatoire

F4 **29 Rue Pasquier 75008** **Madeleine** **01 42 65 35 80** **Apr-Sep: 10am-12:30pm & 1:30-6:30pm Tue-Sat; Oct-Mar: 10am-12:30pm & 1:30-5pm**

King Louis XVIII dedicated this chapel in 1816 to the memory of his brother King Louis XVI and sister-in-law Marie-Antoinette. The pair were buried in a cemetery here after being guillotined nearby at Place de la Concorde (p224). The mass grave, known as the Madeleine Cemetery, was one of four to hold the remains of guillotine victims. Marie-Antoinette and Louis XVI were moved to the Basilica of Saint-Denis (p305) in the 19th century. The chapel merely hints at this turbulent history with a modest Neo-Classical memorial. The tiny garden contains cenotaphs to those who were buried here, including victims of the fireworks disaster at Marie and Louis's wedding in 1770.

8

Église Saint-Augustin

F3 **8 Ave César Caire 75008** **St-Augustin** **10am-4:30pm Mon-Fri, 10am-noon Sat** **saintaugustin.net**

This church is located in one of Paris's most exclusive neighbourhoods. Designed by Victor Baltard, the architect of Les Halles, and completed in 1868 at the intersection of sweeping new boulevards, the building initially drew criticism for its oversized dome and curious red turret. Large quantities of metal were used in the church's construction, and its cast iron framework provides a decorative feature of the interior, complete with iron angels at the tops of the pillars.

9

Gare Saint-Lazare

G3 **13 Rue d'Amsterdam 75008** **Gare Saint-Lazare**

Europe's second-busiest train station after the Gare du Nord, the Gare Saint-Lazare is probably the most celebrated in art. Opened in 1837, it sends trains to the station closest to Giverny, where Claude Monet painted his famous water lilies. The artist was just one of many 19th-century painters to immortalize the Saint-Lazare station in his canvases. Renowned painters Caillebotte and Manet also lived near the station, and their depictions of it hang in galleries around the world. The station has recently undergone major renovations, with new shopping and dining areas.

← A statue of Marie-Antoinette in the Chapelle Expiatoire

↑ A rooftop view of the Art Nouveau Printemps department store

Printemps

📍 G4 🏠 64 Blvd Haussmann 75009 Ⓜ Havre Caumartin 🕐 9:35am–8pm Mon-Sat (to 8:45pm Thu), 11am–7pm Sun 🌐 printemps.com

A stunning Art Nouveau palace dedicated to shopping, the Printemps department store dates back to 1865. High fashion fills the floors, and it feels slightly more elegant and refined than neighbouring Galeries Lafayette. The brasserie under the massive stained-glass dome is a resplendent spot for lunch, while the rooftop café offers great views of the Sacré-Coeur.

Musée Grévin

📍 J4 🏠 10 Blvd Montmartre 75009 Ⓜ Grands Boulevards 🕐 9am–7pm daily (times can vary, check website) 🌐 grevin.com

This waxworks museum was founded in 1882 and is now a Paris landmark, on a par with Madame Tussauds in London. It contains tableaux of vivid historical scenes (such as the arrest of Louis XVI), the Palais des Mirages (a giant walk-in kaleidoscope) and the Cabinet Fantastique, which features regular conjuring shows given by a live magician. Famous figures from the worlds of art, sport and politics are also on show, with new celebrities constantly replacing faded and forgotten stars.

Le Grand Rex

📍 K4 🏠 1 Blvd Poissonnière 75002 Ⓜ Bonne Nouvelle 🌐 legrandrex.com

A national monument, as well as an innovative example of Art Deco architecture, Le Grand Rex, built in 1932, was long touted as Europe's most opulent cinema, hosting many red-carpet events. One of the largest of its kind in Europe, the Grand Rex is a fading but beautiful symbol of the history of cinema. The auditorium has a starred ceiling, 2,800 seats and an enormous screen. Every December, the cinema hosts the Féerie des Eaux, a family-film event featuring an on-stage water show.

STAY

W Hôtel

Chic and modern, the W brand's stylish hotel overlooking the Opéra National de Paris Garnier doesn't disappoint.

📍 H4 🏠 4 Rue Meyerbeer 75009 🌐 wparisopera.com.

€€€

Hôtel Chopin

Hidden away in a 19th-century covered *passage*, this well-located hotel has charm in spades.

📍 J4 🏠 46 Passage Jouffroy 75009 🌐 hotelchopin-paris-opera.com

€€€

Hôtel Parister

Quiet and calm with contemporary décor, this is a wonderful retreat, with its own swimming pool, and very reasonably priced.

📍 J3 🏠 19 Rue Saulnier 75009 🌐 hotelparister.com

€€€

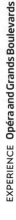
A SHORT WALK
OPÉRA

Distance 1.5 km (1 mile) **Nearest metro** Madeleine
Time 15 minutes

It has been said that if you sit for long enough at the Café de la Paix (opposite the Opéra National de Paris Garnier) the whole world will pass by. During the day, the area is a mixture of commerce – France's top three banks are based here – and tourism. A profusion of shops, ranging from the chic, exclusive and expensive to popular department stores, draws the crowds. In the evening, the theatres and cinemas attract a totally different clientele, and the cafés along the Boulevard des Capucines throb with life.

← The exquisite high altar of La Madeleine

On the north side of Place de la Madeleine the windows of the Fauchon shop are filled with exquisite delicacies.

PL DE LA MADELEINE

RUE TRONCHET

RUE VIGNON

RUE GODOT DE MAUROY

RUE CAUMARTIN

RUE

BLVD DE LA MADELEINE

BLVD DE

Ⓜ **START**

Metro Madeleine

The church of La Madeleine, is dedicated to Mary Magdalene and is one of the best-known in Paris (p174).

Did You Know?
George Gershwin is said to have composed *An American in Paris* at Harry's New York Bar.

← The opulent Opéra National de Paris Garnier, sometimes described as an enormous wedding cake

OPÉRA AND GRANDS BOULEVARDS

Locator Map
For more detail see p170

With a mixture of styles ranging from Classical to Baroque, the Opéra National de Paris Garnier of 1875 has come to symbolize the opulence of the Second Empire (p172).

The world of opera is celebrated at the Bibliothèque-Musée de l'Opéra.

Metro Chaussée d'Antin

The Place de l'Opéra was designed by Baron Haussmann and is one of Paris's busiest intersections.

PL DIAGHILEV

RUE GLUCK

RUE HALEVY

PL J ROUCHE

RUE SCRIBE

RUE

AUBER

PL CH GARNIER

PL DE L'OPERA

FINISH

The Café de la Paix maintains its old-fashioned ways and still has its 19th-century decor, designed by Garnier. Their vanilla slices are legendary.

Metro Opéra

CAPUCINES

RUE DAUNOU

AVE DE L'OPERA

At No. 14 Boulevard des Capucines, a plaque tells of the world's first public screening of a movie, by the Lumière brothers in 1895; it took place in the Salon Indien, a room in the Grand Café.

Harry's New York Bar was named after Harry MacElhone, a bartender who bought the bar in 1913. Past regulars have included F Scott Fitzgerald and Ernest Hemingway (p175).

0 metres   100   N
0 yards   100   ↑

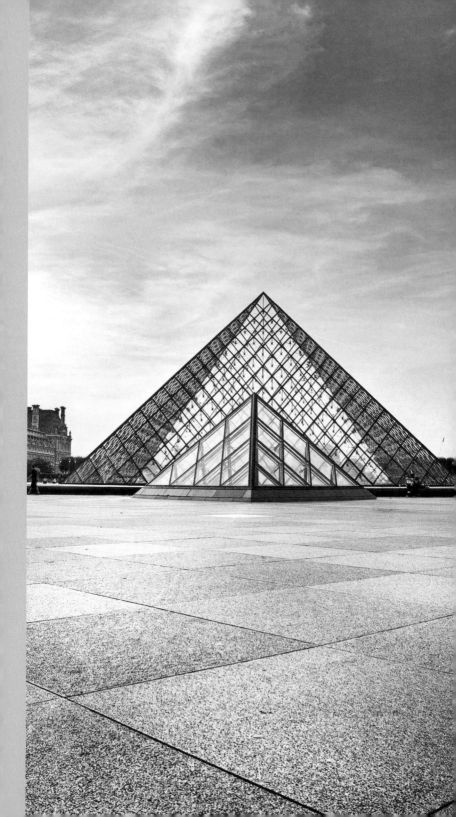

LOUVRE AND LES HALLES

Today the heart of the city, this area lay on the outskirts of Paris in the Middle Ages. Its vulnerable position led Philippe Auguste to build a defensive fortress here in 1190, around which grew up a dense urban district. In 1528, François I took up residence in the Louvre, marking the start of centuries of royal redevelopment and the construction of numerous grand buildings and gardens. The area remained affluent following the downfall of the monarchy in 1789, and is still home to many exclusive shops and luxury hotels.

Les Halles, meanwhile, has much more humble origins. For 800 years the "Belly of Paris" was the site of the central food market in the city. Housed from the late 19th century in 12 magnificent iron-and-glass pavilions designed by Victor Baltard, the market was demolished in 1971 and transformed into a huge underground mall called the Forum des Halles. Deeply unpopular, it was redeveloped as part of a €1 billion infrastructure project and reopened in 2016.

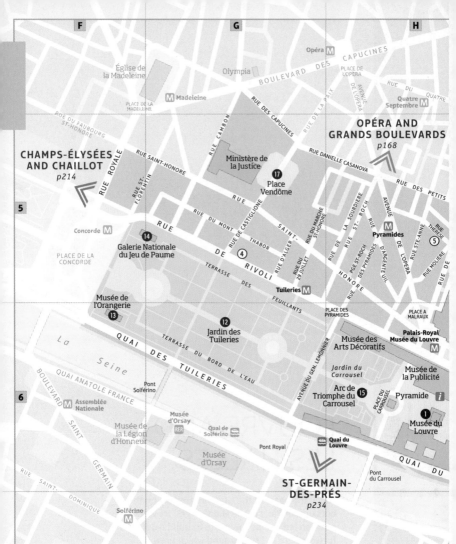

LOUVRE AND LES HALLES

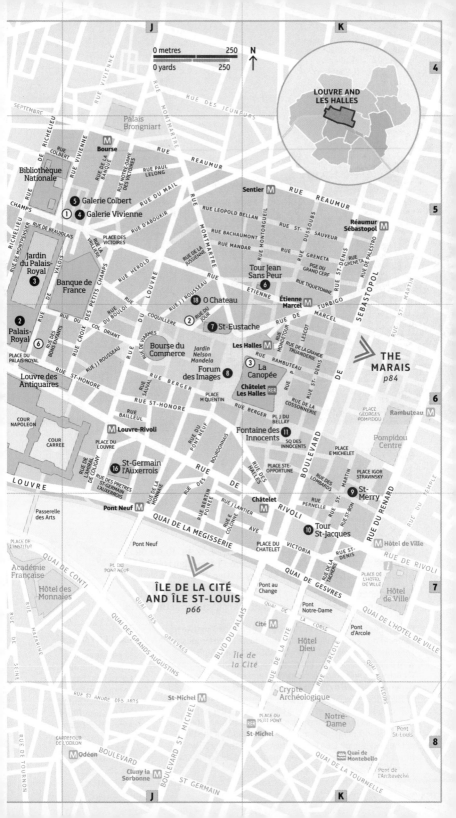

0 metres 250
0 yards 250

N

**LOUVRE AND
LES HALLES**

4

RUE VIVIENNE

RUE SEPTEMBRE

RUE DES JEUNEURS

Palais
Brongniart

RUE MONTMARTRE

RUE RICHELIEU

RUE DE RICHELIEU

RUE COLBERT

Ⓜ
Bourse

RUE
REAUMUR

RUE VIVIENNE

RUE DE LA BANQUE

RUE NOTRE-DAME
DES VICTOIRES

RUE PAUL
LELONG

Sentier Ⓜ

RUE REAUMUR

5

**Bibliothèque
Nationale**

CHAMPS

RUE DE BEAUJOLAIS

Ⓢ Galerie Colbert

① ④ **Galerie Vivienne**

RUE DU MAIL

RUE LEOPOLD BELLAN

RUE MONTORGUEIL

RUE ST-
SAUVEUR

DUSSOUBS

**Réaumur
Sébastopol** Ⓜ

RUE DE PALESTRO

RICHELIEU

RUE DE MONTPENSIER

RUE VIVIENNE

RUE DE LA
VRILLIERE

PLACE DES
VICTOIRES

RUE D'ABOUKIR

RUE BACHAUMONT

RUE MANDAR

RUE
ST-DENIS

RUE GRENETA

PGE DU
GRAND CERF

RUE GRENETA

SEBASTOPOL

RUE ST-MARTIN

**Jardin
du Palais-
Royal**
③

**Banque de
France**

RUE HEROLD

RUE DE LA
JUSSIENNE

RUE MONTMARTRE

RUE DU
LOUVRE

RUE
ETIENNE

**Tour Jean
Sans Peur**
⑥

RUE TIQUETONNE

**Étienne
Marcel** Ⓜ

RUE DE
MARCEL

TURBIGO

②
**Palais-
Royal**
⑥

RUE ST-HONORE

RUE DU
BOULOI

RUE CROIX
DES PETITS CHAMPS

RUE DU
COL DRIANT

RUE
COQUILLERE

RUE J J ROUSSEAU

⑱ **O Chateau**

RUE DU
FOUR

② RUE DU FOUR

⑦ **St-Eustache**

RUE
MONTDETOUR

RUE DE LA GRANDE
TRUANDERIE

LESCOT

RUE DE

MARCEL

THE
MARAIS
p84

PLACE
DU PALAIS-ROYAL

RUE DES
BONS ENFANTS

**Bourse du
Commerce**

RUE DE VIARMES

RUE J J ROUSSEAU

Jardin
Nelson
Mandela

Les Halles Ⓜ

③ **La
Canopée**

RAMBUTEAU

RUE ST-DENIS

DE

6

**Louvre des
Antiquaires**

RUE ST-HONORE

RUE
SAUVAL

RUE BERGER

**Forum
des Images**
⑧

PLACE
M QUENTIN

RUE BERGER

**Châtelet
Les Halles** ℝℰℛ

RUE DE LA
COSSONNERIE

PL J DU
BELLAY

PLACE
GEORGES
POMPIDOU

Rambuteau Ⓜ

Pompidou
Centre

COUR
NAPOLEON

COUR
CARREE

Ⓜ **Louvre-Rivoli**

PLACE
DU LOUVRE

RUE
BAILLEUL

RUE DU
PONT NEUF

RUE
BOURDONNAIS

**Fontaine des
Innocents** ⑪

SQ DES
INNOCENTS

PLACE
E MICHELET

RUE DES
LOMBARDS

PLACE IGOR
STRAVINSKY

⑨ **St-
Merry**

RUE ST-MARTIN

RUE DU RENARD

LOUVRE

RUE DE L'AMIRAL
DE COLIGNY

⑯ **St-Germain
l'Auxerrois**

RUE DES PRETRES
ST-GERMAIN
L'AUXERROIS

RUE DE LA
MONNAIE

RUE DES
HALLES

PLACE STE-
OPPORTUNE

RUE
PERNELLE

RUE ST-BON

RUE DE RIVOLI

RUE DU TEMPLE

**Passerelle
des Arts**

Pont Neuf Ⓜ

QUAI DE LA MEGISSERIE

RUE
BERTIN
POIREE

RUE DES
HALLES

RUE J LANTIER

AVE

RUE E
COLONNE

Châtelet
Ⓜ

RIVOLI

RUE ST-
DENIS

⑩ **Tour
St-Jacques**

Ⓜ **Hôtel de Ville**

RUE DE RIVOLI

PLACE DE
L'HOTEL DE VILLE

ℹ

7

PLACE DE
L'INSTITUT

**Académie
Française**

**Hôtel des
Monnaies**

QUAI DE CONTI

RUE
MAZARINE

RUE
DE
SEINE

QUAI DES GRANDS AUGUSTINS

Pont Neuf

PL DU
PONT NEUF

Pont Neuf

**ÎLE DE LA CITÉ
AND ÎLE ST-LOUIS**
p66

BLVD DU PALAIS

QUAI DES
ORFEVRES

**Île de
la Cité**

**Pont au
Change**

QUAI DE
GESVRES

PLACE DU
CHATELET

VICTORIA

**Pont
Notre-Dame**

Cité Ⓜ

LA CORSE

RUE DE
LA CITE

**Hôtel
Dieu**

RUE D'ARCOLE

QUAI DE L'HOTEL DE VILLE

QUAI AUX FLEURS

**Pont
d'Arcole**

**Hôtel
de Ville**

RUE DE TOURNON

RUE ST ANDRE DES ARTS

St-Michel Ⓜ

BOULEVARD ST MICHEL

CARREFOUR
DE L'ODEON

Ⓜ **Odéon**

BOULEVARD

**Cluny la
Sorbonne**

ST GERMAIN

PLACE DU
PETIT PONT

ℝℰℛ
St-Michel

**Crypte
Archéologique**

**Notre-
Dame**

🚌 **Quai de
Montebello**

QUAI DE LA TOURNELLE

**Pont
St-Louis**

**Pont de
l'Archevêché**

8

The unmistakable glass pyramid of the Louvre in the Cour Napoleon ↓

1 🏛 🎨 🍴 🛍

MUSÉE DU LOUVRE

📍 H6 Ⓜ Palais-Royal Musée du Louvre 🚌 21, 24, 27, 39, 48, 68, 69, 72, 81, 95 🚆 Châtelet-Les-Halles Ⓜ Louvre 🕐 9am–6pm Wed–Mon (to 9:45pm Wed & Fri) 📅 1 Jan, 1 & 8 May, 25 Dec 🌐 louvre.fr

First opened to the public in 1793 after the Revolution, the Louvre contains one of the most important art collections in the world.

Constructed as a fortress in 1190 by King Philippe-Auguste to protect Paris against Viking raids, the Louvre lost its imposing keep during the reign of François I (1514–47), who replaced it with a Renaissance-style building. Thereafter, four centuries of French kings and emperors improved and enlarged it. A glass pyramid designed by I M Pei was added to the main courtyard in 1989, from which all of the galleries can be reached.

The Louvre's treasures can be traced back to the 16th-century collection of François I, who purchased many Italian paintings, including the *Mona Lisa (La Gioconda)*. At the time of Louis XIV's reign (1643–1715) there were a mere 200 works, but donations and purchases augmented the collection and it has been continually enriched ever since.

GALLERY GUIDE

There are eight departments over four floors: Near Eastern antiquities; Egyptian antiquities; Greek, Etruscan and Roman antiquities; Islamic art; sculptures; decorative arts; paintings; and prints and drawings.

① This sculptural spiral staircase forms part of the modern entrance hall designed by I M Pei.

② The Marly Horses by Guillaume Coustou once stood near the Place de la Concorde.

③ *The Coronation of Napoleon* by Jacques-Louis David is an impressive 6.2 m (20½ ft) high by 9.8 m (32 ft) wide.

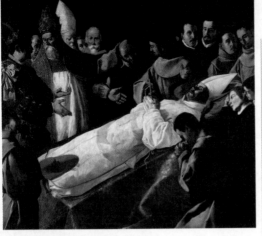

↑ *Lying-in-State of St Bonaventura*
(c 1629) by Francisco de Zurbarán

EUROPEAN PAINTING: 1200 TO 1850

Painting from northern Europe is well covered, with Flemish, Dutch, German and English works by artists including Jan van Eyck, Vermeer, Hans Holbein and J M W Turner. The Spanish collection tends towards depictions of the tragic side of life, although several portraits by Goya are in a lighter vein.

The large collection of Italian paintings covers the period 1200 to 1800. Key figures of the Renaissance are here, including Giotto and Raphael. Several paintings by Leonardo da Vinci are as enchanting as his *Mona Lisa*.

The French collection ranges from the 14th century to 1848. There are superb works by Jean Fouquet, Georges de la Tour and Jean Watteau, as well as J H Fragonard, master of the Rococo.

MONA LISA: WHY DO WE CARE?

Acquired by King François I, this portrait of a mysterious woman was one of the first paintings displayed in the Louvre when the museum opened. For many years it was simply one da Vinci work among many, but that all changed when the painting was stolen in 1911. The much-publicized theft pushed the artwork into the public eye, with reproductions appearing around the world. Its popularity has not dwindled since.

EUROPEAN SCULPTURE: 1100 TO 1850

←

Saint Mary Magdalene
by Gregor Erhart
(c 1515–20)

Early Flemish and German sculpture in the collection has many masterpieces, including an unusual life-size nude figure of the penitent Mary Magdalen by Gregor Erhart (early 16th century). The French section opens with early Romanesque works, such as a Figure of Christ by a 12th-century Burgundian sculptor and a Head of St Peter. With its eight black-hooded mourners, the Tomb of Philippe Pot is one of the more unusual pieces.

The works of Pierre Puget have been assembled inside the Cour Puget, while the Cour Marly houses the Marly Horses and other master-pieces of French sculpture.

The Italian sculpture collection includes pre-Renaissance work by Duccio and Donatello, and later masterpieces such as Michel-angelo's *Slaves* and Cellini's *Nymph of Fontainebleau*.

DECORATIVE ARTS

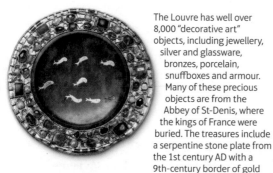

↑ Serpentine stone
plate (1st century/
9th century AD)

The Louvre has well over 8,000 "decorative art" objects, including jewellery, silver and glassware, bronzes, porcelain, snuffboxes and armour. Many of these precious objects are from the Abbey of St-Denis, where the kings of France were buried. The treasures include a serpentine stone plate from the 1st century AD with a 9th-century border of gold and precious stones, and the golden sceptre made for King Charles V in about 1380.

The French crown jewels include the coronation crowns of Louis XV and Napoleon, and the Regent, one of the purest diamonds in the world.

The large collection of French furniture ranges from the 16th to the 19th centuries. On display are important pieces by prominent furniture-makers such as André-Charles Boulle, who was cabinet-maker to Louis XIV.

In 2012, the Islamic Art Department opened in the Cour Visconti, with around 18,000 objects on display covering 3,000 years of history from three continents. The museum also recently installed decorative art galleries dedicated to objects from the reign of Louis XIV and the 18th century.

> **The French crown jewels include the coronation crowns of Louis XV and Napoleon, and the Regent, one of the purest diamonds in the world.**

NEAR EASTERN, EGYPTIAN, GREEK, ETRUSCAN AND ROMAN ANTIQUITIES

The range of antiquities is impressive, with objects from the Neolithic period to the fall of the Roman Empire. Important works of Mesopotamian art include the seated figure of Ebih-il, from 2400 BC, while the warlike Assyrians are represented by delicate carvings and a spectacular reconstruction of part of Sargon II's (722–705 BC) palace. A fine example of Persian art is the enamelled brickwork depicting the king of Persia's personal guard of archers (5th century BC).

Most Egyptian art was made for the dead to take to the afterlife. One exquisite example is the tiny carved funeral chapel built for a high official in about 2500 BC. A special crypt dedicated to the god Osiris contains some colossal sarcophagi and mummified animals.

The department of Greek, Roman and Etruscan antiquities contains some exceptional pieces. The two most famous Greek statues in the Louvre, the *Winged Victory of Samothrace* and the *Venus de Milo*, belong to the Hellenistic period (late 3rd to 2nd century BC), when more natural-looking human forms were beginning to be produced. The star of the Etruscan collection is the terracotta *Sarcophagus of the Cenestian Couple*, while the many fine pieces in the Roman section include a bust of Agrippa and a splendid, powerful bronze head of Emperor Hadrian from the 2nd century AD.

→

*Winged Victory of
Samothrace* (c 190 BC)

EXPERIENCE MORE

❷ Palais-Royal

📍H6 🏠Pl du Palais-Royal 75001 Ⓜ Palais-Royal
🌐domaine-palais-royal.fr

This former royal palace, closed to the public, has had a turbulent history. Starting out in the early 17th century as Richelieu's Palais Cardinal, it passed to the Crown on his death and was the childhood home of Louis XIV. Under the control of the 18th-century royal dukes of Orléans, it was the scene of brilliant gatherings, as well as periods of debauchery and gambling. The cardinal's theatre, where Molière had performed, burned down in 1763, but was replaced by the Comédie Française. After the Revolution, the palace became a gambling house. In 1815, it was reclaimed by the future King Louis-Philippe, one of whose librarians was Alexandre Dumas.

After being restored again between 1872 and 1876, the palace reverted to the state, and it now houses the Council of State, the supreme legal body for administrative matters, and the Constitutional Council. Another wing of the palace is occupied by the Ministry of Culture.

❸ Jardin du Palais-Royal

📍H5 🏠6 Rue de Montpensier, Pl du Palais-Royal 75001 Ⓜ Palais-Royal 🕐Apr-Sep 8am-10.30pm daily; Oct-Mar 8am-8:30pm daily
🌐domaine-palais-royal.fr

The current garden is about one-third smaller than the original one, laid out by the royal gardener for Cardinal Richelieu in the 1630s. This is due to the construction, between 1781 and 1784, of 60 uniform houses bordering three sides of the square. Today, restaurants, art galleries and specialist shops line the square, which has numbered Jean Marais, Jean Cocteau and Colette among its famous former residents.

The courtyard contains the controversial black-and-white striped stone columns that form conceptual artist Daniel Buren's *Les Deux Plateaux*.

The columns were installed in the pedestrianized Palais-Royal courtyard in 1986, despite vociferous opposition about their suitability for the space. Today, they are loved by children and skateboarders alike.

❹ Galerie Vivienne

📍J5 🏠4 Rue des Petits Champs 75002 Ⓜ Bourse, Pyramides 🕐Generally 8:30am-8:30pm daily
🌐galerie-vivienne.com

The early 19th century saw the rise of fashionable covered *passages*, reminiscent of the souks explored during Napoleon's conquests in North Africa. At the height of their popularity there were over 100 of them; they were the shopping malls of their day, well before the department stores came of age. Galerie Vivienne, built in 1823, was a particularly sumptuous example of such a covered *passage*. Its lovely décor has been restored, including its atrium ceilings and mosaic floor with

Daniel Buren's columns in the courtyard of the Jardin du Palais-Royal

↑ The lofty, light-filled interior of the elegant Galerie Vivienne

Did You Know?

Most of Paris's covered *passages* disappeared during Haussmann's renovations in the late 1800s.

patterns reminiscent of decorations from Pompeii. It's the perfect all-weather retreat for a glass of wine, a little bit of shopping in the elegant boutiques, or browsing in the Librairie Jousseaume second-hand bookshop.

5

Galerie Colbert

📍 J5 🏠 2 Rue Vivienne 75002 Ⓜ Bourse, Pyramides 🕐 Generally 9am–5pm daily

Unlike nearby Galerie Vivienne, the covered Galerie Colbert, as exquisite as its neighbour and also completed in 1823, is not used for commercial purposes. The two *passages* have historically been in competition to be Paris's favourite. It was in Galerie Colbert that composer Hector Berlioz, famous for *La Symphonie Fantastique*, sang

with crowds at the onset of the July Revolution in 1830. Today, it houses various institutions and parts of the University of Paris, all dedicated to the arts and cultural preservation. The *passage* is typically open to the public and is worth seeing for its lovely glass rotunda, with a statue of Eurydice beneath it. The *passage* can also be viewed from the adjacent brasserie Le Grand Colbert.

6

Tour Jean Sans Peur

📍 K5 🏠 20 Rue Étienne-Marcel 75002 Ⓜ Étienne-Marcel, Sentier 🕐 1:30–6pm Wed–Sun 🌐 tourjean sanspeur.com

The Duc de Bourgogne feared reprisals after the Duc d'Orléans was assassinated on his orders in 1408. To protect himself, he had this 27-m (88-ft) tower built onto his home, the Hôtel de Bourgogne, and moved his bedroom up to the fourth floor (reached by a flight of 140 steps). The fine vaulted ceiling is decorated with stone carvings of oak leaves, hawthorn and hops, symbols of the Burgundys.

EAT

Le Grand Colbert
This old-world brasserie still charms, and the traditional French food still pleases.

📍 J5 🏠 2 Rue Vivienne 75002 🌐 legrandcolbert.com

€€€

Au Pied de Cochon
Onion soup is a staple of this Les Halles institution, which is open all night.

📍 J6 🏠 6 Rue Coquillière 75001 🌐 pieddecochon.com

€€€

Champeaux
Alain Ducasse's casual-yet-chic eatery under the new canopy at Forum des Halles serves French classics done just right.

📍 K6 🏠 La Canopée, Forum des Halles 75001 🌐 restaurant-champeaux.com

€€€

7

St-Eustache

📍 J6 🏠 2 Impasse St-Eustache, Pl du Jour 75001 Ⓜ Les Halles 🚇 Châtelet-Les-Halles 🕐 9:30am-7pm Mon-Fri, 10am-7:15pm Sat, 9am-7:15pm Sun 🌐 saint-eustache.org

With its Gothic plan and Renaissance decoration, St-Eustache is one of the most beautiful churches in Paris. Its interior plan is modelled on Notre-Dame *(p70)*, with five naves and side and radial chapels. The 105 years (1532–1637) it took to complete the church saw the flowering of the Renaissance style, which is evident in the arches, pillars and columns. The stained-glass windows in the chancel are created from cartoons by Philippe de Champaigne.

The church has associations with many famous figures: Molière was buried here; and the Marquise de Pompadour, official mistress of Louis XV, was baptized here, as was Cardinal Richelieu. Don't miss a chance to hear the fine organ at one of the regular recitals that take place.

8

Forum des Images

📍 J6 🏠 2 Rue du Cinéma, Forum des Halles 75001 Ⓜ Les Halles 🚇 Châtelet-Les-Halles 🕐 Collections: 2-9pm Wed-Sun; café & information: 12:30-9pm Tue-Fri, 2-9pm Sat & Sun 🌐 forumdesimages.fr

At the forum, you can choose from thousands of cinema, television and amateur films, many featuring the city of Paris. There is footage on the history of Paris since 1895,

→

A mild summer evening in the Jardin des Tuileries

including a remarkable newsreel of General de Gaulle avoiding sniper fire during the Liberation of Paris in 1944. There are countless movies, too, such as François Truffaut's *Baisers Volés*. On Friday evenings the forum hosts "Cours de Cinéma", when classic films are analysed. There are also regular film festivals and screenings.

9

St-Merry

📍 K7 🏠 76 Rue de la Verrerie 75004 Ⓜ Hôtel de Ville 🕐 Apr-Oct: 3-7pm Mon-Sat; Nov-Mar: 2-6pm Mon-Sat 🌐 saintmerry.org

The site of this church dates back to the 7th century. St Médéric, the abbot of St-Martin d'Autun, was buried here at the beginning of the 8th century; he died while on pilgrimage in Paris. Construction of the church – in the Flamboyant Gothic style – took place in 1500–1550.

The west front is especially rich in decoration, and the northwest turret contains the oldest bell in Paris, dating from 1331. St-Merry was the wealthy parish church of the Lombard money-lenders, who gave their name to the nearby Rue des Lombards. Guided tours usually take place after concerts on the first and third Sundays of the month.

10

Tour St-Jacques

📍 K7 🏠 Square de la Tour St-Jacques, corner of Rue de Rivoli and Blvd de Sebastopol 75004 Ⓜ Châtelet, Hôtel de Ville 🕐 Gardens: year-round; tower: Jun-Aug: 10am-5pm Fri-Sun

This imposing late-Gothic tower, dating from 1523, is all that remains of an ancient church that was a rendezvous for pilgrims setting out on long journeys. The church was destroyed after the Revolution. Earlier, Blaise Pascal, the 17th-century mathematician, physicist, philosopher and writer, used the tower for experiments. Queen Victoria passed by on her state visit in 1854, giving her name to the nearby Avenue Victoria. The tower can be visited in the summer only; book ahead on the site desmotsetdesarts.com.

Statues set into the façade of the Gothic church of St-Merry ↑

⑪
Fontaine des Innocents

📍 K6 📌 Pl Joachim-du-Bellay 75001 Ⓜ Les Halles 🚉 Châtelet-Les-Halles

This carefully restored Renaissance fountain is a popular meeting place and a Les Halles landmark. It stands in the Place Joachim-du-Bellay, the area's main crossroads. Erected in 1549 on the Rue St-Denis, it was moved to its present location in the 18th century, when the square was constructed on the site of a former graveyard.

Originally set into a wall, the fountain had only three sides so a fourth had to be constructed. It is decorated with mythological figures.

⑫
Jardin des Tuileries

📍 G6 📌 Pl de la Concorde 75001 Ⓜ Tuileries, Concorde 🕐 Apr-Sep: 7am-9pm (to 11pm Jun-Aug); Oct-Mar: 7:30am-7:30pm

Once belonging to the old Palais des Tuileries, these gardens form part of the landscaped area between the Louvre and the Champs-Élysées. They were laid out in the 17th century by royal gardener André Le Nôtre, and later filled with striking sculptures. A staggering 125,000 plants are replanted annually.

STAY

Le Meurice
A mighty palace hotel, it has all the amenities a luxury traveller could want, including a Michelin-starred restaurant.

📍 G5 📌 228 Rue de Rivoli 75001 🌐 dorchester collection.com

€€€

Hôtel Thérèse
A chic boutique-hotel alternative to the big-name hotels in the area, with individually decorated rooms.

📍 H5 📌 5 Rue Thérèse 75001 🌐 hoteltherese.fr.

€€€

Grand Hôtel du Palais Royal
Tucked behind the Palais-Royal and overlooking its garden, this luxury property is central but has a secluded feel.

📍 H6 📌 4 Rue de Valois 75001 🌐 grandhoteldupalais royal.com.

€€€

JEU DE PAUME

Nobles used to play a version of handball, *jeu de paume*, in the former royal court that today houses the Galerie Nationale du Jeu de Paume. French players would yell "*tenez*" or "take it" to their opponents. As the game evolved, the word did, too, and the English began to call it tennis, or real tennis, and used rackets instead of their hands. Later, the Jeu de Paume became a storehouse during World War II, where Nazis stashed stolen art. Those deemed offensive, for example many Picasso and Dalí paintings, were burned in front of it in 1942.

Stained glass at St-Germain l'Auxerrois ↑

Pierre-Auguste Renoir is represented by 27 canvases, including *Les Fillettes au Piano (Young Girls at the Piano)*. There are early Picassos, works by Henri Rousseau – notably *La Carriole du Père Junier (Old Junier's Cart)* – and Matisse, and a portrait of Paul Guillaume by Modigliani. All are bathed in the natural light that flows through the windows. Temporary exhibitions are shown on the lower ground floor.

---

13 🎨 Ⓜ️ 🏛️

Musée de l'Orangerie

📍 F6 🏛️ Jardin des Tuileries, Pl de la Concorde 75001 Ⓜ️ Concorde 🕐 9am–6pm Wed–Mon 🚫 1 May, 14 Jul am & 25 Dec 🌐 musee-orangerie.fr

Claude Monet's crowning work, the water lily series, or *Nymphéas*, can be found here. The series was painted in his garden at Giverny, near Paris, and presented to the public in 1927. These superb large-scale canvases are complemented well by the outstanding Walter-Guillaume collection of artists of the École de Paris, from the late Impressionist era to the inter-War period. This is a remarkable concentration of masterpieces, including a room of dramatic works by Soutine and some 14 works by Cézanne – still lifes, portraits (*Madame Cézanne*) and landscapes, such as *Dans le Parc du Château Noir*.

---

14 🎨 Ⓜ️ 💬 🏛️

Galerie Nationale du Jeu de Paume

📍 F5 🏛️ Jardin des Tuileries, 1 Pl de la Concorde 75008 Ⓜ️ Concorde 🕐 11am–7pm Tue–Sun (to 9pm Tue) 🚫 1 Jan, 1 May & 25 Dec and in between exhibitions 🌐 jeudepaume.org

The Jeu de Paume – or *réal* tennis court – was built by Napoleon III in 1851. When *réal* (royal) tennis was replaced in popularity by lawn tennis, the court was used to exhibit art. Eventually, an Impressionist museum was founded here. In 1986, the collection moved to the Musée d'Orsay (*p238*). The Jeu de Paume now houses the Centre National de la Photographie, and shows exhibitions of contemporary photography and art from both established and emerging artists.

15

Arc de Triomphe du Carrousel

📍 H6 🏛️ Pl du Carrousel 75001 Ⓜ️ Palais-Royal

Built by Napoleon in 1806–8 as an entrance to the former Palais des Tuileries, this vast pink marble arch, inspired by ancient Roman triumphal arches, was originally topped by the so-called Horses of St Mark's from Venice's St Mark's cathedral. They were returned, however, in 1815 after Napoleon's defeat at Waterloo and replaced by copies.

16

St-Germain l'Auxerrois

📍 J6 🏛️ 2 Pl du Louvre 75001 Ⓜ️ Louvre, Pont-Neuf 🕐 9am–7pm Tue–Sat, 9am–8pm Sun (Jul & Aug: 9:30am–7pm Tue–Sun) 🌐 saintgermainauxerrois.fr

This church has been built in a combination of Renaissance and Gothic

Did You Know?

The façade of St-Germain l'Auxerrois is mirrored by the nearby town hall of the 1st arrondissement.

styles. The first church on the site was constructed in the 12th century, of which only the foundations of the bell tower remain. The splendid rose stained-glass windows date from the Renaissance period.

After the Valois Court decamped to the Louvre in the 14th century, this became the favoured church of kings. The church's many historical associations include the horrific St Bartholomew's Day Massacre on 24 August 1572, the eve of the royal wedding of Henri of Navarre and Marguerite de Valois. Thousands of Huguenots who had been lured to Paris for the wedding were murdered as the church bell tolled. Later, after the Revolution, the church was used as a barn and as a police station. Despite many restorations, it is a jewel of Gothic architecture. Check the website for details of the regular concerts held here.

_____

17 (🛍)

Place Vendôme

📍 G5 🏛 75001 Ⓜ Tuileries

Perhaps the best example of 18th-century elegance in the city, the architect Jules Hardouin-Mansart's royal square was begun in 1698. The original plan was to house academies and embassies behind the arcaded façades. However, bankers moved in and created opulent homes. Miraculously, the square has remained virtually intact, and is home to jewellers and bankers. Among the famous, Frédéric Chopin died here in 1848 at No. 12, and César Ritz established his luxury hotel at the turn of the 20th century at No. 15.

18 (🛍)(🎵)(🍴)(🖥)(🛍)

O Chateau

📍 J5 🏛 68 Rue Jean-Jacques Rousseau 75001 Ⓜ Louvre-Rivoli, Étienne Marcel 🕐 4pm–midnight Mon–Sat 🌐 O-chateau.com

With 50 wines served by the glass, this wine-tasting bar in the heart of Les Halles is one of the best places to learn about your soon-to-be favourite vintages *(p53)*. You can stop in for a few drinks, or take a class or even a trip. They can organize outings to Champagne for tastings or prepare a multi-course meal served in one of their vaulted dining rooms. A sommelier pairs each dish with wine, explaining the particularities of French viticulture. English-speakers are catered for, so there's no chance of losing anything in translation.

←

The Galerie Nationale du Jeu de Paume

A SHORT WALK
TULIERIES QUARTER

Distance 2 km (1.25 miles) **Nearest metro** Pyramides
Time 20 minutes

Elegant squares, formal gardens, street arcades and courtyards give this part of Paris its special character. Monuments to monarchy and the arts coexist with contemporary luxury: sumptuous hotels, world-famous restaurants, fashion emporiums and jewellers of international renown. Combine a walk around the area with a visit to the world-famous Louvre, and end the day with a well-deserved sit-down in the Jardin des Tuileries.

The Paris Convention and Visitors' Bureau

Metro Pyramides

START

St-Roch is a remarkably long 17th-century church, unusually set on a north-south axis, and a treasure house of religious art.

The Normandy is an elegant hotel in the belle époque style, a form of graceful living that prevailed in Paris at the turn of the 20th century.

In Place des Pyramides is Frémiet's gilded statue of Joan of Arc, a focus of pilgrimage for royalists.

A highlight of the Musée des Arts Décoratifs' displays of art and design is the Art Nouveau collection.

The formal Jardin des Tuileries were designed by royal gardener André Le Nôtre in the 17th century.

RUE DES PYRAMIDES

RUE ST HONORE

RUE DE L'ECH

AVE DU GL LEMONNIER

RUE

DE

FINISH

| 0 metres | 100 | N |
| 0 yards | 100 | ↑ |

←
Taking a break in the sunshine at the verdant Jardin des Tuileries

↑ The elegant interior of the renowned restaurant Le Grand Véfour

The 18th-century decor makes Le Grand Véfour one of the most beautiful restaurants in Paris. Napoleon and Victor Hugo were two of the many famous people who dined here.

Locator Map
For more detail see p182

With a fountain pool and benches, the Jardin du Palais-Royal is a city haven, bordered by arcades housing restaurants, art galleries and shops (p188).

France's national theatre, the Comédie Française is the setting for the works of great dramatists, such as Molière.

In the 18th century, the Palais-Royal was a setting for brilliant gatherings, debauchery and gambling. Today, modern sculptures grace its square (p188).

Three floors of a former department store house the Louvre des Antiquaires, a chic art and antiques supermarket for the rich collector.

Metro Palais-Royal, Musée du Louvre

Home to French kings for almost four centuries, the Musée du Louvre is now host to one of the world's greatest art collections (p184).

EIFFEL TOWER AND INVALIDES

On the Left Bank of the Seine, this quarter in the 7th arrondissement is monumental in scale. The construction of the Hôtel des Invalides in the late 17th century brought with it the urbanization of the surrounding area, and the neighbourhood quickly became popular with the city's nobles, who wanted more space for their palaces. Many wealthy residents of the Marais moved here in the early 18th century, building the aristocratic town houses that line the Rue de Varenne and Rue de Grenelle. Some of these were destroyed during the Revolution, while others were subsequently converted into national institutions, such as the Assemblée Nationale Palais-Bourbon, or embassies.

The quarter has long had a strong military connection as the home of the École Militaire. In 1889, the school's former parade ground, the Champ-de-Mars, was chosen as the site of a Universal Exhibition to commemorate the 100th anniversary of the Revolution. The centrepiece of that exhibition, the Eiffel Tower, is today the main draw for most visitors to the area.

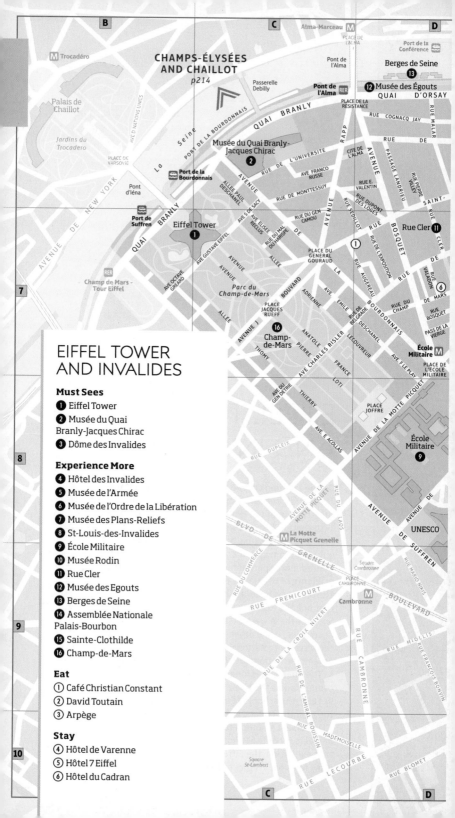

EIFFEL TOWER
AND INVALIDES

Must Sees

1 Eiffel Tower

2 Musée du Quai
Branly-Jacques Chirac

3 Dôme des Invalides

Experience More

4 Hôtel des Invalides

5 Musée de l'Armée

6 Musée de l'Ordre de la Libération

7 Musée des Plans-Reliefs

8 St-Louis-des-Invalides

9 École Militaire

10 Musée Rodin

11 Rue Cler

12 Musée des Egouts

13 Berges de Seine

14 Assemblée Nationale
Palais-Bourbon

15 Sainte-Clothilde

16 Champ-de-Mars

Eat

1 Café Christian Constant

2 David Toutain

3 Arpège

Stay

4 Hôtel de Varenne

5 Hôtel 7 Eiffel

6 Hôtel du Cadran

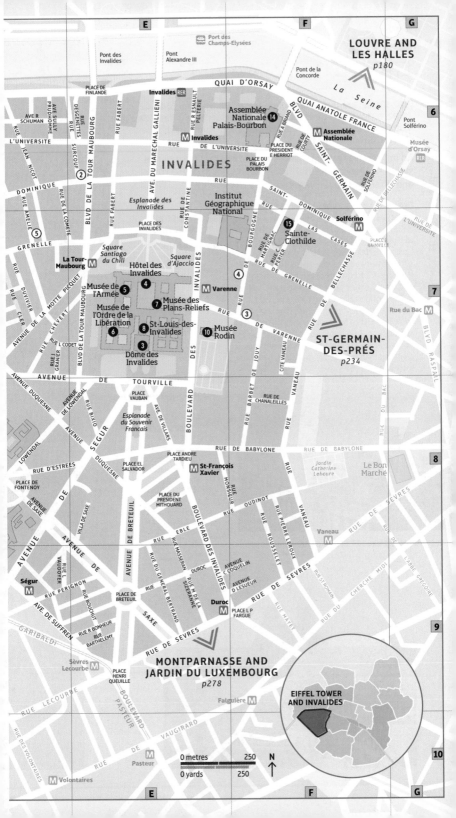

● ⬨ 🛍 🍽

EIFFEL TOWER

📍B7 🚇Quai Branly and Champ-de-Mars Ⓜ Bir Hakeim 🚌42, 69, 72, 82, 87 to Champ-de-Mars 🚆Champ-de-Mars Tour Eiffel ⏰Sep-Jun: 9:30am-11:45pm daily (6:30pm for stairs); Jul-Aug: 9am-12:45am 🗓14 Jul 🌐toureiffel.paris

An impressive feat of engineering and the most distinctive symbol of Paris, the Eiffel Tower stands 324 m (1,063 ft) tall and offers unrivalled views over the city.

Originally built to impress visitors to the 1889 Universal Exhibition, the Eiffel Tower (Tour Eiffel) was meant to be a temporary addition to the Paris skyline. Built by the engineer Gustave Eiffel, it was fiercely decried by 19th-century aesthetes – the author Guy de Maupassant frequently ate lunch at the tower as it was the only place he could avoid seeing it. The world's tallest structure until 1931, when New York's Empire State Building was completed, the tower is now an icon of Paris and attracts 7 million visitors a year. The glass-floored first level houses a modern visitors' centre and an interactive museum chronicling the history of the tower.

THE TOWER IN FIGURES

276 m (905 ft): the height of the viewing gallery on the third level

1,665: the number of steps to the third level

2.5 million: the number of rivets holding the tower together

7 cm (2.5 in): the maximum amount that the tower ever sways

10,100 tonnes: the tower's total weight

60 tonnes: the amount of paint needed to decorate the ironwork

18 cm (7 in): how far the top can move in a curve under the effect of heat

↑ The view from the tower, ranging up to 72 km (45 miles)

← The Eiffel Tower under construction in April 1888, less than halfway complete

Did You Know?

Franz Reichelt died in 1912 after attempting to fly from the parapet using a modified cape as wings.

↑ A view of the Eiffel Tower from the Jardins du Trocadéro *(p222)*

2 ⊘ Ⓜ ▭ ⬔ ⓦ

MUSÉE DU QUAI BRANLY-JACQUES CHIRAC

📍C6 🏠37 Quai Branly Ⓜ Alma-Marceau, Bir-Hakeim, Iéna
🚌 42, 63, 72, 80, 82, 92 🚉 Pont de l'Alma 🕐 11am–7pm Tue, Wed & Sun,
11am–9pm Thu–Sat 🚫 Mon (except during all school hols besides
summer hols), 1 Jan, 1 May, 25 Dec 🌐 quaibranly.fr

This rich collection of artifacts from Africa, Asia, Oceania and the Americas resides in a striking building that uses surrounding greenery as a natural backdrop to the art.

Widely regarded as former President Jacques Chirac's legacy to Paris's cultural scene, quai Branly has proved a major tourist pull since it opened in 2006. The stylish Jean Nouvel building displays 3,500 exhibits from the French state's vast non-Western art collection, one of the world's most prolific. Items include an array of African instruments, Gabonese masks, Aztec statues and painted animal hides from North America. Outside, the grounds offer visitors breathing space, and in summer the museum's 500-seat auditorium opens onto an outdoor theatre for music and dance. The rooftop restaurant boasts breathtaking views.

GALLERY GUIDE

Tickets are bought outside the main building. Inside, a ramp around a large glass tower displaying musical instruments leads to the main collection level, where a suggested route passes through four colour-coded zones of Oceania, Asia, Africa and the Americas. Three mezzanine galleries house temporary exhibitions.

↑ The museum's eyecatching exterior, with a glass wall and thickets of trees in the surrounding gardens

🔍 HIDDEN GEM
Key Object

The Africa collection houses a striking 1.91 m (6 ft 3 in) androgynous wooden statue from Mali, which combines a regal male head with the breasts of a woman.

Sculpted hook (Papua New Guinea, early 20th century)

→ A sculpted female figure on which tribal men would hang ritual offerings

↑ Jean Nouvel's elegant building, an exhibit in itself from the inside and out *(inset)*

③ DÔME DES INVALIDES

◉ E7 ◉ 6 Blvd des Invalides, Esplanade des Invalides ◉ La Tour-Maubourg, Varenne ◉ 28, 63, 69, 80, 82, 83, 87, 92, 93 to Les Invalides ◉ Invalides ◉ Tour Eiffel ◉ Hôtel National des Invalides: Apr-Oct: 10am-6pm daily (Jul & Aug: to 7pm; Apr-Sep: to 9pm Tue); Nov-Mar: 10am-5pm daily ◉ 1st Mon of month, 1 Jan, 1 May, 25 Dec ◉ musee-armee.fr

Built on the orders of Louis XIV, this church with its magnificent gilded dome is the final resting place of Napoleon Bonaparte and a host of other great French military men.

The Dôme des Invalides was designed in 1676 by Jules Hardouin-Mansart for the exclusive use of Louis XIV and for the location of royal tombs. Slotted among the existing buildings of the Invalides military complex, the resulting masterpiece complements the surrounding structures and is one of the greatest examples of 17th-century French architecture. After Louis XIV's death, plans to bury the royal family in the church were abandoned, and it became a monument to Bourbon glory. In 1840, Louis-Philippe decided to install Napoleon's remains in the crypt, and the addition of the tombs of Vauban, Marshal Foch and other figures of military prominence have since turned this church into a French military memorial.

←

Charles de la Fosse's circular painting (1692) on the ceiling of the dome, showing the *Glory of Paradise*, with Saint Louis presenting his sword to Christ

NAPOLEON'S RETURN

King Louis-Philippe decided to bring the Emperor Napoleon's body back from St Helena as a gesture of reconciliation to the Republican and Bonapartist parties contesting his regime. The Dôme des Invalides, with its historical and military associations, was an obvious choice for Napoleon's final resting place. His body was encased in six coffins and finally placed in the crypt in 1861, at the culmination of a grand ceremony which was attended by Napoleon III.

Did You Know?

The dome stands 107 m (351 ft) high and was first gilded in 1706.

↑ The church with its glittering dome, which required 12 kg (26 lb) of gold to re-gild in 1989

EXPERIENCE MORE

④

Hôtel des Invalides

📍 E7 📌 Place des Invalides 75007 Ⓜ La Tour-Maubourg, Varenne 🚉 Invalides 🕐 7:30am-7pm daily (Apr-Sep: to 9pm Tue) 🚫 Jan, 1 May, 25 Dec 🌐 musee-armee.fr

Founded by Louis XIV, this was France's first military hospital and became home to French war veterans and disabled soldiers, who had hitherto been reduced to begging. It was designed by Libéral Bruand and completed in 1675.

Today, the classical façade is one of the most impressive sights in Paris, with its four storeys, cannon in the fore-court, garden and tree-lined esplanade stretching to the Seine. The south side leads to St-Louis-des-Invalides, the soldiers' church, which backs on to the magnificent Dôme des Invalides of Jules Hardouin-Mansart (p204). The dome was regilded in 1989.

---

⑤

Musée de l'Armée

📍 E7 📌 Hôtel des Invalides, 129 Rue de Grenelle, 75007 Ⓜ La Tour-Maubourg, Varenne 🚉 Invalides 🕐 10am-6pm (to 9pm Tue) daily (Nov-Mar: to 5pm). Times may vary; check website 🚫 1st Mon of month (except Jul-Sep), 1 Jan, 1 May, 25 Dec 🌐 musee-armee.fr

This is one of the world's most comprehensive museums of military history, with exhibits ranging from the Stone Age to the final days of World War II.

Situated in the northeast refectory, the Ancient Armoury department is worth visiting for the collection on display, one of the largest in the world, as much as for the 17th-century murals by Joseph Parrocel adorning the walls. These celebrate Louis XIV's military conquests.

The life of Charles de Gaulle and his role in World War II are documented in the *Historial de Gaulle*, a film and interactive multimedia attraction (closed Mon). The Département Moderne is in two parts: the first (1648–1792) covers the reign of Louis XIV, while the second (1792–1871) displays a collection of Napoleon's mementos. Items include his campaign bed, famous frock coat and felt hats, and his stuffed dog.

---

⑥

Musée de l'Ordre de la Libération

📍 11 A3 📌 Hôtel des Invalides, 129 Rue de Grenelle/Place Vauban 75007 Ⓜ La Tour-Maubourg 🚉 Invalides 🕐 Apr-Oct: 10am-6pm daily (to 9pm Tue); Nov-Mar: 10am-5pm daily 🚫 1st Mon of month, public hols 🌐 ordredelaliberation.fr

This museum is devoted to the wartime Free French and their leader, General Charles

The splendid Hôtel des Invalides seen from Pont Alexandre III

↑ The magnificent organ of St-Louis-des-Invalides, dating from the 17th century

STAY

Hôtel de Varenne

A hotel with traditional, refined décor and a private garden in the chic 7th arrondissement.

♀F7 ▢44 Rue de Bourgogne 75007 Ⓦhotelde varenne.com

€€€

Hôtel 7 Eiffel

A modern option near the Eiffel Tower, with a rooftop terrace to boot.

♀D7 ▢17 bis Rue Amélie 75007 Ⓦhotel-7eiffel-paris.com

€€€

Hôtel du Cadran

A stylish boutique hotel with contemporary interior design, also featuring a vaulted breakfast room.

♀D7 ▢10 Rue du Champ de Mars 75007 Ⓦcadranhotel.com

€€€

---

de Gaulle, as well as to the Resistance movement within France and the Resistance fighters who were captured and deported.

The Order of Liberation was created by De Gaulle in 1940. It is France's highest honour and was bestowed on those who made an outstanding contribution to the final victory in World War II. Among the recipients of the honour are French civilians and members of the armed forces, plus a number of overseas leaders such as King George VI, Winston Churchill and Dwight Eisenhower.

Musée des Plans-Reliefs

♀E7 ▢Hôtel des Invalides, 129 Rue de Grenelle 75007 ⓂLa Tour-Maubourg, Varenne ▨Invalides Ⓒ10am–6pm daily (Nov–Mar: to 5pm) Ⓒ1st Mon of month (except Jul, Aug, Sep), 1 Jan, 1 May, 1 Nov, 25 Dec Ⓦmuseedesplansreliefs. culture.fr

The detailed models of French forts and fortified towns, some dating back to Louis XIV's reign, were considered top secret until the 1950s, when they were put on public display. They were created between the reigns of Louis XIV and Napoléon III in order to plan town defences and plot artillery positions. Out of a total of 260, around 100 of these three-dimensional maps are on display in the museum. The oldest model is that of Perpignan, dating from 1686. It shows the fortifications drawn up by the legendary 17th-century military architect Vauban, who built the defences around several French towns, including Briançon.

8

St-Louis-des-Invalides

♀E7 ▢Hôtel des Invalides, 129 Rue de Grenelle 75007 ⓂLa Tour-Maubourg, Varenne ▨Invalides Ⓒ10am–6pm daily (Nov–Mar: to 5pm) Ⓒ1 Jan, 1 May, 25 Dec Ⓦmusee-armee.fr

The "soldiers' church" was built in 1679–1708 by Jules Hardouin-Mansart from original designs by Libéral Bruand. The imposing, but stark, interior is decorated with banners seized in battle.

The first performance of Berlioz's *Requiem* was given on the fine 17th-century organ in 1837, with an orchestra accompanied by a battery of outside artillery.

> 💬 INSIDER TIP
> ### Combined Ticket
>
> Entrance to the Musée de l'Armée, the Musée de l'Ordre de la Libération and the Musée des Plans-Reliefs is all included on one ticket.

9 École Militaire

D8 **1 Pl Joffre 75007**
01 80 50 14 00 **École Militaire**

Founded in 1751 to educate 500 sons of impoverished officers, the Royal Military Academy was designed by architect Jacques-Ange Gabriel. The central pavilion, a magnificent example of the French classical style, is graced with eight Corinthian pillars and a quadrangular dome. The ornate interior is decorated in Louis XVI style; of main interest are the chapel and a Gabriel-designed wrought-iron banister on the main staircase.

One of the academy's early cadets was Napoleon Bonaparte, whose passing-out report stated that "he could go far if the circumstances are right". Today, the academy is used as a cavalry training ground and isn't generally open to the public.

---

10 Musée Rodin

E7 **79 Rue de Varenne 75007** **Varenne**
10am–5:45pm Tue–Sun
1 Jan, 1 May, 25 Dec
musee-rodin.fr

Auguste Rodin, widely regarded as one of the greatest French sculptors of the 19th century, lived and worked in the elegant 18th-century Hôtel Biron from 1908 until his death in 1917. In return for a state-owned flat and studio, Rodin agreed to leave his work to the nation. Some 300 works from Rodin's collection can now be seen in the museum. The attractive grounds consist of a rose garden, an ornamental garden and a relaxation area with benches, and contain some

The grandiose classical façade of the École Militaire ↓

EAT

Café Christian Constant

Classic and reasonable French fare near the Eiffel Tower – a rarity.

D7 **139 Rue Saint-Dominique 75007**
maisonconstant.com

€€€

David Toutain

This relaxed one-star Michelin experience is great value. It's worth booking at lunch.

E6 **29 Rue Surcouf 75007** **Sat, Sun**
davidtoutain.com

€€€

Arpège

Alain Passard's three-star restaurant, with a focus on fresh produce, is a worthwhile treat.

F7 **84 Rue de Varenne 75007**
Sat, Sun
alain-passard.com

€€€

The market street Rue Cler, with its many fine food shops ↑

of Rodin's most celebrated sculptures: *The Thinker*, *The Burghers of Calais*, *The Gates of Hell* and *Balzac*. Spread across 18 rooms, the museum combines a chronology of Rodin's creative development with a thematic exploration of his workshop. It has even re-created a space exactly as it was when Rodin lived and worked here. The outdoor café makes a lovely spot for a drink in warmer weather.

⑪ Rue Cler

📍D7 📮75007 Ⓜ École Militaire, La Tour-Maubourg ⊙Market: all day Tue-Sat & Sun am

This is the street market of the 7th arrondissement, the richest in Paris. The bulk of senior civil servants, wealthy expatriates, business leaders and many diplomats live in this residential neighbourhood. The market area occupies a cobblestoned pedestrian precinct stretching south from Rue de Grenelle. Popular with locals, the vibrant market is frequented by the best-dressed shoppers in town. The produce is excellent, especially the pâtisseries and cheese shops.

⑫ Musée des Égouts

📍D6 📮Pont Alma, opposite 93 Quai d'Orsay 75007 📞01 53 68 27 81 Ⓜ Alma-Marceau 🚌Pont de l'Alma ⊙11am-5pm Sat-Wed (to 6pm May-Sep) 🚫1 Jan, 2 weeks Jan, 25 Dec

One of Baron Haussmann's finest achievements, the majority of Paris's sewers (*égouts*) date from the Second Empire (1852–70). In the 20th century, surprisingly the sewers became a popular attraction. Visits are limited to a small area around the Quai d'Orsay entrance and the sewers may be closed after heavy rain. Display boards explain the history of Paris's water supply and waste management. Reserve in advance if you wish to take a guided tour.

Did You Know?

If laid end to end, the city's 2,100 km (1,300 miles) of sewers would stretch from Paris to Istanbul.

→ Auguste Rodin's famed sculpture *The Three Shades* at the Musée Rodin

⑬ 🍴 🖥 🛍
Berges de Seine

**📍 D6 🏛 Quai d'Orsay 75007
Ⓜ Assemblée Nationale,
Invalides**

In 2013, this former busy roadway along the river bank was revamped for pedestrians, turning it into one of Paris's loveliest promenades. As well as offering spectacular views of the Louvre, Jardin des Tuileries and other monuments along the way, the 2.3-km (1½-mile) walkway is studded with activities for children, like mini playgrounds, climbing walls and floating gardens. The promenade also has an athletics track, a fitness course (check out the daily programme of free exercise classes) and Vélib' bikes for all ages. Cyclists and joggers zigzag between pedestrians taking advantage of a traffic-free stroll. There are cafés and restaurants both on land and aboard boats, especially around Pont Alexandre III. Picnickers and evening revellers often crowd the banks during the summer, making the Berges de Seine one of the liveliest places for evening tipples on the Left Bank.

Did You Know?
—
Pont de la Concorde was built using stones from the Bastille fortress destroyed during the French Revolution.

---

⑭ 🎭 🛍
Assemblée Nationale Palais-Bourbon

**📍 F6 🏛 126 Rue de
l'Université 75007
Ⓜ Assemblée Nationale
🚇 Invalides 🌐 assemblee-nationale.fr**

Built in 1722 for the Duchesse de Bourbon, daughter of Louis XIV, the Palais-Bourbon was confiscated during the Revolution. It has been home to the lower house of the French Parliament since 1830. During World War II, the palace became the Nazi administration's seat of government. The grand Neo-Classical façade with its fine columns was added in 1806, partly to mirror the façade of La Madeleine church facing it across the Seine. The adjacent Hôtel de Lassay is the residence of the president of the National Assembly. Group tours can be organized for a maximum of 50 people on the invitation of a member of parliament, with several months' prior notice.

---

⑮ 🛍
Sainte-Clotilde

**📍 F7 🏛 12 Rue de
Martignac 75007
Ⓜ Solférino, Varenne,
Invalides 🕐 9am-7:30pm
Mon-Fri, 10am-8pm Sat &
Sun. Times vary for Jul &
Aug; check website
🚫 Non-religious public hols
🌐 sainte-clotilde.com**

Designed by the German architect François-Christian Gau and the first of its kind

→
The Assemblée Nationale on the Left Bank of the Seine

←

The pretty Champ-de-Mars gardens at the foot of the Eiffel Tower

Picnickers and evening revellers crowd the banks during the summer evenings, making the Berges de Seine one of the liveliest places for evening tipples on the Left Bank.

to be built in Paris, this church, in Neo-Gothic style, was inspired by the mid-19th-century enthusiasm for the Middle Ages, made fashionable by such writers as Victor Hugo. The church is noted for its imposing twin towers, visible from across the Seine, and there are sculptures of the Stations of the Cross inside. The composer César Franck was the organist here.

16

Champ-de-Mars

C7 75007 Ⓜ École Militaire Champ de Mars-Tour Eiffel

The gardens stretching from the Eiffel Tower to the École Militaire were originally a parade ground for the officer cadets of the École Militaire (p208). The area has since been used for horse-racing, hot-air balloon ascents and the mass celebrations for 14 July, the anniversary of the Revolution. The first Bastille Day ceremony was held in 1790 in the presence of a glum, captive Louis XVI. Vast exhibitions were held here in the late 19th century, including the 1889 World Fair for which the Eiffel Tower was erected. *Le Mur de la Paix*, Clara Halter and Jean-Michel Wilmotte's symbolic monument to world peace, stands at one end.

The park is popular with Parisian families and tourists, who come here to relax, walk their dogs (it is one of the few parks in Paris where dogs are allowed) and to participate in the numerous activities for children, which include playgrounds, pony rides, puppet shows and a carousel. There is also an outdoor café.

A SHORT WALK
INVALIDES

Distance 1.5 km (1 mile) **Nearest metro** La Tour Maubourg **Time** 15 minutes

This walk concentrates on the imposing Hôtel des Invalides, from which the area takes its name. The hôtel was built from 1671 to 1676 by Louis XIV for his wounded and homeless veterans and as a monument to his own glory. At its centre, the glittering golden roof of the Sun King's Dôme des Invalides marks the final resting place of Napoleon Bonaparte. The emperor's body was brought here from St Helena in 1840, 19 years after he died, and placed inside the majestic sarcophagus, designed by Joachim Visconti, that lies at the centre of the Dôme's circular glass-topped crypt. Just to the east of the hôtel on the corner of the Boulevard des Invalides, the superb Musée Rodin offers artistic relief from the pomp and circumstance of the surrounding area.

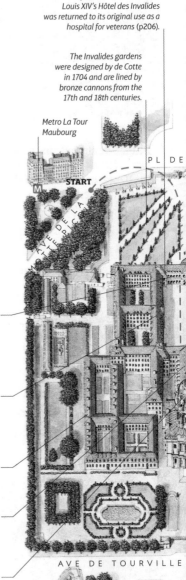

After the two World Wars, Louis XIV's Hôtel des Invalides was returned to its original use as a hospital for veterans (p206).

The Invalides gardens were designed by de Cotte in 1704 and are lined by bronze cannons from the 17th and 18th centuries.

Metro La Tour Maubourg

START

The façade of the hôtel is 196 m (645 ft) long and is topped by dormer windows, each decorated in the shape of a different trophy. A head of Hercules sits above the central entrance.

The vast Musée de l'Armée covers military history from the Stone Age to World War II. It contains the third-largest collection of armoury in the world (p206).

The Musée de l'Ordre de la Libération was set up to honour feats of heroism during World War II (p206).

From St-Louis-des-Invalides, the soldier's chapel, it is possible to see into the Dôme (below), which was built as Louis XIV's private chapel.

In the crypt of the Dôme des Invalides lies Napoleon, whose final wish was to have his ashes "rest on the banks of the Seine" (p204).

AVE DE TOURVILLE

AVE DE SEGOR

Did You Know?

In 1789 rioters stormed the hôtel and seized cannons and muskets to use against the Bastille.

↑ Relaxing in the gardens that surround the Hôtel des Invalides on a sunny afternoon

Locator Map
For more detail see p198

Metro
Varenne

The Musées des Plans-Reliefs contains military models of forts and towns, as well as a display on model-making (p207).

The Cour d'Honneur is still used for military parades. Seurre's statue of Napoleon, known as the Little Corporal, stands above the south side.

Auguste Rodin's key works, including The Thinker (c 1880), are on display at the Musée Rodin (p208).

INVALIDES
RUE DE GRENELLE

FINISH

BLVD DES INVALIDES

AVE DE VILLARS

0 metres 100
0 yards 100

N

↑ Visitors exploring fine sculpture at the excellent Musée Rodin

CHAMPS-ÉLYSÉES AND CHAILLOT

This area radiates wealth and power, but it was once little more than open fields lying on the outskirts of Paris. In 1616, Marie de Medici, wife of Henri IV, commissioned a tree-lined approach road through here to the Tuileries Palace, which was expanded in the late 17th century by Louis XIV's landscape designer, André Le Nôtre. The avenue was christened Champs-Élysées in the 18th century, and became a fashionable location for the nobility to build grand town houses.

The nearby Chaillot Quarter, however, remained just a village before becoming absorbed into the city of Paris in the 19th century. Bestowed with similarly wide avenues and grand mansions, it became one of the city's most elegant neighbourhoods. The districts' allure has not faded, and today they are home to numerous embassies and *haute couture* fashion houses, as well as five-star hotels and fine restaurants.

CHAMPS-ÉLYSÉES AND CHAILLOT

	A	B	C

4

5

6

7

8

EIFFEL TOWER AND INVALIDES
p196

0 metres 300
0 yards 300

N

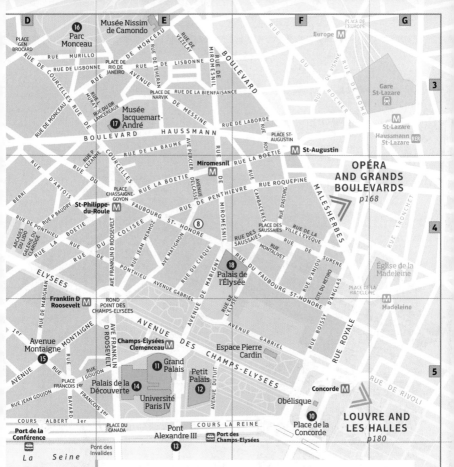

CHAMPS ÉLYSÉES AND CHAILLOT

30

shields just below the Arc's roof each bear the name of a victorious Napoleonic battle.

The golden tones ↑
of the Arc's stonework,
highlighted by the sunset

ARC DE TRIOMPHE

C4 Pl Charles de Gaulle **M**/**RER** Charles de Gaulle-Étoile 22, 30, 31, 52, 73, 92 to Pl Charles de Gaulle Apr-Sep: 10am–11pm daily; Oct–Mar: 10am–10:30pm daily am only 8 May, 14 Jul, 11 Nov; all day 1 Jan, 1 May, 25 Dec **W** paris-arc-de-triomphe.fr

Situated at the heart of Place Charles de Gaulle, overlooking the Champs-Élysées, the Arc de Triomphe was commissioned by Napoleon to celebrate France's military might. The exterior is adorned with sculptures depicting various battles, while the viewing platform at the top affords one of the best views in Paris.

After his greatest victory, the Battle of Austerlitz in 1805, Napoleon promised his men, "You shall go home beneath triumphal arches." The first stone of what was to become the world's most famous triumphal arch was laid the following year, but disruptions to architect Jean Chalgrin's plans and the demise of Napoleonic power delayed the completion of this monumental building until 1836. Standing 50 m (164 ft) high, the Arc is now the customary starting point for victory celebrations and parades.

← The twelve avenues radiating from Place Charles de Gaulle

→ The symbolic torch at the Tomb of the Unknown Soldier

NUPTIAL PARADE

Napoleon divorced Josephine in 1809 because she was unable to bear him children. A diplomatic marriage was arranged in 1810 with Marie-Louise, daughter of the Austrian emperor. Napoleon was determined to impress his bride by going through the Arc on their way to the wedding, but work had barely started so Chalgrin built a full-scale mock-up of the arch on the site for the couple to pass beneath.

Timeline

1806
▽ Napoleon commissions Chalgrin to build the triumphal Arc following the Battle of Austerlitz in the previous year

1815
Napoleon abdicates after defeat at the Battle of Waterloo, causing work on the Arc to cease

1836
King Louis-Philippe completes the Arc during the Bourbon Restoration

1919
Victory parade of Allied armies through the Arc to celebrate the end of World War I

1944
△ De Gaulle leads the crowd from the Arc following the liberation of Paris

 2

PALAIS DE CHAILLOT

B6 Pl du Trocadéro 75016 Trocadéro

The Palais, with its huge, curved colonnaded wings each culminating in an immense pavilion, was designed in Neo-Classical style for the 1937 Paris Exhibition by Léon Azéma, Louis-Hippolyte Boileau and Jacques Carlu. Today it houses three major museums: the Cité de l'Architecture et du Patrimoine, the Musée de l'Homme and the Musée National de la Marine.

The present Palais replaced the Trocadéro palace built for the World's Fair of 1878. It is adorned with sculptures and bas-reliefs, and on the walls of the pavilions are gold inscriptions by the poet and essayist Paul Valéry. The *parvis*, or square, situated between the two pavilions, is decorated with large bronze sculptures and ornamental pools. On the terrace in front of the *parvis* stand two bronzes, *Apollo* by Henri Bouchard and *Hercules* by Albert Pommier. Stairways lead from the terrace to the Théâtre National de Chaillot, which, since World War II, has enjoyed huge fame for its avant-garde productions.

↑ One of the galleries at the Cité de l'Architecture et du Patrimoine *(p222)*

←
View of the Palais de Chaillot from the Eiffel Tower

THÉÂTRE NATIONAL DE CHAILLOT

In addition to being a prestigious performance venue, the Théâtre National de Chaillot has also played an important role in world history. It was here that the Universal Declaration of Human Rights was signed in 1948.

Exhibits from the anthropology and ethnology collection of the Musée de l'Homme *(p222)* ↑

> ◎ PICTURE PERFECT
> **Eiffel Tower**
>
> The palace's terrace boasts magnificent views of the Eiffel Tower. Head here to get a panoramic shot of the Iron Lady.

←
The bronze *Hercules* statue on the terrace

EXPERIENCE MORE

③ Cité de l'Architecture et du Patrimoine

📍B6 🏛Palais de Chaillot, Pl du Trocadéro 75016
Ⓜ Trocadéro 🕐11am-7pm Wed-Mon (to 9pm Thu)
🚫1 Jan, 1 May, 25 Dec
🌐citedelarchitecture.fr

In the east wing of the Palais de Chaillot, this museum charts the development of French architecture through the ages. Among the unmissable displays is the Galerie des Moulages, which covers the period from the Middle Ages to the Renaissance. Here, you will find three-dimensional models of great French cathedrals, such as Chartres. Also worth a look is the Galerie Moderne et Contemporaine, with a reconstruction of an apartment designed by Le Corbusier.

④ Musée de l'Homme

📍A6 🏛Palais de Chaillot, Pl du Trocadéro 75016
Ⓜ Trocadéro 🕐10am-6pm Wed-Mon 🚫1 Jan, 1 May, 25 Dec 🌐museedelhomme.fr

Situated in the west wing of the Chaillot palace, this museum traces the process of human evolution, from prehistoric times to the present, through anthropological exhibits from around the world. Reopened in 2015 after five years of renovations, it houses one of the world's most comprehensive prehistoric collections. Displays show how humans have adapted to the environment, and there is also a focus on the development of language and culture.

⑤ Musée National de la Marine

📍B6 🏛Palais de Chaillot, Pl du Trocadéro 75016
Ⓜ Trocadéro 🌐musee-marine.fr

Closed for renovation until 2021, this museum recounts French maritime history from the days of the royal wooden warships to today's aircraft carriers and nuclear submarines through wonderfully exact scale models (most of them two centuries old), mementos of naval heroes, paintings and navigational instruments. The museum was set up by Charles X in 1827, and was moved to the Chaillot palace in 1943. Exhibits include Napoleon's barge and models of the fleet he assembled at Boulogne-sur-Mer in 1805 for his planned invasion of Britain.

↑ Henri Bouchard's *Apollo* statue outside the Musée de l'Homme

⑥ Jardins du Trocadéro

📍10 D2 🏛75016
Ⓜ Trocadéro

These charming gardens were created for the Universal Exhibition in 1937, at the same time as the Palais de Chaillot (p220). Their centrepiece is a long rectangular ornamental pool, bordered by stone and bronze-gilt statues, which look spectacular at night when the fountains are illuminated. The statues include *Man* by Pierre Traverse and *Woman* by Georges Braque, *Bull* by Paul Jouve and *Horse* by Georges Guyot. On either side of the pool, the slopes of the Chaillot hill lead down to the Seine and the Pont d'Iéna. The 10-ha (25-acre) park is laid out with flowering trees, small

WORLD FAIR

In 1889, the World Fair (or Exposition Universelle) saw the construction of the Eiffel Tower (p200). The 1937 edition led to the building of the Palais de Chaillot (p220), which replaced the exotic-looking Palais du Troacadéro, itself erected for the 1878 World's Fair. Numerous other temporary structures dotted the area around the Champs de Mars, but today, only the Iron Lady remains. If it weren't for the fact that the Eiffel Tower proved useful as a radio tower, it, too, would have been dismantled.

 PICTURE PERFECT
Eiffel Tower

Visit the Eiffel Tower by taking the metro to the Trocadéro stop, on line 6 or 9. This allows for postcard-perfect photographs from the terrace at the Palais de Chaillot looking across the river with Paris's most iconic landmark in the background.

streams and bridges, and is a romantic place for a stroll. There is an aquarium in the northeast corner of the gardens and in December a lovely Christmas market takes place.

7

Aquarium de Paris - Cinéaqua

B6 **5 Ave Albert de Mun 75016** **Trocadéro, Iéna** **10am-7pm daily** **14 Jul** **cineaqua.com**

Originally built in 1878 for the Universal Exhibition, this is now a state-of-the-art aquarium which is home to over 500 species of sea creatures from around the world, including seahorses, clownfish, stonefish and some spectacular sharks and rays.

The building is located in a former quarry and has been designed to blend in entirely with the Chaillot hillside. Cinema screens showing cartoons and animal documentaries are interspersed with the aquariums, and there are art exhibitions and shows for children in the theatre. The aquarium regularly runs special late night openings; check the website for details.

→

The Eiffel Tower seen from the Jardins du Trocadéro

One of the ornamental fountains in the huge Place de la Concorde

⑧ 🍴 🖥 🏛

Avenue des Champs-Élysées

📍 D4 📮 75008
Ⓜ Franklin D. Roosevelt, George V

Paris's most famous and popular thoroughfare had its beginnings in about 1667, when the royal landscape garden designer André Le Nôtre extended the royal view from the Tuileries by creating a tree-lined avenue which eventually became known as the Champs-Élysées (Elysian Fields). It has been France's national "triumphal way" ever since the homecoming of Napoleon's body from St Helena in 1840. With the addition of cafés and restaurants in the second half of the 19th century, the Champs-Élysées became the place in which to see and be seen. The Rond-Point des Champs-Élysées is the prettiest part, with chestnut trees and flowerbeds. A number of major brands, such as Banana Republic, H&M and Abercrombie & Fitch, have their flagship stores here, while fast-food cafés jostle for space with more upmarket establishments such as Fouquet's Brasserie. In December, the avenue hosts a huge Christmas market and holiday light show.

⑨ Place Charles de Gaulle (l'Étoile)

📍 C1 📮 75008 Ⓜ Charles de Gaulle-Étoile

Known as the Place de l'Étoile until the death of Charles de Gaulle in 1969, the area is still referred to simply as l'Étoile, the star. The present *place* was laid out in accordance with Baron Haussmann's plans of 1854 (*p55*). For motorists, it is the ultimate challenge.

⑩ Place de la Concorde

📍 1F5 📮 75008
Ⓜ Concorde

One of Europe's most magnificent and historic squares, Place de la Concorde covers more than 8 ha (20 acres) in the middle of Paris. Starting out as Place Louis XV, displaying a statue of the eponymous king, it was built in the mid-18th century by architect Jacques-Ange Gabriel, who chose to make it an open

One of the most magnificent and historic squares in the whole of Europe, Place de la Concorde covers more than 8 ha (20 acres) in the middle of Paris.

octagon with only the north side containing mansions. In the square's next incarnation, as the Place de la Révolution, the statue was replaced by the guillotine. The death toll in the square in two and a half years was 1,119, and victims included Louis XVI, Marie-Antoinette (who died in view of the secret apartment she kept at No. 2 Rue Royale) and the Revolutionary leaders Danton and Robespierre.

In the spirit of reconciliation, the square was then renamed Concorde (originally by chastened Revolutionaries). Its grandeur was enhanced in the 19th century by the arrival of the 3,200-year-old Luxor obelisk – a gift from Egypt, 23-m (75-ft) tall and covered in hieroglyphics – as well as two fountains and eight statues personifying French cities. It has become the culminating point of triumphal parades down the Champs-Élysées each 14 July, most notably on the memorable Bastille Day of 1989 when the Revolution's bicentenary was celebrated by a million people, including many world leaders.

Grand Palais

⑪

⑨ E5 🚪 Porte A, Ave Général Eisenhower 75008 Ⓜ Champs-Élysées-Clemenceau 🕐 1 May, 25 Dec 🌐 grandpalais.fr

Built at the same time as the Petit Palais and the Pont Alexandre III, the exterior of this massive palace combines an imposing classical stone façade with a riot of Art Nouveau ironwork. The enormous glass roof (15,000 sq m/ 160,000 sq ft) has Récipon's colossal bronze statues of flying horses and chariots at its four corners. The metal structure supporting the glass weighs 8,500 tonnes, some 500 tonnes more than the Eiffel Tower. Today, the restored Grand Palais hosts art exhibitions and other events. During the winter, the nave turns into the world's biggest indoor ice rink. Major temporary and touring exhibitions are held at the Galeries Nationales in the same building; these are often very popular and it's worth booking ahead. Check the website for details of what's on.

Petit Palais

⑫

⑨ E5 🚪 Ave Winston Churchill 75008 Ⓜ Champs-Élysées-Clemenceau 🕐 10am–6pm Tue–Sun (to 9pm Fri for temporary exhibitions) 🚫 Public hols 🌐 petit palais.paris.fr

Built for the Universal Exhibition in 1900, this jewel of a building now houses the Musée des Beaux-Arts de la Ville de Paris. Arranged around a pretty courtyard, the palace is similar in style to the Grand Palais, and is graced with Ionic columns, a grand porch and a dome. The wing nearest the river is used for temporary exhibitions, while the Champs-Élysées side of the palace houses the permanent collections: Greek and Roman artifacts; medieval and Renaissance ivories and sculptures; Renaissance clocks and jewellery; and 17th-, 18th-, and 19th-century art and furniture. There are also many works by the Impressionists.

↓ The Neo-Classical entrance to the Petit Palais

EAT

L'Astrance
Go for broke at this three-Michelin-star restaurant with epic tasting menus.

⑨ B7 🚪 4 Rue Beethoven 75016 🌐 astrance restaurant.com

€€€

Pierre Gagnaire
One of Paris's best chefs wows diners with a contemporary dining experience.

⑨ C4 🚪 6 Rue Balzac 75008 🌐 pierre-gagnaire.com

€€€

Relais de l'Entrecôte
Steak, chips and nothing else. It's a family favourite; just go early to queue up – it doesn't take long to get a table.

⑨ D5 🚪 15 Rue Marbeuf 75008 🌐 relaisentrecote.fr

€€€

↑ A ceiling painting by Maurice Denis inside the Petit Palais

The Avenue de la Grande Armée, looking towards the Arc de Triomphe

⑬ Pont Alexandre III

📍 E5 🏠 75008
Ⓜ Champs-Élysées-Clemenceau

This is Paris's prettiest bridge with its exuberant Art Nouveau decoration of lamps, cherubs, nymphs and winged horses at either end. It was built between 1896 and 1900, in time for the Universal Exhibition, and it was named after Tsar Alexander III of Russia, whose son Nicholas II laid the foundation stone in October 1896.

The style of the bridge reflects that of the Grand Palais, to which it leads on the Right Bank. The construction of the bridge is a marvel of 19th-century engineering, consisting of a 6-m- (18-ft-) high single-span steel arch that stretches across the Seine. The design was subject to strict controls that prevented the bridge from obscuring the view of the Champs-Élysées (p224) or the Dôme des Invalides (p204) so, today, you can still enjoy magnificent views from here.

⑭ Palais de la Découverte

📍 E5 🏠 Ave Franklin D Roosevelt 75008
Ⓜ Franklin D. Roosevelt
🕐 9:30am–6pm Tue–Sat, 10am–7pm Sun 🚫 1 Jan, 1 May, 25 Dec 🌐 palais-decouverte.fr

Opened in a wing of the Grand Palais (p225) for the World's Fair of 1937, this science museum is a Paris institution. Demonstrations and displays, including a planetarium, cover many subjects and explain such phenomena as electromagnetism.

⑮ Avenue Montaigne

📍 D5 🏠 75008
Ⓜ Franklin D. Roosevelt

In the 19th century, this avenue was famous for its dance halls and its Winter Garden, where Parisians went to hear Adolphe Sax play his newly invented saxophone. Today, it is still one of Paris's most fashionable streets, bustling with restaurants, cafés, hotels and designer boutiques. At one end lies the beautiful Art Deco Théâtre de Champs-Élysées, built in 1913.

⑯ Parc Monceau

📍 D3 🏠 35 Blvd de Courcelles 75017
Ⓜ Monceau, Courcelles
🕐 7am–8pm daily (to 10pm summer)

This green haven dates back to 1778 when the Duc de Chartres (later Duc d'Orléans) commissioned the painter-writer and amateur landscape designer Louis Carmontelle to create a magnificent garden. Also a theatre designer, Carmontelle created a "garden of dreams", an exotic landscape full of architectural follies in imitation of English and German fashions of the time. In 1783, the Scottish landscape gardener Thomas Blaikie laid out an area of the garden in English style. The park was the scene of the first recorded parachute landing,

The ornamental pond in the charming Parc Monceau ↑

made by André-Jacques Garnerin on 22 October 1797. Over the years, the park changed hands and in 1852 it was acquired by the state and half the land sold off for property development. The remaining land was made into public gardens. These were restored and new buildings erected by Adolphe Alphand, architect of the Bois de Boulogne (p292) and the Bois de Vincennes (p294).

The park, one of the most chic in Paris, has lost many of its early features. A *naumachia* basin – an ornamental version of a Roman pool used for simulating naval battles – remains, flanked by Corinthian columns. Other remaining features include a Renaissance arcade, pyramids, statues, a river and the Pavillon de Chartres, a charming rotunda designed by Nicolas Ledoux which was once used as a tollhouse. Just south of here is a huge red Chinese pagoda, which now houses a gallery devoted to Asian art.

17

Musée Jacquemart-André

▢E3 ⌂158 Blvd Haussmann 75008 Ⓜ Miromesnil, St-Philippe-du-Roule Ⓞ10am–6pm daily (to 8:30pm Mon) Ⓦmusee-jacquemart-andre.com

This museum is known for its collection of Italian Renaissance and French 18th-century works of art, as well as its beautiful frescoes by Tiepolo. Highlights include works by Mantegna, Uccello's masterpiece *St George and the Dragon* (c1435), paintings by Boucher and Fragonard, and 18th-century tapestries.

←

Pont Alexandre III, with its flamboyant Art Nouveau decoration

STAY

Four Seasons Hotel George V

A perennial favourite, this landmark luxury hotel is a true treat for those willing to pay the price.

▢C5 ⌂31 Ave George V 75008 Ⓦfourseasons.com

€€€

Hôtel Barrière Le Fouquet's

A hotel this close to the Champs-Élysées doesn't come cheap, but nor does it disappoint.

▢C4 ⌂46 Ave George V 75008 Ⓦhotelsbarriere.com

€€€

Shangri-La

A luxury hotel with all the trimmings, and a fantastic Chinese restaurant.

▢B6 ⌂10 Ave d'Iéna 75116 Ⓦshangri-la.com.

€€€

18
Palais de l'Élysée

📍E4 🏠55 Rue du Faubourg-St-Honoré 75008 Ⓜ St-Philippe-du-Roule

Backing onto splendid English-style gardens, the Élysée Palace, closed to the public, was built for the Comte d'Evreux in 1718 and has been the official residence of the President of the Republic since 1873. From 1805 to 1808, it was occupied by Napoleon's sister, Caroline, and her husband, Joachim Murat. Two charming rooms have been preserved from this period: the Salon Murat and the Salon d'Argent. General de Gaulle gave press conferences in the Hall of Mirrors. Today, the president's modernized apartments are located on the first floor in the east wing, opposite the Rue de l'Élysée.

The imposing Art Deco Palais de Tokyo, housing two galleries of modern art →

19
Cimetière de Passy

📍A6 🏠2 Rue du Commandant-Shloesing 75016 Ⓜ Trocadéro ⏰8am–5:30pm Mon–Sat, 9am–5:30pm Sun (to 6pm 16 Mar–5 Nov)

This small cemetery, opened in 1820, is packed with the graves of eminent Parisians. Figures buried here include the composers Claude Debussy, Gabriel Fauré and Jacques Ibert, and renowned painter Edouard Manet, as well as many politicians and aristocrats, such as Ghislaine Dommanget, Princess of Monaco; Leila Pahlavi, daughter of the Shah of Iran; and Michel Droit, writer and journalist.

←

Edouard Manet's gravestone in the Cimetière de Passy

20
Musée d'Art Moderne de la Ville de Paris

📍C6 🏠11 Ave du Président-Wilson 75116 Ⓜ Iéna, Alma Marceau ⏰10am–6pm Tue–Sun (to 10pm Thu) 🚫Public hols 🌐mam.paris.fr

This large lively museum houses the city of Paris's own renowned collection of modern art. It has about 10,000 works representing major 20th- and 21st-century artistic movements and artists. Established in 1961, the museum is one of two within the vast Palais de Tokyo, which was built for the 1937 World's Fair.

One of the museum's highlights is Raoul Dufy's gigantic mural *The Spirit of Electricity*, which traces the history of electricity through the ages. It was designed for the Electricity Pavilion in the 1937 World's Fair. One of the

largest paintings in the world, measuring 600 sq metres (6,500 sq ft), this curved mural takes up a whole room of the museum. Also notable are the Cubists, Amedeo Modigliani, George Rouault, Duchamp, Klein and the Fauves. This group of avant-garde artists, including Dufy and Derain, was dominated by Matisse, whose celebrated mural, *La Danse*, is on display here; you can see both the incomplete early version and the finished version. Entry to the permanent exhibition is free, while the frequent temporary exhibitions require a ticket.

Did You Know?

Passy was a small town, integrated into Paris only in 1860.

21

Palais de Tokyo

C5 · 13 Ave du Président-Wilson 75116 · Iéna, Alma Marceau · Noon–midnight Wed-Mon · 1 Jan, 1 May, 25 Dec, 2 weeks in Dec · palaisde tokyo.com

This enormous modern art gallery is adjacent to the Musée d'Art Moderne de la Ville de Paris within the imposing 1937 Palais de Tokyo. It presents an innovative, changing programme of contemporary art exhibitions, fashion shows and avant-garde performances. Installations by artists such as Pierre Joseph, Wang Du and Frank Scurti have earned the Palais de Tokyo a reputation as one of the most cutting-edge art houses in Europe. It also has a good bookshop and two restaurants, while club nights regularly take place in its basement space, Yoyo.

DRINK

Here are five of the best hotel bars for enjoying a decadent sundowner around Champs-Élysées.

Le Bar at the Four Seasons Hotel George V
C5 · 31 Ave George V 75008 · fourseasons.com

Bar de l'Hôtel Belmont
C5 · 30 Rue de Bassano, 75116 · belmont-paris-hotel.com

Bar Kléber at the Peninsula
B4 · 19 Ave Kléber 75116 · paris.peninsula.com

Le Bar Botaniste at the Shangri-La
B6 · 10 Ave d'Iéna 75116 · shangri-la.com

Le Bar du Bristol
E4 · 112 Rue du Faubourg-St-Honoré 75008 · oetkercollection.com

A SHORT WALK
CHAMPS-ÉLYSÉES

Distance 2 km (1.25 miles) **Nearest metro** Invalides
Time 20 minutes

The formal gardens that line the Champs-Élysées from the Place de la Concorde to the Rond-Point have changed little since they were laid out by the architect Jacques Hittorff in 1838. The Grand Palais and Petit Palais, which were created as a showpiece of the Third Republic for the Universal Exhibition of 1900, sit on either side of an impressive vista that stretches from Place Clémenceau across the elegant curve of the Pont Alexandre III to the Invalides.

There are plaques on the back door of the Théâtre du Rond-Point representing Napoleon's campaigns.

Metro Franklin D Roosevelt

AVE DES CHAMP

AVE FRANKLIN D ROOSEVELT

AVE G. EISENHOWER

Christian Dior and other haute couture houses are based on the chic Avenue Montaigne.

RUE JEAN GOUJON

Designed by Charles Girault, the 19th-century Grand Palais is still used for major exhibitions (p225).

RUE FRANÇOIS PREMIER

The Lasserre restaurant is decorated in the style of a luxurious ocean liner from the 1930s.

Outside the Palais de la Découverte is a pair of equestrian statues (p228).

PL DU CANADA

COURS L

PONT DES INVALIDES

← The interior of the Palais de la Découverte, a museum of scientific discoveries

Avenue des Champs-Élysées was the setting for the victory parades following the two World Wars, and for the bicentennial parade in 1989 (p224).

Metro Champs-Élysées-Clemenceau

Locator Map
For more detail see p216

The Jardins des Champs-Élysées, with their fountains, flower beds, paths and pleasure pavilions, became very popular towards the end of the 19th century. Fashionable Parisians, including Marcel Proust, often came here.

FINISH

↑ Strolling through the tree-lined Jardin des Champs-Élysées

Lit by natural light, Petit Palais is as much a work of art as the wide-ranging collections it contains, from antiquity to the belle époque (p225).

START

Pont Alexandre III's four columns help to anchor the piers that absorb the immense forces generated by such a large single-span structure (p228).

0 metres 100
0 yards 100

N

The interior of St-Germain-des-Prés church

ST-GERMAIN-DES-PRÉS

Named after a Benedictine abbey that was
founded here in the 6th century, St-Germain-
des-Prés came to prominence in the 1950s as
the nucleus of the city's intellectual life. Largely
working class, the neighbourhood attracted
numerous writers and philosophers with its
non-conformist atmosphere and profusion of
bookshops and publishing houses. Leading figures
such as Jean-Paul Sartre and Simone de Beauvoir
held court at the district's celebrated cafés, most
notably Café de Flore, Les Deux Magots and
Le Procope. They and their disciples may have
left, but this area is still renowned for its youthful
student atmosphere and literary traditions.
Since the 1970s the neighbourhood has become
progressively more upmarket, with the emergence
of numerous fashionable boutiques. Rue de Seine
is lined with charming restaurants and contains
many high-end galleries where the smart set
purchase their art.

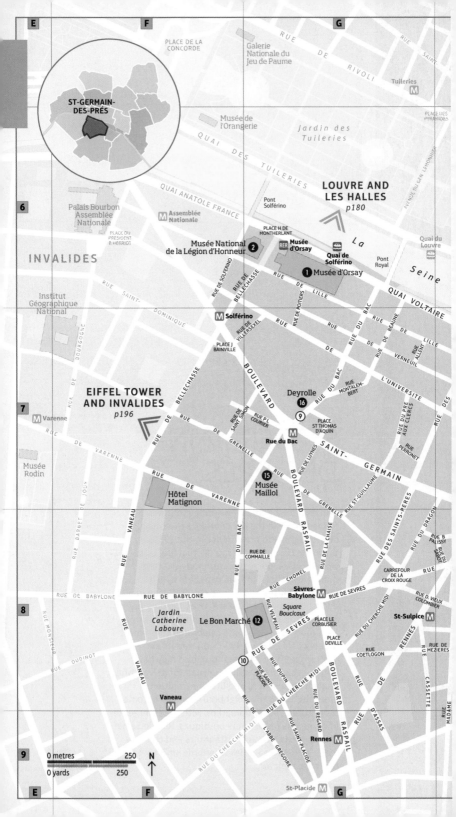

ST-GERMAIN-DES-PRÉS

Must See
1. Musée d'Orsay

Experience More
2. Musée National de la Légion d'Honneur
3. Académie Française
4. École Nationale Supérieure des Beaux Arts
5. Musée Eugène Delacroix
6. St-Germain-des-Prés
7. Monnaie de Paris
8. Rue St-André-des-Arts
9. Cour du Commerce St-André
10. Le Procope
11. St-Sulpice
12. Le Bon Marché
13. Café de Flore
14. Les Deux Magots
15. Musée Maillol
16. Deyrolle
17. Pont des Arts

Eat
1. Semilla
2. Le Comptoir du Relais
3. Ze Kitchen Galerie

Stay
4. Hôtel d'Aubusson
5. Relais Christine
6. Hôtel Récamier

Shop
7. Rue Lobineau
8. Rue Bonaparte
9. Rue du Bac
10. Rue de Sèvres
11. Rue de Buci

MUSÉE D'ORSAY

G6 · 1 Rue de la Légion d'Honneur · Solférino · 24, 68, 69, 84 to Quai A
France; 73 to Rue Solférino; 63, 83, 84, 94 to Bd St-Germain · Musée d'Orsay
9:30am–6pm Tue–Sun (to 9:45pm Thu) · 1 Jan, 1 May, 25 Dec · musee-orsay.fr

The Musée d'Orsay picks up where the Louvre ends, showing a variety of
art forms from 1848 to 1914. Its star attraction is a superb collection of
Impressionist art, which includes famous works by Monet, Renoir, Manet
and Degas, as well as pieces by Georges Seurat, Gaugin and Van Gogh.

In 1986, 47 years after it had closed as a
mainline railway station, Victor Laloux's superb
late-19th-century building was reopened as
the Musée d'Orsay. Originally commissioned
by the Orléans railway company to be its Paris
terminus, the structure avoided demolition in
the 1970s after being classified as a historical
monument. During the conversion into a
museum, much of the original architecture
was retained. The collection was set up to
present each of the arts of the period from
1848 to 1914 in the context of contemporary
society and other forms of creative activity
happening at the time. Renovations to the
upper levels have expanded exhibition spaces
to improve the display of works.

↑ The light and spacious entrance hall,
with curved glass ceiling

GREAT VIEW
City Panorama

Make your way to the rear escalator, ride it all the way up, and head to the small rooftop terrace for a great bird's-eye view of the city.

1 The clock face on the fifth floor provides views over the Seine to the Jardin des Tuileries.

2 *Le Déjeuner sur l'herbe* (1863) by Manet caused a scandal when it was first exhibited.

3 Monet's *Le Déjeuner sur l'herbe* (1865–6) was a tribute to the work of the same name by Manet.

GALLERY GUIDE

The collection occupies three levels. On the ground floor, there are works from the mid- to late 19th century. The middle level features Art Nouveau decorative art and a range of paintings and sculptures from the second half of the 19th century to the early 20th century, as well as Neo-Impressionist art. The upper level has an outstanding collection of Impressionist art.

←

The former railway station, designed by Victor Laloux for the Universal Exhibition in 1900

EXPERIENCE MORE

2

Musée Nationale de la Légion d'Honneur

📍 G6 🏠 2 Rue de la Légion d'Honneur (Parvis du Musée d'Orsay) 75007 Ⓜ Solférino 🚇 Musée d'Orsay 🕐 1–6pm Wed–Sun 🗓 1 Jan, 1 May, 15 Aug, 1 Nov, 25 Dec 🌐 musee-legiondhonneur.fr

Next to the Musée d'Orsay is the truly massive Hôtel de Salm. It was one of the last great mansions to be built in the area (1782). The first owner was a German count, Prince de Salm-Kyrbourg, who was guillotined in 1794.

Today, the building contains a museum where you can learn all about the Legion of Honour, a decoration launched by Napoleon I. Those awarded the honour wear a small red rosette in their buttonhole. The impressive displays of medals and insignia are complemented by paintings. In one of the rooms, Napoleon's Legion of Honour is on display with his sword and breastplate.

The museum also contains examples of decorations from most parts of the world, among them the British Victoria Cross and the American Purple Heart.

3

Académie Française

📍 H7 🏠 23 Quai de Conti 75006 Ⓜ Pont Neuf, St-Germain-des-Prés 🌐 academie-francaise.fr

This striking Baroque edifice was built as a school for young noblemen in 1688 and given over to the Institut de France in 1805. Its cupola was designed by architect Louis Le Vau to harmonize with the Palais du Louvre.

The Académie Française is the oldest of the five academies of the institute. Founded in 1635 by Cardinal Richelieu, it is charged with regulating the French language by deciding acceptable grammar and vocabulary, and with the compilation of an official

> **INSIDER TIP**
> **Macaron Mecca**
>
> Sample the city's most innovative macarons, such as jasmine and wild strawberry, at Pierre Hermé's flagship, on Rue Bonaparte.

dictionary of the French language. From the beginning, membership has been limited to 40 scholars, who are entrusted with a lifelong commitment to working on the dictionary. The building is only open to the public during the Journées du Patrimonie (Heritage Days) on the third weekend of September.

4

École Nationale Supérieure des Beaux-Arts

H7 13 Quai Malaquais & 14 Rue Bonaparte 75006 St-Germain-des-Prés beauxartsparis.com

The main French school of fine arts occupies an enviable position at the corner of Rue Bonaparte and the riverside Quai Malaquais. The school is housed in several buildings, the most imposing being the 19th-century Palais des Études. A host of budding French and foreign painters and architects have crossed the large courtyard to study in the ateliers of the school. Young American architects, in particular, have frequented the halls since the late 19th century. Works from its collections can be viewed in regular exhibitions; see website.

← The Académie Française, ultimate arbiter of French language and grammar

---

5

Musée Eugène Delacroix

H7 6 Rue de Fürstenberg 75006 St-Germain-des-Prés, Mabillon 9:30am-5:30pm Wed-Mon 1 Jan, 1 May, 25 Dec musee-delacroix.fr

The leading non-conformist Romantic painter Eugène Delacroix, known for his passionate and highly coloured canvases, lived and worked here from 1857 to his death in 1863. Here, he painted *The Entombment of Christ* and *The Way to Calvary* (which now hang in the museum). He also created superb murals for the Chapel of the Holy Angels in the nearby St-Sulpice church *(p243)*, which is part of the reason why he moved to this area. The first-floor apartment and garden studio now form a national museum, where regular exhibitions of Delacroix's work are held. The apartment has portraits, studies for future works and artistic memorabilia.

The charm of Delacroix's garden is reflected in the tiny Fürstenberg square. With its pair of rare catalpa trees and old-fashioned street lamps, the square is one of Paris's most romantic corners.

6

St-Germain-des-Prés

H7 3 Pl St-Germain-des-Prés 75006 St-Germain-des-Prés 8am-7:45pm daily eglise-saintgermaindespres.fr

This is the oldest church in Paris, originating in 543 when King Childebert built a basilica to house holy relics. It became a powerful Benedictine abbey, which was suppressed during the French Revolution, when most of the buildings were destroyed by a fire in 1794. The present church dates from about the 11th century and was restored in the 19th century. The interior is a mix of architectural styles, with a number of 6th-century marble columns, Gothic vaulting and Romanesque arches. Famous tombs include those of René Descartes.

TOP 5 SHOPPING STREETS

Rue Lobineau
H8
Home of the St-Germain food market.

Rue Bonaparte
H8
Full of swanky shops, including the Pierre Hermé flagship.

Rue du Bac
G7
Full of pastry shops and other confections.

Rue de Sèvres
G8
The location of Le Bon Marché *(p243)*, Paris's first department store.

Rue de Buci
H8
A former market street that today houses cafés and cute shops.

7

Monnaie de Paris

Q H7 **🏠** 11 Quai de Conti 75006 **Ⓜ** Pont Neuf, Odéon **🕐** 11am–7pm daily (to 9pm Wed) **🌐** monnaiedeparis.fr

In the late 18th century, when Louis XV decided to rehouse the Mint, he launched a design competition for the new building. The Hôtel des Monnaies is the result. It was completed in 1775, and the architect, Jacques Antoine, lived here until his death.

Coins were minted in the mansion until 1973, when the process was moved to Pessac in the Gironde. Until recently only a small part of the building was accessible to the public, but after major renovation, the whole complex can now be visited, including its interior courtyards and a garden, as well as its revamped museum, the Musée du 11 Conti.

Centred around a tranquil public space and surrounded by artists' workshops, the permanent gallery focuses on the history of coins and minting. Regular exhibitions of contemporary art are also staged here. Plus, there are shops selling work by resident artisans, a gastronomic restaurant run by chef Guy Savoy and a more casual café.

←

A coin press at the newly revamped Musée du 11 Conti

Did You Know?
—
Remnants of the old Paris wall can be found in the chocolate shop on Cour du Commerce St-André.

8

Rue St-André-des-Arts

Q J8 **🏠** 75006 **Ⓜ** St-Michel, Odéon

Extending from Place St-André-des-Arts, where the square's namesake church once stood, this little street boasts numerous historical monuments. Dating back to 1179, it once led to the gate of the city in the former Philippe Auguste wall. The mansion at No. 27 was owned by Louis XIII's geographer in the 1600s, while grammarian and encyclopaedist Pierre Larousse lived at No. 49 in the 19th century. Peeling south off Rue St-André-des-Arts is the cobbled Cour du Commerce.

9

Cour du Commerce St-André

Q J8 **🏠** 75006 **Ⓜ** Odéon

No. 9 in this historic passage has a particularly grisly past, because it was here that Dr Guillotin is supposed to have perfected his "philanthropic decapitating machine". In fact, although the idea was Guillotin's, it was Dr Antoine Louis, a Parisian surgeon, who was responsible for putting

The picturesque Cour du Commerce St-André ↑ enchants at twilight

the "humane" plan into action. When the guillotine was first used for execution in 1792, it was known as a *Louisette*.

10

Le Procope

Q J8 **🏠** 13 Rue de l'Ancienne-Comédie 75006 **Ⓜ** Odéon **🕐** 11:30am–midnight daily (to 1am Thu–Sat) **🌐** procope.com

Founded in 1686 by the Sicilian Francesco Procopio dei Coltelli, this claims to be the world's first coffee house. It quickly became popular with the city's political and cultural elite.

Its illustrious patrons have included the philosopher Voltaire – who supposedly drank 40 cups of his favourite mixture of coffee and chocolate every day – and the young Napoleon, who would leave his hat as security while he went searching for the money to pay the bill. Le Procope is now an 18th-century-style restaurant run by the famous Frères Blanc group.

13

Café de Flore

⊙ H7 **⌂** 172 Blvd St-Germain 75006 **Ⓜ** St-Germain-des-Prés **⊙** 7:30am-1:30am daily **Ⓦ** cafedeflore.fr

The classic Art Deco interior of this café has changed little since the War. Like its neighbouring rival Les Deux Magots (p244), Café de Flore has hosted most of the French intellectuals during the post-War years.

EAT

Semilla
Sharing plates and fresh, innovative cooking with local ingredients are on the menu here.

⊙ H7 **⌂** 54 Rue de Seine 75006 **Ⓦ** semillaparis.com

€€€

Le Comptoir du Relais
This bistro is a staple of the area for inventive French cooking at lunch and dinner.

⊙ H8 **⌂** 9 Carrefour de l'Odéon 75006 **Ⓦ** hotel-paris-relais-saint-germain.com

€€€

Ze Kitchen Galerie
French cooking infused with international inspirations; the tasting menu at this former canteen is good value.

⊙ J7 **⌂** 4 Rue des Grands Augustins 75006 **⊙** Sat, Sun **Ⓦ** zekitchengalerie.fr

€€€

11

St-Sulpice

⊙ H8 **⌂** 2 Rue Palatine, Pl St-Sulpice 75006 **Ⓜ** St-Sulpice **⊙** 7:30am-7:30pm daily **Ⓦ** pss75.fr/saint-sulpice-paris

It took over a century, from 1646, for this imposing church to be built. The result is a simple two-storey west front with two tiers of elegant columns. The overall harmony of the building is marred only by the towers, one at each end, which do not match.

Large arched windows fill the interior with light. By the front door are two huge shells given to François I by the Venetian Republic – they rest on bases sculpted by Jean-Baptiste Pigalle.

In the side chapel to the right of the main door are three magnificent murals by Eugène Delacroix: *Jacob Wrestling with the Angel*, *Heliodorus Driven from the Temple* and *St-Michael Killing the Dragon*. If you are lucky, you can catch an organ recital. Regular guided tours of the church take place at 2:30pm every Sunday.

12

Le Bon Marché

⊙ G8 **⌂** 24 Rue de Sèvres 75007 **Ⓜ** Sèvres-Babylone **⊙** 10am-8pm Mon-Sat (to 9pm Thu), 11am-8pm Sun **Ⓦ** 24sevres.com

Welcoming as many as 15,000 customers per day, "The Good Market" (or "The Good Deal") is the swankiest department store in Paris, selling luxury goods as well as gourmet foods in its annexe La Grande Epicerie on Rue du Bac. The designer clothing section is well-sourced, the high-end accessories are excellent, and the own-brand linen has a good quality-to-price ratio.

Le Bon Marché is also the world's oldest department store, founded in 1852 by Aristide Boucicaut and his wife. The Boucicauts used their keen sense of commerce to introduce innovative practices – fixed prices, sales, home delivery, advertising and guarantees – that became the standard for other *grands magasins*. Designed by Louis-Charles Boileau and Gustave Eiffel, it is an architectural landmark.

14 🖵
Les Deux Magots

📍H7 🏠6 Pl St-Germain-des-Prés 75006 Ⓜ St-Germain-des-Prés ⏰7:30am–1am daily 🗓One week in Jan 🌐lesdeuxmagots.com

Established in 1914, this café still trades on its reputation as the meeting place of the city's literary and intellectual elite. This derives from the patronage of Surrealist artists and writers, including Ernest Hemingway, in the 1920s and 1930s, and existentialist philosophers and writers in the 1950s.

The present clientele is more likely to consist of publishers or people-watchers than the new Hemingway. The café's name comes from the two wooden statues of Chinese commercial agents (*magots*) that adorn one of the

pillars. This is a good place for enjoying an old-fashioned hot chocolate and watching the world go by. On Thursdays, there's a live jazz session between 7:30 and 10pm.

15 🎨🖵🏛
Musée Maillol

📍G7 🏠59/61 Rue de Grenelle 75007 Ⓜ Sèvres-Babylone, Rue du Bac ⏰10:30am–6:30pm daily (to 9:30pm Fri) 🗓1 Jan, 25 Dec 🌐museemaillol.com

Once the home of novelist Alfred de Musset, this museum was created by Dina Vierny, former model of Aristide Maillol. All aspects of the artist's work are here: drawings, engravings, paintings, sculpture and decorative objects. Also displayed is Vierny's private collection, including works

STAY

Hôtel d'Aubusson
A cosy lobby and refined rooms define this Left Bank favourite.

📍J7 🏠33 Rue Dauphine 75006 🌐hoteldaubusson.com

€€€

Relais Christine
This luxury property includes a spa for guests who are after a bit of pampering.

📍J7 🏠3 Rue Christine 75006 🌐relais-christine.com

€€€

Hôtel Récamier
Elegance and comfort are on order at this tiny property tucked behind St-Sulpice.

📍H8 🏠3B Place St-Sulpice 75006 🌐hotelrecamier.com

€€€

At night, illuminated every so often by the Bateaux Mouches cruising underneath, the Pont des Arts is an especially romantic place to walk or picnic in warmer months.

by Matisse, Picasso and Rodin. The museum stages regular temporary art exhibitions, which are usually on themes and artists associated with Maillol. Note that it is closed in between exhibitions, so it is best to check the website before visiting.

Large allegorical figures of the city of Paris, the River Seine and the four seasons decorate Edme Bouchardon's fountain, La Fontaine des Quatre Saisons, built in 1739–45, in front of the house.

16
Deyrolle

📍 G7 🏠 46 Rue du Bac 75005 Ⓜ Rue du Bac
🕐 10am–1pm Mon, 10am–7pm Tue–Sat
🌐 deyrolle.com

A Parisian institution since 1831, Deyrolle is a cabinet of curiosities that continues to delight all who enter its doors. Originally a taxidermy shop, it has evolved over the years, and now part of its mission is to raise awareness about wildlife conservation. The

← The Pont des Arts with its prime views of the Île de la Cité

casual visitor, however, can simply enjoy the collection of taxidermied animals, from giant elephants and rhinos to the most delicate birds and crustaceans. There is a wide range of insects housed in drawers. Iridescent beetles and colourful butterflies sit alongside terrifying tarantulas and scorpions. Everything is for sale, mostly at decent prices considering the quality.

17
Pont des Arts

📍 H7 🏠 75006
Ⓜ Louvre-Rivoli

Sometimes referred to as the Passerelle des Arts, this picturesque iron bridge, part of the UNESCO-listed Parisian riverfront, has more often been called the "Love Lock Bridge" in recent years. The nickname refers to the now-forbidden practice of couples fixing padlocks to the bridge to signify their love; the practice had to be stopped because the locks exerted too much weight on the structure and started to destroy it. Now revived and restored – following the removal of almost a million locks weighing 45 tonnes – this pedestrian bridge, built under Napoleon from 1801 to 1804, has been returned to its 19th-century splendour. The first iron bridge in Paris, it links the Institut de France with the Louvre, offering resplendent views of the Île de la Cité from above the river. At night, illuminated every so often by the Bateaux Mouches cruising gently underneath, the Pont des Arts is an especially romantic place to walk or picnic in warmer months.

THE CELEBRATED CAFÉS OF PARIS

One of the most enduring images of Paris is the café scene. For the visitor, it is the romantic vision of great artists, writers or eminent intellectuals consorting in one of the Left Bank's celebrated cafés. For the Parisian, the café is one of life's constants, an everyday experience, providing people with a place to tryst, drink and meet friends, to conclude business deals, or to simply watch the world go by.

The most famous cafés are on the Left Bank, in St-Germain and Montparnasse. Sartre and his intellectual peers, among them the writers Simone de Beauvoir and Albert Camus, gathered to work and discuss their ideas in Les Deux Magots and Café de Flore.

↑ Les Deux Magots, where the literary and intellectual elite used to gather

A SHORT WALK
ST-GERMAIN-DES-PRÉS

Distance 1.5 km (1 mile) **Nearest metro** St-Germain-des-Prés
Time 15 minutes

A walk around this area is to follow in the footsteps of some of Paris's most iconic inhabitants. After World War II, St-Germain-des-Prés became synonymous with intellectual life centred on bars and cafés. Philosophers, writers, actors and musicians mingled in the cellar nightspots and brasseries, where existentialist philosophy co-existed with American jazz. The area is now smarter than in the heyday of Jean-Paul Sartre and Simone de Beauvoir, but the writers are still around, enjoying the pleasures of café-life.

Descartes and Casimir, king of Poland, are among the notables buried in Paris's oldest church, St-Germain-des-Prés (p241).

In the 1950s, French intellectuals wrestled with new philosophical ideas in the Art Deco interior of the Café de Flore (p243).

The Les Deux Magots is famous for its celebrity patrons such as Ernest Hemingway (p244).

Colourful ceramics decorate the famous Brasserie Lipp, once frequented by politicians.

BLVD ST - GERMAIN

RUE DU DRAGON

RUE DU SABOT

RUE DE RENNES

RUE BONAPARTE

RUE DU FOUR

START

0 metres   100
0 yards   100
N

Café terraces, boutiques, cinemas, restaurants and bookshops characterize the central section of the Left Bank's Boulevard St-Germain.

← Les Deux Magots, on the pleasant Boulevard St-Germain

↑ Admiring the works of the Romantic painter at the Musée Eugène Delacroix

Locator Map
For more detail see p236

Picasso's sculpture *Homage to Apollinaire is a tribute to the artist's friend, the poet Guillaume Apollinaire. It was erected in 1959, near the Café de Flore.*

The tiny square of Rue de Fürstenberg, with its old-fashioned street lamps, is often used as a film set.

The Musée Eugène Delacroix is dedicated to the life and works of the Romantic painter (p241).

Rue de Buci was once the site of some real tennis courts. It now holds a lively daily market.

Palais Abbatial was the residence of abbots from 1586 till the 1789 Revolution.

Danton's statue (1889), by Auguste Paris, is a tribute to the Revolutionary leader.

Metro Odéon

Marché St-Germain is an old covered food market which opened in 1818, taking over the site of a former fairground.

Metro Mabillon

FINISH

RUE MAZARINE

RUE DE BUCI

BLVD ST-GERMAIN

RUE DE SEINE

RUE DE L'ANCIENNE COMEDIE

RUE MABILLON

RUE DE MONTFAUCON

RUE FELIBIEN

CARREFOUR DE L'ODEON

LATIN QUARTER

Located on the Left Bank, the Latin Quarter spreads over the 5th and 6th arrondissements. One of the oldest and best-known areas of Paris (the Rue St-Jacques is probably the oldest street in the city), this lively neighbourhood exudes a bohemian charm. It emerged in the Middle Ages as a student quarter, with the celebrated Sorbonne University attracting scholars from all over Europe. Much of the area's character was established at this time, as it grew up into a maze of tiny cobblestoned streets leading to gardens or churches. The Latin Quarter was at the centre of the riots that erupted out of the student protests and workers strike in May 1968, but since then the Boulevard St-Michel, the area's spine, has turned increasingly to commerce, not demonstrations. Today there are cheap shops and fast-food outlets, and the cobbled streets are now pedestrianized and filled with small cafés, ethnic boutiques and second-hand bookshops.

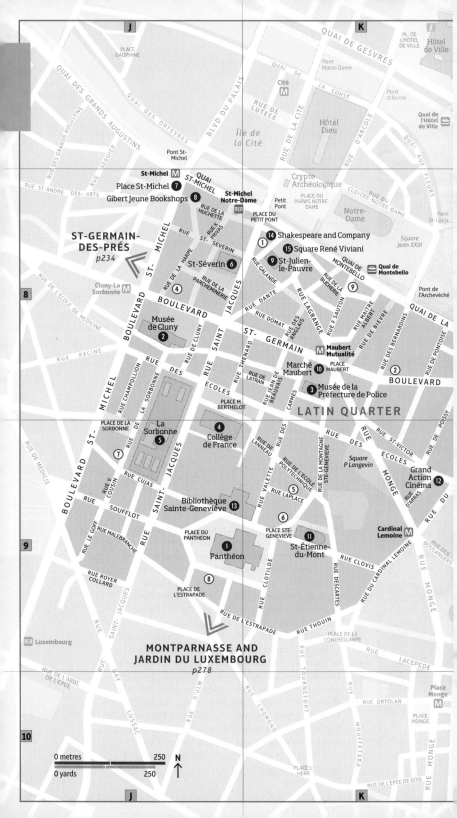

LATIN QUARTER

Must See
1 Panthéon

Experience More
2 Musée de Cluny
3 Musée de la Préfecture de Police
4 Collège de France
5 La Sorbonne
6 St-Séverin
7 Place St-Michel
8 Gibert Jeune Bookshops
9 St-Julien-le-Pauvre
10 Marché Maubert
11 St-Étienne-du-Mont
12 Grand Action Cinéma
13 Bibliothèque Sainte-Geneviève
14 Shakespeare and Company
15 Square René Viviani

Eat
1 Shakespeare and Co Café
2 Chez Gladines
3 La Tour d'Argent

Drink
4 Monk Le Taverne de Cluny
5 Le Piano Vache
6 Le Bombardier

Stay
7 Hôtel Design Sorbonne
8 Hôtel des Grands Hommes
9 Les Degrés de Notre-Dame

1 ✍ Ⓜ

PANTHÉON

📍 J9 🏛 Pl du Panthéon Ⓜ Cardinal Lemoine, Maubert-Mutualité
🚌 84 to Panthéon; 21, 27, 38, 82, 84, 85, 89 to Gare du Luxembourg
🚉 Luxembourg 🕐 10am–6:30pm daily (Oct–Mar: to 6pm)
🚫 1 Jan, 1 May, 25 Dec 🌐 paris-pantheon.fr

Inspired by the Pantheon in Rome, Paris's Panthéon was originally built as a church. Today a public building, it provides a fitting final resting place for the nation's great figures.

When Louis XV recovered from desperate illness in 1744, he was so grateful to be alive that he conceived a magnificent church to honour Sainte Geneviève. The design was entrusted to the French architect Jacques-Germain Soufflot, who planned the church in Neo-Classical style. Work began in 1757 and was completed in 1790, ten years after Soufflot's death, under the supervision of Guillaume Rondelet. But with the Revolution under way, the church was soon turned into a pantheon – a location for the tombs of France's great and good. Napoleon returned it to the Church in 1806, but it was secularized and then desecularized once more before finally being made a civic building in 1885.

←

The colonnade encircling the dome, both decorative and part of an ingenious supporting system

THE PANTHÉON'S ENSHRINED

The first of France's great men to be entombed here (though later removed on the orders of Robespierre) was the popular orator Honoré Mirabeau. Voltaire followed, as did other literary notables, including Jean-Jacques Rousseau, Victor Hugo and Émile Zola. In the 1970s, the remains of the wartime Resistance leader Jean Moulin were reburied here. Pierre and Marie Curie's remains were transferred here in 1995, followed by Alexandre Dumas in 2002. In 2015, four more Resistance fighters – two of them women – took their place in the Panthéon.

Pediment relief _____

Entrance _____

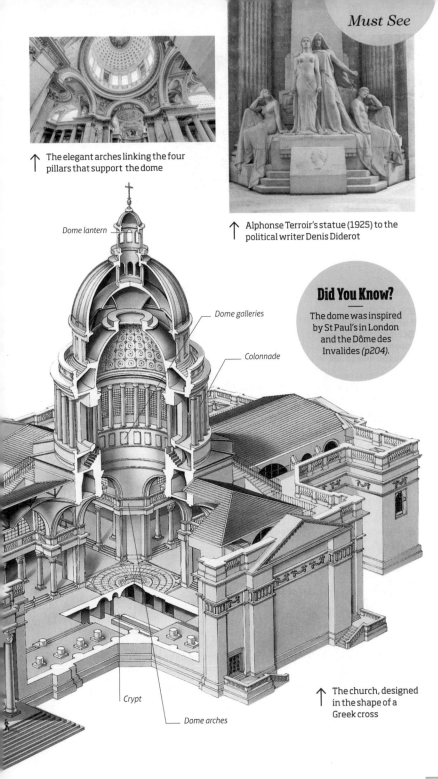

The elegant arches linking the four pillars that support the dome

↑ Alphonse Terroir's statue (1925) to the political writer Denis Diderot

Dome lantern

Dome galleries

Colonnade

Did You Know?

The dome was inspired by St Paul's in London and the Dôme des Invalides *(p204)*.

↑ The church, designed in the shape of a Greek cross

Crypt

Dome arches

← A collection of exquisitely decorated medieval armour and shields at the Musée de Cluny

Curiosities on show include arrest warrants for figures such as the famous Revolutionary Danton, and a rather sobering display of weapons and tools used by famous criminals. There is also a section on the part that the police played in the Resistance and subsequent liberation of Paris.

EXPERIENCE MORE

2

Musée de Cluny

⚑ J8 🏠 6 Pl Paul-Painlevé 75005
Ⓜ Cluny-La Sorbonne, Odéon, St-Michel
🌐 musee-moyenage.fr

This museum is housed in the former town house of the abbots of Cluny, the Hôtel de Cluny. Surrounded by imaginatively recreated medieval gardens, it is a unique combination of Gallo-Roman ruins incorporated into a medieval mansion, and contains one of the world's finest collections of medieval art. Highlights include the *Lady with the Unicorn*, an outstanding series of six tapestries, and the Gallery of the Kings, which contains 22 of the 27 stone heads of the Kings of Judah (carved around 1220 and removed from Notre-Dame in the 18th century). The museum is partially closed until 2020 while it undergoes renovation; check the website for details before planning a visit.

3 🎒

Musée de la Préfecture de Police

⚑ K8 🏠 4 Rue de la Montagne Ste-Geneviève 75005 📞 01 44 41 52 50
Ⓜ Maubert-Mutualité
🕐 9:30am–5pm Mon–Fri, 10:30am–5:30pm 3rd Sat of month 🚫 Sun & public hols

A darker side to Paris's history is exposed in this small, rather old-fashioned museum. Created in 1909, the collection traces the development of the police in Paris from the Middle Ages to the 20th century.

← A statue of Guillaume Budé, Collège de France

4

Collège de France

⚑ J9 🏠 11 Pl Marcelin-Berthelot 75005
Ⓜ Maubert-Mutualité
🕐 Sep–Jun: 9am–6pm Mon–Fri 🚫 School hols
🌐 college-de-france.fr

One of Paris's great institutes of research and learning, the college was established in 1530 by François I. Guided by the great humanist Guillaume Budé, the king aimed to counteract the rigidity and traditionalism of the Sorbonne. A statue of Budé stands in the west courtyard, and the unbiased approach to learning is reflected in the inscription on the old college entrance: *docet omnia* (all are taught here). Lectures are free and open to the public, depending on availability.

🔍 HIDDEN GEM
Thermes de Cluny

These Roman baths were built at the end of the 1st century AD. In the 14th century the Cluny monks built their abbey over the ruins and today they can be seen as part of a visit to the Musée de Cluny.

5 (M)

La Sorbonne

📍 J9 🏠 1 Rue Victor
Cousin 75005 Ⓜ Cluny-
La Sorbonne, Maubert-
Mutualité ⓦ sorbonne.fr

The Sorbonne, seat of the
University of Paris, was established in 1253 by Robert de
Sorbon, confessor to Louis IX,
for 16 poor students to study
theology. The college soon
became the centre of schol-
astic theology. In 1469, the
rector had three printing
machines brought over from
Mainz, thereby founding the
first printing house in France.
The college's opposition to
liberal 18th-century philosophy led to its suppression
during the Revolution. It was
re-established by Napoleon
in 1806. The buildings built
by Richelieu in the early
17th century were replaced
by the ones seen today, with

→

The chapel of
La Sorbonne, with
its elegant dome

the exception of the chapel.
You can book onto a guided
tour by emailing ahead.

6

St-Séverin

📍 J8 🏠 3 Rue des Prêtres-
St-Séverin 75005 Ⓜ St-
Michel 🕐 11am–7:30pm
Mon-Sat, 9am–8pm Sun
ⓦ saint-severin.com

One of the most beautiful
churches in Paris and a
popular venue for concerts,
St-Séverin, named after a
6th-century hermit who lived
in the area, is a perfect example of the Flamboyant Gothic
style. Construction finished
during the early 16th century
and included a remarkable
double ambulatory circling
the chancel. In 1684, the
Grande Mademoiselle,
cousin to Louis XIV,
adopted St-Séverin after
breaking with St-Sulpice
and had the church's
chancel modernized.

EAT

Shakespeare
and Co Café
Sip coffee and nibble
cakes outside the iconic
bookshop (p258).

📍 K8 🏠 37 Rue de la
Bûcherie 75005
ⓦ shakespeareand
company.com

Chez Gladines
Hearty and affordable
no-frills French meals.

📍 H8 🏠 44 Blvd St-
Germain 75005
ⓦ chezgladines-
saintgermain.fr

La Tour d'Argent
Dine where French
royalty first used
a fork. Try the
legendary duck.

📍 L8 🏠 17 Quai de la
Tournelle 75005 🚫 Sun,
Mon ⓦ tourdargent.com

€€€

❼ Place St-Michel

◙ J8 **🏛 75005**
Ⓜ St-Michel

This square at a busy intersection is a popular meeting place for Parisians and tour groups. Created in 1855, it's defined by the statue of Saint Michael the archangel slaying Satan, part of the monumental fountain built into the side of an adjacent building. The mix of colours and motifs earned it some criticism initially, and it was the last monumental wall fountain to be built in the city, ending the Renaissance-era trend brought to Paris by Catherine de Medici. Originally the fountain was meant to honour Napoleon Bonaparte, but the city council thought better of it and opted not to ruffle the feathers of anti-Bonaparte reactionaries. Nowadays, the fountain is a memorable welcome to the Latin Quarter for visitors entering the district from Île St-Louis. It is surrounded by cafés and bookshops which are popular with local university students.

❽ 🛍 Gibert Jeune Bookshops

◙ J8 **🏛 Multiple locations, Place St-Michel 75005**
Ⓜ St-Michel **🕐 9.30am–7.30pm** **✖ Sun** **🌐 gibert jeune.fr**

A former professor, Joseph Gibert opened his first shop in 1886. He sold books on the Quai St-Michel along with the other *bouquinistes* (used-book sellers who ply their wares out of green boxes along the Seine). Gibert's sons continued the family business, opening separate outposts under the name. Gibert Jeune is the original bookshop, while Gibert Joseph is a newer space, with a number of other outlets all dotted around the Place St-Michel, a stone's throw from the Sorbonne. Inside, customers will find academic books, maps of Paris, novels, travel guides and much else. At No. 10 there is a large collection of travel- and tourism-related books.

300,000
—
books are held in the green boxes of the *bouquinistes* along the river.

❾ St-Julien-le-Pauvre

◙ K8 **🏛 79 Rue Galande 75005** **Ⓜ St-Michel**
🚆 St Michel-Notre-Dame
🕐 9:30am–1:30pm, 3–6:30pm daily
🌐 sjlpmelkites.fr

At least three saints can claim to be patron of this church, but the most likely is St Julian the Hospitaller. The church, together with St-Germain-des-Prés, is one of the oldest in Paris, dating from between 1165 and 1220. The university held its official meetings in

→
The monumental fountain in Place St-Michel

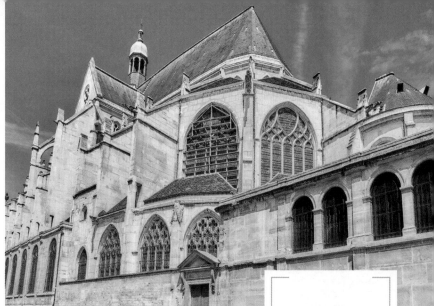

↑ The Gothic-Renaissance church of St-Étienne-du-Mont

the church until 1524, when a student protest created so much damage that meetings were barred from the church by parliament. Since 1889, it has belonged to the Melchite sect of the Greek Orthodox Church, and it is now the setting for chamber and religious music concerts.

Marché Maubert

Q K8 **A** Place Maubert 75005 **C** 7am-2.30pm Tue, Thu & Sat **M** Maubert-Mutualité

Popular with locals, this is one of the city's oldest outdoor markets, dating back to 1547. In earlier times the square was a place where carriage drivers emptied their waste, creating a truly gut-wrenching stench that drove out many inhabitants. Eventually the city cleaned up the mess and repurposed the square as a place for public executions, installing breaking wheels and gibbets here in the 16th century. By the 19th century

the square had returned to commercial use, and included a unique market where beggars would sell unused tobacco that they collected from the streets. Today the market is entirely wholesome, and you can browse stalls selling organic strawberries, cheese and dried hams.

St-Étienne-du-Mont

Q K9 **A** 30 Rue Descartes, Pl Ste-Geneviève 75005 **M** Cardinal Lemoine **C** Opening hours vary; check website for details **W** saintetiennedumont.fr

This remarkable church houses the shrine of Sainte Geneviève, patron saint of Paris, as well as the remains of the great literary figures Racine and Pascal. Some parts are in the Gothic style and others date from the Renaissance, including a magnificent rood screen that crosses the nave like a bridge. The stained-glass windows are also of note.

STAY

Hôtel Design Sorbonne

Stylish and central, this boutique hotel is a good deal given its location.

Q J9 **A** 6 Rue Victor Cousin 75005 **W** hotelsorbonne.com

€€€

Hôtel des Grands Hommes

Sleep in 19th-century grandeur at this tasteful property.

Q J9 **A** 17 Place du Panthéon 75005 **W** hoteldesgrands hommes.com

€€€

Les Degrés de Notre-Dame

Good-value simplicity in central Paris, right across from Notre-Dame.

Q K8 **A** 10 Rue des Grands Degrés 75005 **W** les-degres-de-notre-dame.com

€€€

12 🏷️ Grand Action Cinéma

📍 K9 🏠 5 Rue des Écoles 75005 Ⓜ Cardinal Lemoine, Jussieu 🌐 legrandaction.com

Located in the heart of the Latin Quarter, this tiny two-theatre operation is one of the most exciting cinematic experiences in Paris. The site has been a handball court, a Revolutionaries' meeting place and a dance hall over the years. Today it welcomes all sorts of films and retrospectives, ranging from niche independent films to Oscar-nominated pictures. The director and local student clubs regularly host industry professionals for talks to the public on themes such as science-fiction movies or Russian films. There are just two theatres with rows of red-cushioned seats, but the Grand Action perseveres even as multiplexes have risen in popularity.

13 Bibliothèque Sainte-Geneviève

📍 J9 🏠 10 Place du Panthéon 75005 Ⓜ Maubert-Mutualité 🕙 10am–10pm 🗓️ Sun 🌐 bsg.univ-paris3.fr

This massive, sober-looking library houses some two million documents salvaged from the nearby abbey of Sainte-Geneviève. Visitors to the neighbourhood may completely overlook it, as the enormous dome of the Pantheon tends to command more attention. It was, however, the first French library that was built without any connection to a palace or school building. It opened to the public in 1851, and architect Henri Labrouste incorporated a soaring glass-and-iron ceiling into the main reading room. There is usually a queue to enter the library, and visitors may be required to register at the front desk, but it is worth it to work in such a grand setting.

14 📖 🛍️ Shakespeare and Company

📍 K8 🏠 37 Rue de la Bûcherie 75005 🕙 10am–10pm daily Ⓜ St-Michel, Maubert-Mutualité 🌐 shakespeareand company.com

George Whitman opened this now-iconic shop in 1951. Originally called Le Mistral, it was renamed Shakespeare and Company in 1964 after the renowned bookshop run by Sylvia Beach on nearby Rue de l'Odéon, which closed in 1941 during the Occupation. Whitman sought to emulate the spirit of Beach's shop, attracting expat writers like Henry Miller and Anaïs Nin. Over the years, the owner

Did You Know?
—
This district was the scene of violent clashes between angry students and police in the riots of May 1968.

↑ The legendary American-run English-language bookshop Shakespeare and Company

allowed young writers to sleep in the shop for free, asking them only to read, pitch in at the shop and write a page-long autobiography. The shop continues Whitman's traditions, and his daughter Sylvia – named after Beach – maintains the ethos. There are always literary events taking place, some featuring big names like David Sedaris. The shop is tiny, but well-stocked with contemporary literature, Paris-themed books and a healthy selection of English travel books. Next door is a coffee shop (p255), where you can settle down with a book at one of the outdoor tables facing Notre-Dame.

15

Square René Viviani

◉ K8 ⌂ 25 Quai Montebello 75005 Ⓜ St-Michel, Maubert-Mutualité ⊙ 9.30am–5pm (to 8.30pm in summer)

One of many little green oases in Paris, Square René Viviani has views of Notre-Dame that beat all others. The park was once a graveyard belonging to the 6th-century basilica that formerly stood here. Now, the church St Julien-le-Pauvre (p256), begun in the 12th century, sits adjacent to the park. Its most notable feature is a black locust tree

(Robinia pseudoacacia), allegedly planted in 1601. Held up by a couple of concrete stilts, it is generally accepted to be the oldest tree in Paris. A World War I shell damaged the upper part of it, but it continues to grow. The square owes its name to France's first Labour Minister, René Viviani, who once spoke out in support of women's suffrage – albeit, in a limited fashion.

DRINK

Monk le Taverne de Cluny
Craft beer has infiltrated the Parisian scene, and this is the place for it on the Left Bank.

◉ J8 ⌂ 51 Rue de la Harpe 75005 Ⓦ latavernede cluny.com

€€€

Le Piano Vache
Students and locals hit the bar at this rowdy watering hole.

◉ K9 ⌂ 8 Rue Laplace 75005 🗓 Sun Ⓦ lepianovache.com

€€€

Le Bombardier
Paris has a few pubs worthy of the name, but this one has earned its stripes.

◉ K9 ⌂ 2 Place du Panthéon 75005 Ⓦ bombardierpub.fr

€€€

← Square René Viviani, a perfect retreat from the bustle of the city

A SHORT WALK
LATIN QUARTER

Distance 2 km (1.25 miles) **Nearest metro** Cluny La Sorbonne
Time 20 minutes

This riverside quarter, dating back to the Roman times, acquired its name from early Latin-speaking students. The area is generally associated with artists, intellectuals and the bohemian way of life but it also has a history of political unrest. In 1871, the Place St-Michel became the centre of the Paris Commune, and in May 1968, it was the site of the student uprisings. Though now sufficiently chic to contain the homes of some of the establishment, the quarter is still full of bookshops and cafés, perfect for an afternoon of browsing.

Place St-Michel contains a fountain by Davioud. The bronze statue by Duret shows St Michael killing the dragon.

Metro St-Michel

No. 22 Rue St-Séverin is the narrowest house in Paris and used to be the residence of Abbé Prévost, author of Manon Lescaut.

The northern end of the Boulevard St-Michel is a lively mélange of cafés, book and clothes shops, with bars and experimental cinemas nearby.

Begun in the 13th century, the beautiful St-Séverin took three centuries to build and is a fine example of the Flamboyant Gothic style (p255).

Metro Cluny La Sorbonne

One of the finest collections of medieval art in the world is kept at the superb Musée de Cluny (p254).

START

↑ Davioud's decorative fountain, found in Place St-Michel

↑ The iconic Shakespeare and Company bookshop and accompanying café

Locator Map
For more detail see p250

Rue du Chat qui Pêche translates as "street of the fishing cat".

Little Athens is a lively place in the evening, especially at the weekend, when the Greek restaurants situated in the touristy streets around St-Séverin are at their busiest.

Shakespeare and Company at No. 37 Rue de la Bûcherie is a delightful, if chaotic, bookshop. Any books purchased here are stamped with Shakespeare & Co Kilomètre Zéro Paris (p258).

Did You Know?

Rue du Chat qui Pêche is the narrowest street in Paris at just 1.8 m (6 ft) wide.

One of the oldest churches in Paris, St-Julien-le-Pauvre has 13th-century Romanesque architecture. The vault was added in the 17th century (p256).

Rue du Fouarre used to host lectures in the Middle Ages. The students sat on straw (fouarre) in the street.

Metro Maubert Mutualité

Rue Galande was home to the rich and chic in the 17th century, but subsequently became notorious for its taverns.

0 metres 100
0 yards 100
N ↑

JARDIN DES PLANTES AND PLACE D'ITALIE

This is one of the oldest areas in Paris, with a history dating back to ancient times. Part of the Roman settlement of Lutetia, it housed the large Arènes de Lutèce amphitheatre. The Rue Mouffetard was also established during the Roman era, and remained an important market street throughout the ensuing centuries. In 1626, Louis XIII founded the Jardin des Plantes as the royal medicinal plant gardens, and it soon became a scientific laboratory and botanical research centre – in the 18th centry it was the stomping ground of naturalists Georges Louis Leclerc, Comte de Buffon and Jean-Baptiste Lamarck, whose research eventually influenced Charles Darwin and his *On the Origin of Species*. In more recent years the area has become home to a sizable Muslim community, focused on the Grande Mosquée de Paris and the Institut du Monde Arabe cultural centre.

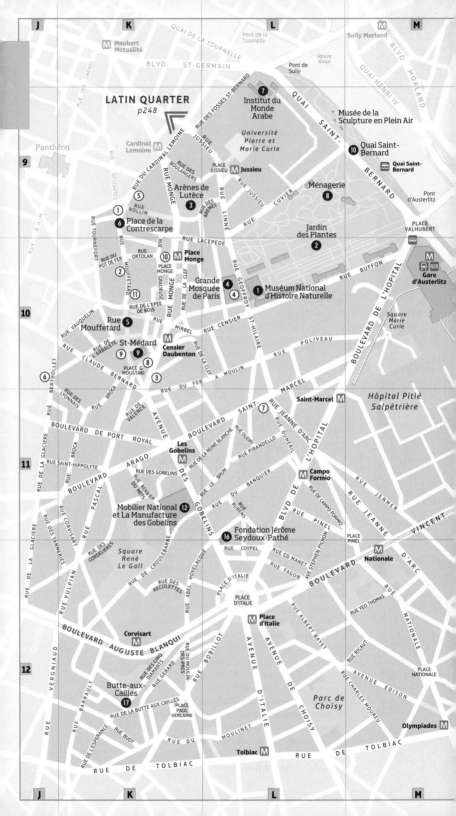

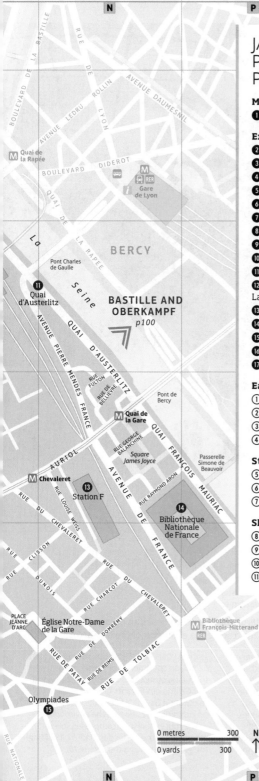

JARDIN DES PLANTES AND PLACE D'ITALIE

Must See

1. Muséum National d'Histoire Naturelle

Experience More

2. Jardin des Plantes
3. Arènes de Lutèce
4. Grande Mosquée de Paris
5. Rue Mouffetard
6. Place de la Contrescarpe
7. Institut du Monde Arabe
8. Ménagerie
9. St-Médard
10. Quai Saint-Bernard
11. Quai d'Austerlitz
12. Mobilier National et La Manufacture des Gobelins
13. Station F
14. Bibliothèque Nationale de France
15. Olympiades
16. Fondation Jérôme Seydoux-Pathé
17. Butte-aux-Cailles

Eat

1. Café Delmas
2. Au P'tit Grec
3. Dans les Landes
4. Café de la Mosquée

Stay

5. Hôtel des Grandes Écoles
6. Seven Hôtel
7. Hôtel Saint Marcel

Shop

8. Carl Marletti
9. Androuet
10. Marché Place Monge
11. Mococha

The spectacular Grande Galerie de l'Évolution ↑

❶ ⊗ 🖵 🛍

MUSÉUM NATIONAL D'HISTOIRE NATURELLE

📍L10 🏠2 Rue Buffon 75005 Ⓜ Jussieu, Austerlitz
🕐10am-6pm Wed-Mon 🚫1 May 🌐mnhn.fr

This collection of galleries in the Jardin des Plantes houses an impressive display of natural history specimens tracing the evolution of life on Earth.

Originally a botany research centre in the 17th century, the museum was founded in 1793 to include the study of animals. It has three galleries in the Jardin des Plantes: the Galerie de Minéralogie et de Géologie, with its crystals, gems and meteorites; the Galeries d'Anatomie Comparée et de Paléontologie, housing dinosaur skeletons and fossils; and the Grande Galerie de l'Évolution, featuring stuffed tigers and elephants. With more than 62 million specimens, the museum has the third-largest research collection in the world. The Galerie des Enfants (Children's Gallery), in the Grande Galerie de l'Évolution, is a hands-on exhibition focusing on the environment.

The museum also encompasses several other sites in the Jardin des Plantes, including the greenhouses and the zoo (p270).

GALERIES D'ANATOMIE COMPARÉE ET DE PALÉONTOLOGIE

Built in 1898 for the Universal Exposition of 1900, the Galeries d'Anatomie Comparée et de Paléontologie mesmerize young visitors with their collection of dinosaur skeletons, including a Triceratops and a Tyrannosaurus rex. Beginning in the Paleozoic Era, the exhibition takes visitors on a 540-million-year journey through each stage in the development of animal life. Keep a special eye out for the skeleton of Louis XV's rhino; one of the museum's longest-held specimens, it once lived at Versailles.

TYRANNOSAURUS REX SKULL

7,000

specimens are on display in the Grande Galerie de l'Évolution.

1 A wide range of flora is on show in the greenhouses.

2 The museum sits amid the glorious Jardin des Plantes.

3 The zoo is famed for its orangutans.

EXPERIENCE MORE

2

Jardin des Plantes

📍 **L9** 🏛 **57 Rue Cuvier/ 2 Rue Buffon 75005**
📞 **01 40 79 56 01** Ⓜ **Jussieu, Austerlitz** 🕐 **7:30am-8pm daily (8am-5:30pm winter)**

A treasure to locals in the 5th arrondissement, the Jardin des Plantes comprises a museum, a zoo, botanical gardens, a science lab and a university research centre. Previously known as the Jardin du Roi, it started life as a medicinal herb garden created by Guy de la Brosse and Jean Hérouard, King Louis XIII's physicians, in 1626. After opening to the public in 1640 and offering a free school of botany, chemistry and anatomy, it quickly attracted renowned scientists, such as the Comte de Buffon, whose studies were to shape Darwin's views on evolution.

Today, this popular botanical garden is home to three galleries of the Muséum National d'Histoire Naturelle (p266). It includes a small zoo (p270), rose garden and a labyrinth that kids adore. As well as beautiful vistas and walkways flanked by ancient trees and punctuated with statues, the park features a remarkable alpine garden with plants from the Alps, the Himalayas, Corsica and Morocco, and an unrivalled display of herbaceous and wild plants. It also has the first cedar of Lebanon to be planted in France, originally from Britain's Kew Gardens.

3

Arènes de Lutèce

📍 **K9** 🏛 **49-59 Rue Monge/ 4 Rue des Arènes 75005**
📞 **01 45 35 02 56** Ⓜ **Jussieu, Cardinal Lemoine**
🕐 **8/9am-6pm, depending on the time of year**

The remains of this vast Roman arena (Lutetia was the Roman name for Paris) date from the late 1st century. Its destruction began towards the end of the 3rd century at the hands of the Barbarians, and later, parts of it were used to build the walls of the Île de la Cité. The arena was then gradually buried and its exact location preserved only in old documents and the local name Clos des Arènes. It was rediscovered in 1869 during the construction of Rue Monge and the allocation of building plots nearby. Action towards its restoration began with the campaigning of Victor Hugo (among others) in the 19th century but work did not get underway until 1918.

With a seating capacity of 15,000, arranged in 35 tiers, the original arena was used both for theatrical performances and as an amphitheatre for gladiator fights. This type of combined use was peculiar to Gaul (France), and the arena is similar to the other ones in Nîmes and Arles.

🔍 **HIDDEN GEM**
Dodo Manège

This unique merry-go-round in the Jardin des Plantes allows you to ride on a host of strange and exotic animals, including a dodo, a triceratops, a horned turtle and even a sivatherium, a giraffe-like animal with antlers.

4

Grande Mosquée de Paris

📍 **L10** 🏛 **2 bis Pl du Puits de l'Ermite 75005 (Turkish baths/tearoom: 39 Rue Geoffroy St-Hilaire)**
Ⓜ **Place Monge** 🕐 **9am-noon, 2-6pm; baths: 9am-9pm Wed-Mon**
🕌 **Muslim hols** 🌐 **mosquee de paris.net**

Built in the 1920s in the Hispano-Moorish style, this complex is the spiritual centre

← People enjoying a stroll on a spring day in the Jardin des Plantes

for Paris's Muslim community and the home of the Grand Imam. It comprises religious, educational and commercial sections; at its heart is a mosque. Each of the mosque's domes is decorated in a different manner, and the minaret stands nearly 33 m (100 ft) high. Inside is a grand patio with mosaics on the walls and tracery on the arches.

Once used only by scholars, the mosque's place in Parisian life has grown over the years. The Turkish baths are strictly for women only. A tearoom and restaurant set in a peaceful tree-shaded courtyard serve Moorish specialities and make a lovely spot for a glass of mint tea and sticky cakes.

The tranquil, tiled gardens at the Grande Mosquée de Paris

⑤
Rue Mouffetard

📍K10 🏠75005 Ⓜ Censier Daubenton, Place Monge ◎Market Place Maubert: 7am-2:30pm Tue, Thu, Sat (to 3pm Sat); Place Monge: 7am-2:30pm Wed, Fri, Sun (to 3pm Sun)

A major thoroughfare since Roman times, when it linked Lutetia (Paris) and Rome, this street is one of the oldest in the city. In the 17th and 18th centuries, it was known as the Grande Rue du Faubourg St-Marcel, and many of its buildings date from that time. Some of the small shops still have ancient painted signs, and some houses have mansard roofs.

Did You Know?

Ernest Hemingway lived in the area in the 1920s, at 74 Rue du Cardinal Lemoine.

No. 125 has an attractive, restored Louis XIII façade, and the entire front of No. 134 is beautifully decorated with wild beasts, flowers and plants. No. 69 sports an old shop sign featuring a carved oak tree, while at No. 60, the *Fontaine de Pot-de-Fer* is a small fountain dating from Roman times. Later on, it was connected to an aqueduct used by Marie de Médicis to take water to the Palais du Luxembourg and its gardens.

The area is known for its open-air markets, especially those in Place Maubert, Place Monge (set around the Monge fountain) and Rue Daubenton, a side street where a lively African market takes place.

At night, the street bustles with people enjoying the Greek, Italian, Argentinian and other cuisines on offer at the many small restaurants.

6 🍴 💻

Place de la Contrescarpe

📍K9 📮75005
Ⓜ Place Monge

At one time, this site lay outside the city walls. It gets its name from the backfilling of the moat that ran along Philippe-Auguste's wall. The present square was laid out in 1852, but the fountain was added in 1994. At No. 1, there is a memorial to the old "pine-cone club"; here, a group of writers known as *La Pléiade* used to meet in the 16th century. Four hundred years later, authors such as Ernest Hemingway, James Joyce and George Orwell also found the streets of this historically working-class neighbourhood a great source of inspiration.

The area has always been used for meetings and festivals. Today, it still embodies old Paris, with its narrow cobblestoned streets and charming cafés, and is very lively at weekends.

7 ✏️ 🎨 🍴 💻

Institut du Monde Arabe

📍L9 📮1 Rue des Fossées St-Bernard, Pl Mohammed V 75005
Ⓜ Jussieu, Cardinal Lemoine ⏰ Museum & temp exhibs: 10am–6pm Mon–Fri, 10am–7pm Sat & Sun 🌐 imarabe.org

This cultural institute was founded in 1980 by France and 20 Arab countries with the intention of fostering cultural links between the Arab world and the West. It is housed in a magnificent building designed by Jean Nouvel (who was also responsible for the Musée du quai Branly and the Philharmonie), combining modern materials with the spirit of traditional Arab architecture. The white marble book tower, which can be seen through the glass of the west wall, spirals upwards, bringing to mind the minaret of a mosque. The emphasis that is traditionally placed on interior space in Arab architecture has been used here to create an enclosed courtyard reached by a narrow gap splitting the building in two.

Flamingos in the Ménagerie, France's oldest public zoo ↑

From floors four to seven, there's a fascinating display of Islamic works of art from the 9th to the 19th centuries, including ceramics, sculpture, carpets and astrolabes. The centre also houses a library and media archive, and puts on a lively programme of lectures and concerts.

8 ✏️ 🎨 🍴 💻 🛍️

Ménagerie

📍L9 📮57 Rue Cuvier/ Rue Buffon 75005
Ⓜ Jussieu, Austerlitz ⏰ 9am–6pm daily (to 6:30pm Sun & public hols) 🌐 zoodujardindes plantes.fr

France's oldest public zoo is situated in the pleasant surroundings of the Jardin des Plantes (*p268*). The Ménagerie was set up during the Revolution to house the survivors from the royal menagerie at Versailles – all

←

St-Médard and a Rue Mouffetard street market

Did You Know?

The old wall of Paris can be seen along Rue Clovis, by the prestigious Henri IV school.

four of them. The state then rounded up animals from circuses, and exotic creatures were sent from abroad. Tragically, during the Prussian siege of Paris (1870–71), most of these animals were slaughtered in order to feed the hungry citizens.

The zoo specializes in small mammals, insects, birds, primates and reptiles. It is a great favourite with children as it allows them to get quite close to the animals, and feeding times are especially popular. The big cat house contains panthers from China, and other attractions include a large monkey house, a waterfowl aviary, and wild sheep and goats. The displays in the vivarium (enclosures of live animals in their natural habitat) are changed at

regular intervals, and there is a permanent exhibition of micro-arthropods (also known as creepy-crawlies!).

9

St-Médard

K10 **141 Rue Mouffetard 75005** **M Censier-Daubenton** **8am–12:30pm & 2:30–7:30pm Tue–Sat; 9am–12:30pm & 4–8:30pm Sun** **saintmedard.org**

The origins of this church go back to the 9th century. St Médard, counsellor to the Merovingian kings, was known for giving a wreath of white roses to young girls noted for their virtue. The churchyard became notorious in the 18th century as the centre of the cult of the Convulsionnaires, whose hysterical fits were brought on by the contemplation of miracle cures. The interior has many fine paintings, including the 17th-century *St Joseph Walking with the Christ Child* by Francisco de Zurbarán and the organ loft is adorned with Renaissance statues.

STAY

Hôtel des Grandes Écoles

A garden terrace and old-world feel make this a perpetual favourite.

K9 **75 Rue du Cardinal Lemoine 75005** **hotel-grandes-ecoles.com**

€€€

Seven Hôtel

Swanky décor sets this modern hotel apart from most in the area.

J10 **20 Rue Berthollet 75005** **sevenhotel paris.com**

€€€

Hôtel Saint Marcel

A great location and amenities such as a wine bar stocked with the family's own wine make this hotel a real bargain.

L11 **43 Blvd St-Marcel 75013** **hotel-saint-marcel-paris.com**

€€€

10
Quai Saint-Bernard

M9 **75005**
Gare d'Austerlitz

Running along the river from the Pont de Sully as far as the Pont d'Austerlitz is the peaceful Quai Saint-Bernard. Not always so sedate, Quai Saint-Bernard was famous during the 17th century as a spot for nude bathing, until scandalized public opinion made it illegal. The quay is studded with contemporary sculptures, but its main draw is the green space known as the Jardin Tino-Rossi, named for the Coriscan singer who recorded "Petit Papa Noël" in 1946, one of France's best-selling songs ever. The park is alive with music in the summer, from French folk to salsa and tango. Dancers of all levels meet here at night, turning the park into an outdoor dance hall.

Butting up to the left-hand corner of the Institut du Monde Arabe, the Pont de Sully links the Île St-Louis with both banks of the Seine. Opened in 1877 and built of cast iron, the Pont de Sully is not an especially beautiful structure. Despite this, it is well worth pausing for a moment on the bridge for a fabulous view of Notre-Dame rising dramatically behind the graceful Pont de la Tournelle.

11
Quai d'Austerlitz

M10 **97013**
Gare d'Austerlitz
citemodedesign.fr

Stretching along the Left Bank from Gare d'Austerlitz towards the Bibliothèque, this riverfront promenade is a little-known part of town. It's closed off to traffic and offers a pleasant stroll with views of the Seine. Several boats host cafés serving coffee and wine. The impressive contemporary cultural centre known as Les Docks, Cité de la Mode et du Design, perches over the Seine, with its green undulating façade looking northwards. Housed in an old industrial warehouse, it is home to an assortment of bars, cafés and restaurants, as well as a fashion institute, and hosts regular exhibitions. Further south is the Port de la Gare where, in the summer, outdoor restaurants and cafés line the riverfront. The Batofar, a floating nightclub, and the Piscine Josephine Baker, a floating public pool, also moor here year-round.

Did You Know?

The Batofar at Quai d'Austerlitz was one of the first floating clubs in Paris.

12
Mobilier National et La Manufacture des Gobelins

K11 **42 Ave des Gobelins 75013** **Gobelins**
11am–6pm Tue–Sun (temporary exhibitions)
1 Jan, 1 May, 25 Dec
mobiliernational.culture.gouv.fr

Originally a dyeing workshop set up in about 1440 by the Gobelin brothers, the building became a tapestry factory

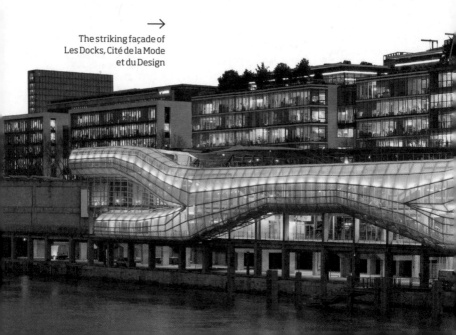

→ The striking façade of Les Docks, Cité de la Mode et du Design

early in the 17th century. Louis XIV took it over in 1662 and gathered together the greatest craftsmen of the day – carpet weavers, cabinet-makers and silversmiths – to furnish his new palace at Versailles (p296). Working under the direction of court painter Charles Le Brun, 250 Flemish weavers laid the foundations for the factory's international reputation. Today, weavers continue to work in the traditional way but with modern designs, including those of Picasso and Matisse. Guided tours on Wednesday afternoons can be booked via the website.

Station F

Q N11 **⌂** 5 Parvis Alan Turing 75013
M Chevaleret **W** stationf.co

This converted train station, which opened in 2017, houses Paris's burgeoning innovation scene. The world's largest start-up campus, Station F is as long as the Eiffel Tower is high. The venue hosts

a variety of events about business and technology, with registration available on its website. Visitors can take a tour of the new ventures or cosy up with entrepreneurs at the public café. A restaurant area featuring refurbished

train cars is open 24 hours for any late-night revellers looking for a place to dine. It features four kitchens, a bar, and an enormous terrace that can seat up to 1,000.

SHOP

Carl Marletti
Daring confectionaries fill Marletti's celebrated pâtisserie, with ephemeral favourites like the *fraisier* popping up each year.

Q K10 **⌂** 51 Rue Censier 75005 **W** carlmarletti.com

Androuet
Expert artisan cheeses from here have pleased Parisians since 1909, including classics such as Camembert.

Q K10 **⌂** 134 Rue Mouffetard 75005
W androuet.com

Marché Place Monge
Vendors stock fresh produce that changes with the seasons at this outdoor market with a focus on quality over quantity.

Q K10 **⌂** 1 Place Monge 75005 **◷** 7am-2:30pm Wed, Fri & Sun

Mococha
Surprising combinations deck the shelves of this boutique, run by a team of inspired chocolatiers.

Q K10 **⌂** 89 Rue Mouffetard 75005
W chocolatsmococha.com

14

Bibliothèque Nationale de France

N11 **Quai François Mauriac 75013** **10am–7pm Tue–Sat, 1–7pm Sun** **Bibliothèque François-Mitterrand** **bnf.fr**

The national library collection dates back to the 1300s, when King Charles V began a library at the Louvre. Kings and queens added to the shelves, even involuntarily, as Revolutionaries confiscated thousands of volumes from aristocrats during the French Revolution. Nowadays, the symbol of the BNF is the ultra-modern building rising over the Quai François Mauriac. The structure looks like four giant glass books opening onto a courtyard and is largely used by scholars. Commissioned by President Mitterrand and completed in 1996, it houses the world's largest selection of medieval manuscripts and boasts over 14 million books in its entire collection. Temporary exhibitions take place throughout the year, as well as in the other BNF sites located around the city.

15

Olympiades

N12 **75013** **Olympiades**

This curious, modern corner of Paris is part of the city's larger vision of

→ A water fountain in Chinatown

urban development. It is marked by the Olympiades towers, an innovative housing complex where each tower is named after a different Olympic host city. Today, the area is largely known as Paris's largest Chinatown, where the annual Chinese New Year parade takes place in February. Parisians head here for delicious Chinese and Vietnamese food, including some of the best *bobun* in the entire city. Its affordable fare and exotic grocery stores, like Tang Frères, are huge draws for anyone interested in a break from *steak-frites* and cheese. The district is bordered on the south by the tramline that stretches around southern Paris.

16

Fondation Jérôme Seydoux-Pathé

L11 **73 Ave des Gobelins 75013** **Place d'Italie, Les Gobelins** **Salle Charles Pathé & Exhibitions: 1–7pm Tue–Fri, 11:30am–7pm Sat; research centre: by appt only; Ciné-Spectacle: 2:30pm Wed** **fondation-jeromeseydoux-pathe.com**

The headquarters of the Fondation Jérôme Seydoux-Pathé sits on the site of a mid-19th-century theatre that was transformed into one of Paris's first cinemas in the mid-1900s. Pathé, a major French film production and distribution company, is the second-oldest operating film company in the world. The foundation is dedicated to the preservation of its legacy and to promoting cinematography. The building has a 68-seat screening room for silent

↑ Dominique Perrault's modern Bibliothèque Nationale de France

Did You Know?

The Bibliothèque Nationale de France is one of the oldest libraries in the world.

films, plus temporary and permanent collections of films, cameras, projectors, programmes and posters dating back to 1896. It is a treasure trove for film enthusiasts and researchers. Guided tours are held on Saturdays at noon.

17

Butte-aux-Cailles

K12 **75013** **Place d'Italie, Corvisart**

Named after landowner Pierre Caille who grew grapes here in the 1500s, this little hill was once an important area for tanneries and other industry. The La Biévre river, which now runs underground, used to run right through it. Limestone quarries

underground made the land unsuitable for Haussmann's large construction projects, and as a result the area has more of a village feel than most parts of Paris – the Rue des Cinq-Diamants is a great example of this. Interestingly, it was in this area, in 1783, that the first official hot-air balloon trip landed successfully. Today the district is full of local character in its bars and cafés; they are relatively cheap, making the area especially popular among young university types. The area is also an excellent place to discover some great street art, with lots of examples of the work of tagger Miss.Tic.

↑ The rooftops of Ste-Anne-de-la-Buttes-aux-Cailles church in the picturesque, Butte-aux-Cailles district

EAT

Café Delmas
Traditional French fare with a side order of people-watching.

📍 K9 🏠 2 Place de la Contrescarpe 75005 🌐 cafedelmas.com

€€€

Au P'tit Grec
A popular spot serving huge take-away crêpes.

📍 K10 🏠 68 Rue Mouffetard 75005 📧 auptitgrec.com

€€€

Dans les Landes
Convivial bistro serving French tapas.

📍 K10 🏠 119 bis Rue Monge 75005 🌐 dansleslandes.fr

€€€

Café de la Mosquée
A lovely tea room attached to the mosque.

📍 L10 🏠 2 bis Place du Puits de l'Ermite 75005

€€€

A SHORT WALK
JARDIN DES PLANTES QUARTER

Metro Cardinal Lemoine

START

Distance 2.5 km (1.5 miles) **Nearest metro** Cardinal Lemoine
Time 25 minutes

A well-to-do residential patchwork of 19th- and early 20th-century buildings, this area also has one or two surprises up its sleeve, including a Roman amphitheatre and a Hispano-Moorish mosque. The area began life in 1626 as a royal medicinal herb garden, the work of two physicians to Louis XIII, Jean Hérouard and Guy de la Brosse. The herb garden and gardens of various religious houses gave the region a rural character. In the 19th century, the population and thus the area expanded and it became more built up, transforming into the area you see today.

The Place de la Contrescarpe is a village-like square filled with restaurants and cafés (p270).

Locals flock to the market street of Rue Mouffetard, one of the oldest in the city, where vendors' displays spill onto the cobblestones in a colourful spread of fresh produce, pastries and wine (p269).

Pot de Fer fountain is one of 14 that Marie de Médici had built on the Left Bank in 1624 as a source of water for her palace. The fountain was rebuilt in 1671.

Metro Place Monge

Passage des Postes is an ancient alley opened in 1830. Its entrance is in the Rue Mouffetard.

The church of St-Médard dates to the mid-1400s. In 1784, the choir was revamped and the nave's windows replaced with contemporary stained glass (p271).

↑ Taking time out on the cobbled square of Place de la Contrescarpe

The Arènes de Lutèce, a Roman amphitheatre, was used for burials in the 4th century (p268).

Rue des Arènes is round the corner from the Arènes de Lutèce. No. 5 is an interesting Gothic Revival house in which the writer Jean Paulhan lived from 1940.

JARDIN DES PLANTES AND PLACE D'ITALIE

Locator Map
For more detail see p264

Cuvier Fountain is a memorial to naturalist Georges Cuvier. It was erected in 1840 by P Vigouroux, with figure carving by Jean-Jacques Feuchère.

RUE DES BOULANGERS

RUE DES ARÈNES

RUE LINNE

RUE DE NAVARRE

FINISH

RUE LACEPEDE

RUE QUATREFAGES

RUE GEOFFROY ST HILAIRE

RUE DE LA CLEF

RUE LARREY

RUE G DESPLAS DU GRIL

RUE D'AUBENTON

RUE DE MIRBE

↑ The Hispano-Moorish Grande Mosquée de Paris and its garden

Did You Know?

The Grande Mosquée honours Muslims who died on French battlefields during World War I.

The Grande Mosquée de Paris, the centre of Paris's Muslim community, includes within its walls a Turkish bath, a Moorish café and restaurant, and an oriental bazaar (p268).

Metro Censier-Daubenton

0 metres 100
0 yards 100

N
↑

The Fontaine Médicis in the Jardin du Luxembourg

MONTPARNASSE AND JARDIN DU LUXEMBOURG

Montparnasse takes its name from the Mount Parnassus of Ancient Greece, the home of Apollo, god of poetry and music. In the first three decades of the 20th century, Montparnasse was a thriving artistic literary centre. Many modern painters and sculptors, new novelists and poets were drawn to this bohemian area, where they would frequent cafés such as La Closerie des Lilas and La Coupole. The great epoch ended with World War II, and change continued with the destruction of many ateliers and the construction of the soaring Tour Montparnasse, Paris's tallest office tower, which heralded the more modern *quartier*.

The Jardin du Luxembourg was initiated by Marie de Médici in 1612, inspired by the Boboli Gardens in her native Florence. Baron Haussmann redeveloped the area around the park in the 19th century; his changes were deeply unpopular with the public for encroaching on the gardens and reducing their size. Nonetheless, the area has retained its own unique charm of winding streets, beautiful buildings, bookshops and art galleries.

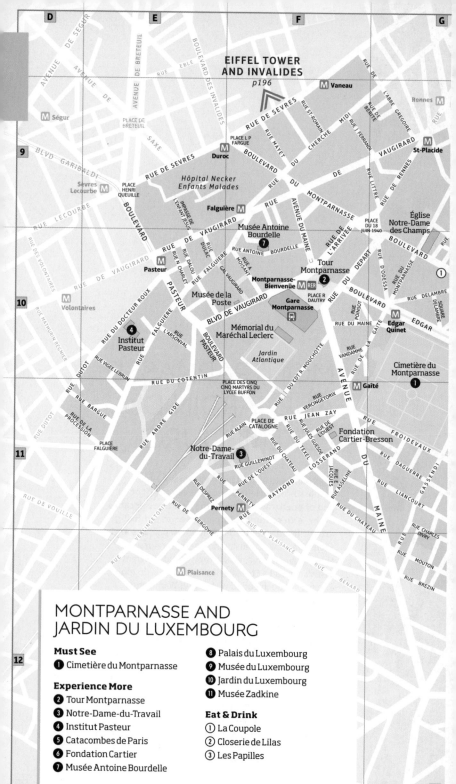

MONTPARNASSE AND JARDIN DU LUXEMBOURG

Must See

❶ Cimetière du Montparnasse

Experience More

❷ Tour Montparnasse
❸ Notre-Dame-du-Travail
❹ Institut Pasteur
❺ Catacombes de Paris
❻ Fondation Cartier
❼ Musée Antoine Bourdelle

❽ Palais du Luxembourg
❾ Musée du Luxembourg
❿ Jardin du Luxembourg
⓫ Musée Zadkine

Eat & Drink

① La Coupole
② Closerie de Lilas
③ Les Papilles

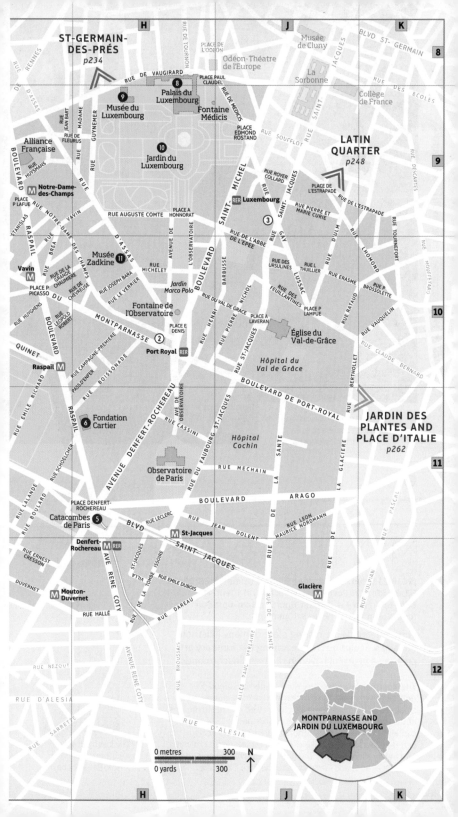

Montparnasse, the second largest cemetery in Paris after Père Lachaise ↑

CIMETIÈRE DU MONTPARNASSE

📍G10 🏠3 Blvd Edgar Quinet Ⓜ️Edgar Quinet 🚌28, 58, 68, 82, 83, 88, 91 to Port Royal 🚉Port Royal 🕐Mid-Mar-mid-Nov: 8am-6pm Mon-Fri, 8:30am-6pm Sat, 9am-6pm Sun (mid-Nov-mid-Mar closes 5:30pm)

This cemetery is the resting place of many illustrious Parisians. Sculptures nestle among the funerary art, creating a peaceful haven in the tree-lined grounds.

The Montparnasse Cemetery was planned by Napoleon outside the city walls to replace the numerous, congested, small cemeteries within the old city, viewed as a health hazard at the turn of the 19th century. It was opened in 1824 and contains the graves of many notable Parisians, particularly Left Bank personalities. Like all French cemeteries, it is divided into rigidly aligned paths. The Rue Émile Richard cuts it into two parts, the Grand Cimetière and the Petit Cimetière.

The Kiss by Brancusi, who is buried just off Rue Émile Richard ↑

Notable Residents

Did You Know?

The cemetery's tower is the remains of a 17th-century windmill.

Jean-Paul Sartre and Simone de Beauvoir

△ The famous existentialist couple, undisputed leaders of the post-War literary scene, lie here close to their Left Bank haunts.

Jean Seberg

▷ The Hollywood actress, chosen by Jean-Luc Godard as the star of his film *À Bout de Souffle*, was the epitome of American blonde beauty, youth and candour.

Serge Gainsbourg

The French singer, composer and pop icon of the 1970s and 80s is best known for his wistful and irreverent songs. He was married to the actress Jane Birkin.

Samuel Beckett

◁ The great Irish playwright, renowned for *Waiting for Godot*, spent most of his life in Paris. He died in 1989.

Man Ray

The American photographer immortalized the Montparnasse artistic and café scene in the 1920s and 30s.

André Citroën

▷ The engineer and industrialist, who died in 1935, founded the famous French car firm.

CHARLES BAUDELAIRE

The cemetery contains the cenotaph of Charles Baudelaire, the great poet and critic. Baudelaire, who was born and died in Paris, shocked the world with his frank and decadent collection of poems *Les Fleurs Mal*, published in 1857. His work has had a widespread literary influence, and has even inspired rock stars such as Mick Jagger.

EXPERIENCE MORE

2 🗺️ 🍴 🖥️

Tour Montparnasse

📍 F10 🏠 33 Ave du Maine 75014 Ⓜ Montparnasse-Bienvenüe 🕐 Apr–Sep: 9:30am–11:30pm daily; Oct–Mar: 9:30am–10:30pm daily (to 11pm Fri & Sat) 🌐 tourmontparnasse 56.com

This was Europe's largest office block when it was built in 1973. At 210 m (690 ft) high, it totally dominates the area's skyline. The lift takes you up to the observation floor with its panoramic bar. For the best views you'll need to climb up the last three floors to the open-air observatory. The views from here are spectacular – up to 40 km (25 miles) on a clear day. The tower will be closed for major renovations in the run-up to the Olympics from 2020 to 2024.

3

Notre-Dame-du-Travail

📍 F11 🏠 36 Rue Guilleminot 75014 Ⓜ Pernety 🕐 7.30am–7.45pm Mon–Fri, 9am–7:30pm Sat, 8:30am–7:30pm Sun 🌐 notredame dutravail.net

This church dates from 1901 and is made of an unusual mix of materials: stone, rubble and bricks over a riveted steel-and-iron framework. It was the creation of Father Soulange-Boudin, a priest who organized cooperatives and sought to reconcile labour and capitalism. Local parishioners raised the money for its construction, but lack of funds meant that many features, such as the bell towers, were never built. On the façade hangs the Sebastopol Bell, a trophy from the Crimean War given to the people of the Plaisance district by Napoleon III. The Art Nouveau interior has been restored and features paintings of saints.

4 🗺️

Institut Pasteur

📍 E10 🏠 25–28 Rue du Docteur Roux 75015 Ⓜ Pasteur 🌐 pasteur.fr

The Institut Pasteur, France's leading medical research centre, was founded by the scientist Louis Pasteur in 1888–9. He discovered the process of milk pasteurization, as well as vaccines against rabies and anthrax. The centre houses a museum that includes a reconstruction of Pasteur's apartment and laboratory. Unfortunately, the museum is currently closed to

→ Tour Montparnasse, as seen from the Eiffel Tower

One of the skull-lined underground passages in the Catacombes de Paris

individuals, though groups of ten or more can apply at least three months in advance to visit; check the website for the latest updates. Pasteur's tomb is in a basement crypt built in the style of a small Byzantine chapel. The tomb of Dr Émile Roux, who discovered the treatment for diphtheria, is in the garden. The institute has laboratories for pure and applied research and a hospital established to apply Pasteur's theories. There is also a library – the institute's original building from 1888 – where research into AIDS is carried out, led by pioneering Professor Luc Montagnier, who discovered the HIV virus in 1983.

5

Catacombes de Paris

📍 H11 🏛 1 Ave du Colonel Henri Rol-Tanguy 75014 Ⓜ Denfert-Rochereau 🕙 10am-8:30pm Tue-Sun 🚫 1 Jan, 1 May 🌐 catacombes.paris.fr

In 1786, a monumental project began here: the removal of the millions of skulls and bones from the unsanitary city cemetery in Les Halles to the quarries at the base of the three "mountains": Montparnasse, Montrouge and Montsouris.

Initially the bones were placed haphazardly, but from the early 19th century they were used to adorn the walls in decorative patterns.

During World War II, the French Resistance set up its headquarters here. Above the door outside are the words "Stop! This is the empire of death." Visiting the catacombs has become very popular, so reserving your ticket in advance is strongly advised. Guided tours in English are held at 3pm on Tuesdays.

6

Fondation Cartier

📍 H11 🏛 261 Blvd Raspail 75014 Ⓜ Raspail 🕙 11am-8pm Tue-Sun (to 10pm Tue) 🚫 1 Jan, 25 Dec 🌐 fondationcartier.com

This foundation for contemporary art and architecture is housed in a building designed by architect Jean Nouvel. He has created an air of transparency and light, as well as incorporating a cedar of Lebanon, which was planted in 1823 by François-René de Chateaubriand. The structure complements the nature of the exhibitions of progressive art, which showcase personal, group or thematic displays, often including works by young unknowns.

EAT & DRINK

La Coupole
An Art Nouveau brasserie serving up meaty classics.
📍 G10 🏛 102 Blvd du Montparnasse 75014 🌐 lacoupole-paris.com
€€€

Closerie des Lilas
A classic brasserie, once frequented by Hemingway.
📍 H10 🏛 171 Blvd du Montparnasse 75006 🌐 closeriedeslilas.fr
€€€

Les Papilles
Wine bottles line the walls of this friendly local.
📍 J9 🏛 30 Rue Gay-Lussac 75005 🚫 Sun, Mon 🌐 lespapillesparis.fr
€€€

Equipment on display at the museum at the Institut Pasteur

7

Musée Antoine Bourdelle

⊙ F10 **⌂ 18 Rue Antoine Bourdelle 75015** **Ⓜ Montparnasse-Bienvenüe** **⊙ 10am-6pm Tue-Sun** **⊘ Public hols** **ⓦ bourdelle.paris.fr**

The prolific sculptor Antoine Bourdelle lived and worked in the studio here from 1884 until his death in 1929. The house, studio and garden are now a museum. Among the 900 sculptures on display are the original plaster casts of his monumental works planned for wide public squares. They include the group of sculptures for the relief decoration of the Théâtre des Champs-Élysées. Frequent temporary exhibitions, for which there is an entry fee, complement the free permanent collection.

← One of the many statues in the Musée Antoine Bourdelle

8

Palais du Luxembourg

⊙ H9 **⌂ 19 Rue de Vaugirard 75006** **Ⓜ Odéon** **ⓡ Luxembourg** **ⓦ senat.fr/visite**

Now the home of the French Senate, this palace was designed by Salomon de Brosse in the style of Florence's Pitti Palace to remind Marie de Médicis, widow of Henri IV, of her native town. By the time it was finished (1631), Marie had been banished, but it remained a royal palace until the Revolution. In World War II, it was the headquarters of the Luftwaffe. Individual visits to the palace are currently suspended (check the website for updates), but the Musée du Luxembourg, in the east gallery, is open.

9

Musée du Luxembourg

⊙ H9 **⌂ 19 Rue de Vaugirard 75006** **Ⓜ St-Sulpice** **ⓡ Luxembourg** **⊙ Times vary depending on exhibitions; check website** **⊘ 1 May & 25 Dec** **ⓦ museeduluxembourg.fr**

Housed in the Palais du Luxembourg, the two adjoining galleries of this museum were created to hang Marie de Médicis' collection of paintings by Rubens. In 1750, the east wing became France's first public gallery, housing works by renowned artists such as Leonardo da Vinci, Van Dyck and Rembrandt. Following extensive renovations, today it hosts impressive temporary exhibitions on leading figures from the art world, including Rubens, Cézanne and Pissaro.

10

Jardin du Luxembourg

⊙ H9 **⌂ Blvd St-Michel/ Rue de Vaugirard/Rue Guynemer 75006** **Ⓜ Odéon** **ⓡ Luxembourg** **⊙ Dawn-dusk daily** **ⓦ senat.fr/visite**

A green oasis covering 25 ha (60 acres) in the heart of the Left Bank, the Jardin du Luxembourg is one of the most popular parks in Paris. The beautifully sculpted gardens are centred around the Palais du Luxembourg and feature an octagonal basin that is often surrounded by children sailing their wooden toy boats.

The Jardin du Luxembourg was created at the request of Marie de Médici, who had it designed as a fitting reminder of the Boboli Gardens at the Pitti Palace, in her home town of Florence. The original garden measured 8 ha (20 acres); what remains of it today are the large pond, the Fontaine Médicis and 2,000 elm trees.

↑ The stately Palais du Luxembourg in the gorgeous Jardin du Luxembourg

A green oasis covering 25 ha (60 acres) in the heart of the Left Bank, the Jardin du Luxembourg is one of the most popular parks in Paris.

Statues were placed throughout the park around 1848. They include those of the queens of France, famous French women – Sainte Geneviève is an impressive example – and, later, famous writers and artists, too, totalling 106 statues.

The garden is a great space for children, with activities such as a puppet theatre starring the famous character Guignol, a fenced-in playground, a carousel and tennis courts. Adults can play chess or bridge, wander through the open-air photography exhibitions or grab a chair and enjoy a free concert.

🟡 ♿ Ⓜ

Musée Zadkine

📍 H10 🏛 100 bis Rue d'Assas 75116 Ⓜ Notre-Dame-des-Champs 🕐 10am–6pm Tue-Sun 🚫 Public hols 🌐 zadkine.paris.fr

The Russian-born sculptor Ossip Zadkine lived here from 1928 until his death in 1967.

The small house, studio and garden contain his works. Here he produced his great commemorative sculpture *Ville Détruite*, commissioned by Rotterdam after World War II, and two monuments to Vincent van Gogh. The museum's works span the development of Zadkine's style, from his Cubist beginnings to Expressionism and Abstractionism.

FONTAINE MÉDICIS

This Baroque fountain, thought to have been designed by Salomon de Brosse, was built in 1624 for Marie de Médici in the style of an Italian grotto. The fountain stands at the end of a long pond filled with goldfish. The mythological figures were added much later by Auguste Ottin (1866) and represent Polyphemus discovering the lovers Acis and Galatea.

A SHORT WALK
MONTPARNASSE

Distance 2.5 km (1.5 miles) **Nearest metro** Gaîté
Time 25 minutes

Renowned for its mix of art and high living (Picasso, Hemingway, Matisse and Modigliani were frequent visitors), Montparnasse is a pleasant mixture of bars, cafés and art galleries. Take a couple of detours on this walk: first, go to the top of the Tour Montparnasse for sweeping views of the city; and second, pay your respects to Parisian icons at the Cimetière du Montparnasse.

Did You Know?

Artists Giacometti and Modigliani were students at the Académie de la Grande-Chaumière

The Tour Montparnasse, one of Europe's tallest tower blocks, rests on 56 piles that extend 62 m (203 ft) below the surface (p284).

↑ Sculpture at the Cimetière du Montparnasse

Metro Edgar Quinet

The Cimetière du Montparnasse is the final resting place of several Parisian icons (p282).

The Théâtre Montparnasse at No. 31 has fully restored original 1880s decor.

START

0 metres 100
0 yards 100

N ↑

EXPERIENCE Montparnasse

↑ The Art Deco-style interior
of the iconic La Coupole

Locator Map
For more detail see p280

MONTPARNASSE AND
JARDIN DU LUXEMBOURG

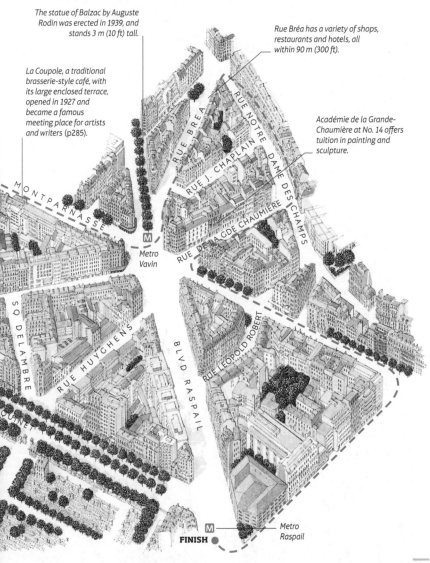

*The statue of Balzac by Auguste
Rodin was erected in 1939, and
stands 3 m (10 ft) tall.*

*Rue Bréa has a variety of shops,
restaurants and hotels, all
within 90 m (300 ft).*

*La Coupole, a traditional
brasserie-style café, with
its large enclosed terrace,
opened in 1927 and
became a famous
meeting place for artists
and writers (p285).*

*Académie de la Grande-
Chaumière at No. 14 offers
tuition in painting and
sculpture.*

RUE BRÉA

RUE NOTRE DAME DES CHAMPS

RUE J. CHAPLAIN

MONTPARNASSE

Ⓜ Metro Vavin

RUE DE LA GDE CHAUMIERE

SQ DELAMBRE

RUE HUYGHENS

BLVD RASPAIL

RUE LEOPOLD ROBERT

QUINET

Ⓜ
FINISH ●

Ⓜ Metro Raspail

The stunning Fondation Louis Vuitton

Must Sees

❶ Bois de Boulogne
❷ Château and Bois de Vincennes
❸ The Palace and Gardens of Versailles
❹ Disneyland® Paris

Experience More

❺ La Défense
❻ Musée Marmottan-Monet
❼ Basilique-Cathédrale de St-Denis
❽ Potager du Roi
❾ Marché aux Puces de St-Ouen
❿ Marché aux Puces de la Porte de Vanves

BEYOND THE CENTRE

The area beyond the Périphérique (ring road) once served as a country retreat for the aristocracy, with the medieval Château de Vincennes as the royal residence. It was usurped in the 17th century by Louis XIV's spectacular palace at Versailles, where the excessive displays of opulence were brought to a violent end during the Revolution of 1789. An industrial boom in the 19th century was followed by a number of large-scale construction projects in the 20th century, including blocks of social housing and the Périphérique. Today the varied neighbourhoods of the suburbs are home to the vast majority of Paris's citizens.

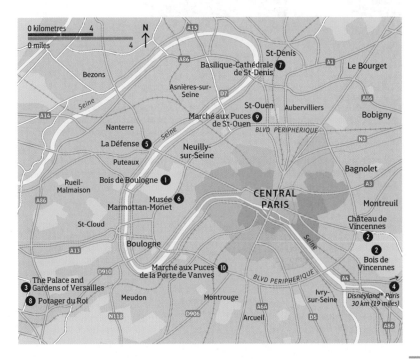

BOIS DE BOULOGNE

□ 75016 Ⓜ Porte Maillot, Porte Dauphine, Porte d'Auteuil, Sablons ⊙ 24 hrs daily; gardens: 9:30am–dusk daily Ⓦ Jardin d'Acclimatation: jardindacclimatation.fr; Théâtre de Verdure du Jardin Shakespeare: jardinshakespeare.com; Fondation Louis Vuitton: fondationlouisvuitton.fr

Between the western edges of Paris and the Seine, this 865-ha (2,137-acre) park offers greenery for strolling and a boating lake, plus opportunities for horse riding, picnicking or a day at the races. It is a favourite outdoor retreat with Parisians, especially on summer weekends.

The remains of a royal hunting ground, the many beautiful areas around the Bois include the Hippodrome de Longchamp racecourse, the Jardin d'Acclimatation amusement park and Roland Garros, home to the French Tennis Open championships. Hidden within its borders is the Théâtre de Verdure, an open-air playhouse that puts on Shakespeare, dance and musical performances in summer. The charming Bagatelle Gardens feature architectural follies and an 18th-century orangery famous for its rose garden. Opened in 2014, Frank Gehry's stunning Fondation Louis Vuitton is a cultural centre dedicated to modern art.

Did You Know?

The orangery was built in 64 days as a bet between the Comte d'Artois and Marie Antoinette.

↑ Boats for hire on the Lac Inférieur, the largest of the two lakes in the park

EAT

Le Franck
A high-end restaurant within the Fondation Louis Vuitton.

🅰 8 Ave du Mahatma Gandhi, 75116
🕐 Tue & Sat–Sun lunch
🌐 restaurantlefrank.fr

€€€

① The "sails" of the Fondation Louis Vuitton are made of 3,600 glass panels.

② The Château de Bagatelle was built by Louis XVI's brother, the Comte d'Artois.

③ A statue of French tennis legend Henri Cochet stands outside Roland Garros.

② 🏛️ 🖼️ 🍴 ☕ 🛍️

CHÂTEAU ET BOIS DE VINCENNES

🏠 Ave de Paris, Vincennes 94300 Ⓜ️ Château de Vincennes 🚇 Vincennes
🕐 Château: mid-May–mid-Sep: 10am–6pm daily (mid-Sep–mid-May: to 5pm daily); Bois de Vincennes: dawn to dusk daily 🚫 Public hols
🌐 chateau-vincennes.fr

Guarded by an imposing medieval keep, the sprawling Bois de Vincennes is a verdant wonderland. With boating lakes, formal gardens and numerous walking and cycling trails, it is the perfect playground in which to escape the city.

The Château de Vincennes was once a royal residence; it was here that Henry V of England died of dysentery in 1422. Abandoned when the Palace of Versailles was completed, the château was subsequently converted into an arsenal by Napoleon.

The 14th-century keep is the tallest in Europe and is a fine example of medieval military architecture. It houses the château's museum. The Gothic chapel features beautiful stone rose windows, while two 17th-century pavilions house a fascinating museum of army insignia.

Once a royal hunting ground, the Bois de Vincennes was given to the City of Paris by Napoleon III in 1860. Baron Haussmann's landscape architect added a number of ornamental lakes and cascades. Among the forest's main attractions is the largest funfair in France (open from Palm Sunday to end of May) and the renovated Parc Zoologique de Paris.

> Once a royal hunting ground, the Bois de Vincennes was given to the City of Paris by Napoleon III in 1860.

The château, used as a prison from the 16th to the 19th centuries ↑

↑ Lake Daumesnil, one of four artificial lakes in the park

EAT

Le Chateau des Vignerons
French dishes with an international twist.

🏠 17 Rue des Vignerons, 94300 Vincennes
🌐 chateau desvignerons.com

€€€

Did You Know?

Henry V's corpse was boiled in the château's kitchen to prepare it for shipping back to England.

The Amazon-Guyana biozone at the Parc Zoologique de Paris ↑

THE PALACE AND GARDENS OF VERSAILLES

Place d'Armes, 78000 Versailles ◼ Versailles Express from Eiffel Tower ◼ Versailles-Château-Rive-Gauche, Versailles Chantiers ◷ Opening hours vary; check website for details ◷ 1 Jan, 25 Dec ◼ chateauversailles.fr

This stunning royal residence is overwhelming in its scale and opulence. The spectacular, lavishly decorated palace and vast gardens, complete with fountains, landscaped topiary and even a model farm, make Versailles the top day trip from the centre of Paris.

The Palace

Starting in 1668 with his father's hunting lodge, Louis XIV built the largest palace in Europe, housing 20,000 people at a time. Architects Louis Le Vau and Jules Hardouin-Mansart designed the buildings, which grew as a series of "envelopes" around the lodge. The Opera House was added by Louis XV in 1770.

The sumptuous main apartments are on the first floor of the vast château complex. These were richly decorated by Charles Le Brun with coloured marbles, stone and wood carvings, murals, velvet, silver and gilded furniture. The climax is the Hall of Mirrors, where 357 great mirrors face 17 tall arched windows.

TOP 5 TOP FIVE PALACE ROOMS

Salon de Vénus
A statue of Louis XIV stands amid this room's rich marble decor.

Salon d'Apollon
Designed by Le Brun and dedicated to the god Apollo, this was Louis XIV's throne room.

Salon de la Guerre
The room's theme of war is dramatically reinforced by the stuccoed relief of Louis XIV riding to victory.

Hall of Mirrors
This glittering room stretches 73 m (240 ft) along the west façade.

Queen's Bedroom
In this room, the queens of France gave birth to the royal children in full public view.

The palace and gardens of Versailles, the epitome of royal grandeur ↓

1 The Marble Courtyard is decorated with marble paving, urns, busts and a gilded balcony.

2 Mansart's last great work, the two-storey Baroque Chapelle Royale was Louis XIV's final addition to Versailles.

3 The South Wing's original apartments for great nobles were replaced by Louis-Philippe's museum of French history.

The formal gardens, complete with geometric paths and shrubberies ↑

The Gardens

The grounds of Versailles are no less impressive than the palace. Designed by the great landscaper André Le Nôtre, the formal gardens are a masterpiece: sculptural fountains and secluded groves sit amid geometric flowerbeds and hedges. The 1.7-km- (1-mile-) long Grand Canal leads from the gardens to the enormous park, which features wooded areas and agricultural fields delineated by a network of footpaths. The grounds also encompass the Grand Trianon and Petit Trianon palaces, built as private apartments for Louis XIV and Louis V, as well as the Queen's Hamlet – a life-size model village built for Marie-Antoinette that was also a functioning farm.

> The formal gardens are a masterpiece: sculptural fountains and secluded groves sit amid geometric flowerbeds and hedges.

↑ The Grand Trianon, built by Louis XIV in 1687 to escape the rigours of court life

EAT

Ore

This Alain Ducasse dining experience in the Pavillon Dufour is as luxurious as the château it occupies.

🏠 Château de Versailles, 78000 Versailles
🌐 ducasse-chateauversailles.com

€€€

Angelina

The iconic tea house has two outposts in Versailles – one in the Pavillon d'Orléans and one at the Petit Trianon – both serving a selection of snacks and delectable pastries.

🏠 Château de Versailles, 78000 Versailles
🌐 angelina-paris.fr

€€€

Did You Know?

One-third of the estate's budget went to the fountains. Today they only go on during the summer months.

1 The cottages in the Queen's Hamlet were inspired by rural French architecture. Although rustic on the exterior, inside they were richly furnished.

2 During the Grands Eaux Nocturnes in the summer, the gardens of Versailles come alive with superb illuminations and installations.

3 Built in 1762 as a retreat for Louis XV, the Petit Trianon became a favourite of Marie-Antoinette.

④ 🛷 Ⓜ 🍴 ☕ 🛍

DISNEYLAND®
PARIS

🏠 Marne-la-Vallée 77777 🚌 Disneyland® Paris Express from Gare du Nord, Opéra and Châtelet 🚆 Marne-la-Vallée/Chessy 🕐 Disneyland® Park: 10am–11pm in high season (closes earlier in low season); Walt Disney Studios® Park: 10am–9pm in high season (closes earlier in low season) 🌐 disneylandparis.com

Unbeatable for complete escapism, combined with vibrant excitement and sheer energy, Disneyland® Paris offers extreme rides, gentle experiences and phenomenal visual effects.

The resort is built on a massive scale – the 2,230-ha (5,510-acre) site encompasses two theme parks; seven hotels; a shopping, dining and entertainment village; an ice-skating rink; a lake; two convention centres; and a golf course. The theme parks are split into Disneyland® Park and the Walt Disney Studios® Park. The former, with more than 60 rides and attractions, celebrates Hollywood folklore and fantasies, while the latter highlights the ingenuity involved in cinema, animation and television production with interactive exhibits and live shows.

DISNEY VILLAGE

The fun does not have to end when the two parks close. Disney Village offers a host of evening entertainment options – including a cinema, concerts and Buffalo Bill's Wild West Show – as well as numerous restaurants and shops. Seasonal events take place all year, including celebrations for Easter, Halloween and New Year.

Did You Know?

Sleeping Beauty's castle was designed to contrast with the grey Parisian skies.

↑ The view from Alice's Curious Labyrinth in Disneyland® Park

1 The entrance to Crush's Coaster® in Walt Disney Studios® Park.

2 The Mad Hatter's Tea Cups in Disneyland® Park's Fantasyland®.

3 The parade in Disneyland® Park features characters from films such as *Toy Story*.

DISNEYLAND® PARK

The Disneyland® Park is comprised of five areas. Main Street represents a fantasy small-town America, its Victorian façades fronting interesting stores and food outlets. Frontierland®, a homage to America's Wild West, hosts some of the park's most popular attractions, while wild rides and Audio-Animatronics are the draw at Adventureland®. The buildings in Fantasyland® are modelled on those in animated movies, and contain many attractions for younger children. Science fiction and the future are the themes at Discoveryland®, home to the popular multi-loop ride Star Wars Hyperspace Mountain.

TOP 3 RIDES IN DISNEYLAND® PARK

Star Wars Hyperspace Mountain
Formerly known as Space Mountain®, this iconic rollercoaster draws crowds from the outset but at the end of the day you can often walk straight on.

Big Thunder Mountain
This wild rollercoaster ride on a speeding runaway mine train is a crowd favourite.

Pirates of the Caribbean
This boat ride takes you on a thrilling journey through underground prisons and past fighting galleons.

← The park, home to rides such as Indiana Jones™ and the Temple of Peril *(below)*

The entrance to Walt Disney Studios® Park, with the Earful Tower ↑

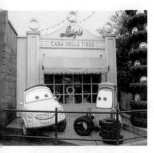

↑ The four-wheeled Cars Quatre Roues Rallye attraction

↑ The underwater animated world of Crush's Coaster®

WALT DISNEY STUDIOS® PARK

The four production zones at Walt Disney Studios® Park reveal the secrets of movie-making. Inside the giant studio gates on the Front Lot, Disney Studio 1 houses a film set boulevard, complete with stylized street façades and venues such as the 1930s-style Club Swankedero. Toon Studio® contains rides and exhibits inspired by various iconic Disney and Pixar characters, and includes La Place de Rémy, home to the 4D experience Ratatouille: A Recipe for Adventure. The Production Courtyard® offers the chance to see behind the scenes on the Studio Tram Tour®, among other attractions, while the Backlot focuses on special effects, film music recording and dare-devil stunts.

→ Mickey Mouse casting his magic over the Toon Studio® zone

EXPERIENCE MORE

5
La Défense

**☖ 1 Parvis de la Défense
Ⓜ/ⓇⒺⓇ La Défense ☉ La
Grande Arche: 10am–7pm
daily Ⓦ grandearche.com**

This skyscraper business district on the western edge of Paris is one of Europe's largest modern office developments and covers 80 ha (198 acres). It was launched in 1958 to create a new home for leading French and multinational companies. Since then, a major artistic scheme has transformed many of the squares into fascinating open-air museums.

In 1989, one of Paris's most striking landmarks, La Grande Arche, was added to the complex – an enormous hollow cube large enough to contain Notre-Dame cathedral. This was designed by Danish architect Otto von Spreckelsen as part of major construction works, or *Grands* *Travaux*, which were initiated by (and are now a memorial to) the late President François Mitterrand. You can take a lift to the top of the arch for some great views. There's also a restaurant and an exhibition space for photojournalism.

6
Musée Marmottan-Monet

**☖ 2 Rue Louis Boilly 75016
Ⓜ Muette ☉ 10am–6pm
Tue–Sun (to 9pm Thu)
☒ 1 Jan, 1 May, 25 Dec
Ⓦ marmottan.fr**

In 1932, art historian Paul Marmottan bequeathed his 19th-century mansion and his Renaissance, Consular and First Empire collections of paintings and furniture to the Institut de France, and a museum was established. The focus of the museum changed in 1934 after the bequest by

↑ Claude Monet's glasses, Musée Marmottan-Monet

Michel Monet of 65 paintings by his father, Claude Monet. Some of his most famous paintings are here, among them *Impression – Sunrise*, a beautiful canvas from the Rouen Cathedral series, and several *Water Lilies*.

In addition, part of Monet's personal art collection passed to the museum, including paintings by Camille Pissarro and works by the Impressionists Pierre Auguste Renoir and Alfred Sisley. The museum also displays some exquisite medieval illuminated manuscripts.

↓ Shiny new office blocks at La Défense business district

→ Tombs within the Basilique-Cathédrale de St-Denis

7

Basilique-Cathédrale de St-Denis

⌂ 1 Rue de la Légion D'Honneur, 93200 St-Denis Ⓜ St-Denis-Basilique ⓇⒺⒷ St-Denis ⏱ Apr-Sep: 10am-6:15pm Mon-Sat, noon-6:15pm Sun; Oct-Mar: 10am-5:15pm Mon-Sat, noon-5:15pm Sun 🔒 1 Jan, 1 May, 25 Dec 🌐 saint-denis-basilique.fr

Constructed between 1137 and 1281, the cathedral is on the site of the tomb of St Denis, the first bishop of Paris, who was beheaded in 250. The building was the original influence for Gothic art. From Merovingian times, it was a burial place for rulers of France. During the Revolution, many tombs were desecrated and scattered, but the best were stored, and now represent a collection of funerary art. Memorials include those of Dagobert, Henri II and Catherine de Medici, and Louis XVI and Marie-Antoinette.

8

Potager du Roi

⌂ 10 Rue du Maréchal-Joffre, 78000 Versailles ⏱ 10am-6pm Tue-Fri (plus Sat & Sun Apr-Oct) ⓇⒺⒷ Versailles-Château-Rive Gauche 🌐 potager-du-roi.fr

When Louis XIV built Versailles, he decided that it would be prudent for a king to have his own vegetable garden (poisoning was a constant threat in the château). Jean-Baptiste de La Quintinie developed the *potager* – vegetable patch – for Louis in 1678. At first, the swampy ground proved difficult to master, but eventually La Quintinie was producing all sorts of fruits and vegetables for the king, including summer produce in the winter. The garden continued to function in several capacities after the Revolution, becoming a centre for education and horticultural schools. In 1991, the Potager du Roi opened up to the public for visits. There is a shop selling seasonal produce pulled from the garden.

9

Marché aux Puces de St-Ouen

⌂ Rue des Rosiers, 75018 St-Ouen Ⓜ Porte-de-Clignancourt, Garibaldi ⏱ 10am-5:30pm Mon-Sat; reduced hours during summer 🌐 marcheaux puces-saintouen.com

This is the oldest, most expensive and largest of the Paris flea markets, covering 6 ha (15 acres). In the 19th century, rag merchants and tramps would gather outside the city limits and offer their

Did You Know?

Less than a quarter of Paris's 10.5 million inhabitants live within the 20 arrondissements.

wares for sale. By the 1920s, there was a proper market here, where masterpieces could sometimes be purchased cheaply from the often uninformed sellers. Today, it is divided into specialist markets. Known especially for its profusion of furniture and ornaments from the Second Empire (1852–70), few bargains are to be found these days, yet some 150,000 treasure-hunters, tourists and dealers still flock here to browse among more than 2,000 stalls.

10

Marché aux Puces de la Porte de Vanves

⌂ 4 Ave Georges Lafenestre 75014 Ⓜ Porte de Vanves ⏱ 7am-7:30pm Sat & Sun 🌐 pucesde vanves.typepad.com

Every Saturday and Sunday, bargain hunters descend on this lively outdoor flea market. Visitors can pick through a wide selection of glassware, furniture, artwork, and a seemingly endless variety of odds and ends. There are always surprises. In 1989, the very first portrait ever taken by Louis Daguerre sold here at this market for the equivalent of €500, a modest sum for such a monumental piece of photographic history. There are real finds to be had if you look hard enough – go early to beat the crowds and prepare to spend a few hours browsing.

NEED TO KNOW

The Metro whizzing across the Pont de Bir Hakeim

BEFORE YOU GO

Forward planning is essential to any successful trip. Be prepared for all eventualities by considering the following points before you travel.

AT A GLANCE

CURRENCY
Euro (EUR)

AVERAGE DAILY SPEND

SAVE	SPEND	SPLURGE
€60	€165	€300+

BOTTLED WATER	COFFEE	BEER	DINNER FOR TWO
€1.00	€2.50	€5.00	€60

ESSENTIAL PHRASES

Hello	Bonjour
Goodbye	Au revoir
Please	S'il vous plaît
Thank you	Merci
Do you speak English	Parlez-vous anglais?
I don't understand...	Je ne comprends pas

ELECTRICITY SUPPLY

Power sockets are type C and E, fitting two-pronged plugs. Standard voltage is 230 volts.

Passports and Visas

For a stay of up to three months for the purpose of tourism, EU nationals and citizens of the US, Canada, Australia and New Zealand do not need a visa. For visa information specific to your home country, consult your nearest French embassy or check online.
France-Visas
w france-visas.gouv.fr

Travel Safety Advice

Visitors can get up-to-date travel safety information from the **UK Foreign and Commonwealth Office**, the **US State Department**, and the **Australian Department of Foreign Affairs and Trade**.
AUS
w smartraveller.gov.au
UK
w gov.uk/foreign-travel-advice
US
w travel.state.gov

Customs Information

An individual is permitted to carry the following within the EU for personal use:
Tobacco products 800 cigarettes, 400 cigarillos, 200 cigars or 1 kg of smoking tobacco.
Alcohol 10 litres of alcoholic beverages above 22% strength, 20 litres of alcoholic beverages below 22% strength, 90 litres of wine (60 litres of which can be sparkling wine) and 110 litres of beer.
Cash If you plan to enter or leave the EU with €10,000 or more in cash (or the equivalent in other currencies) you must declare it to the customs authorities.
If travelling outside the EU limits vary, so always check restrictions before departing.

Insurance

It is wise to take out an insurance policy covering theft, loss of belongings, medical problems, cancellation and delays.

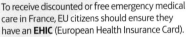

To receive discounted or free emergency medical care in France, EU citizens should ensure they have an **EHIC** (European Health Insurance Card).

Visitors from outside the EU must arrange their own private medical insurance.

EHIC
🆆 gov.uk/european-health-insurance-card

Vaccinations

No inoculations are needed for France.

Money

Most establishments accept major credit, debit and prepaid currency cards, but it's always a good idea to carry some cash too. Contactless payments are widely accepted in Paris.

Booking Accommodation

Paris offers a huge variety of accommodation, comprising luxury five-star hotels, family-run B&Bs, budget hostels and private apartments.

The city is busiest during Christmas, New Year and France's school breaks. Tourists pour in from May to September, but Parisians pour out en masse in August. In times of high demand it is wise to book ahead by at least a month.

Travellers with Specific Needs

Paris's historic buildings and cobbled streets can make the city tricky to navigate. However, there are a number of organizations working to improve accessibility in France's capital.

The **Office du Tourisme et des Congrès** has a useful guide that lists easily accessible sights and routes for visitors with mobility issues, while **Jaccede** has details of accessible museums, hotels, bars, restaurants and cinemas in Paris and other French cities.

The **Vianavigo** website provides detailed information on accessible public transport, including a route planner that can be tailored to your specific needs.

Les Compagnons du Voyage will provide an escort for persons with limited mobility or visibility on any form of public transport, for a small fee.

For further information on accessibility, contact the **GIHP** or consult **ParisInfo** (p315).

Accès Plus
🆆 accessibilite.sncf.com
GIHP
🆆 gihpnational.org
J'accede
🆆 jaccede.com
Les Compagnons du Voyage
🆆 compagnons.com
Office du Tourisme et des Congrès
🆆 parisinfo.com
Vianavigo
🆆 vianavigo.com

Language

Parisians are fiercely proud of their language, but don't let this put you off. Mastering a few niceties goes a long way though you can get by without knowing the language at all.

Closures

Lunchtime Some shops and businesses close for an hour or two from around noon.
Mondays Some museums, small shops, restaurants and bars are closed for the day.
Tuesdays National museums are closed for the day, except Versailles and the Musée d'Orsay, which are closed on Monday.
Sundays Most shops are closed.
Public holidays Public services, shops, museums and attractions are usually closed.

PUBLIC HOLIDAYS 2019	
1 Jan	New Year's Day
22 Apr	Easter Monday
1 May	Labour Day
8 May	Victory 1945
30 May	Ascension Day
10 Jun	Whit Monday
14 July	Bastille Day
15 Aug	Assumption Day
1 Nov	All Saints' Day
11 Nov	Armistice 1918
25 Dec	Christmas Day

GETTING
AROUND

Paris has an efficient public transport system that will allow you to navigate the city's many sights with ease.

PUBLIC TRANSPORT COSTS

Tickets are valid on all forms of public transport.

SINGLE

€1.90

(zones 1-3)

DAY TICKET

€12.00

(zones 1-3)

3-DAY TICKET

€26.65

(zones 1-3)

SPEED LIMIT

MOTORWAY

130 km/h (80 miles/h)

MAJOR ROADS

80 km/h (49 miles/h)

RING ROADS

70 km/h (43 miles/h)

URBAN AREAS

50 km/h (30 miles/h)

Arriving by Air

Paris has two major airports, Charles de Gaulle (also known as Roissy) and Orly, and one secondary airport, Beauvais, which serves mainly budget airlines. All three are well connected to the city centre by train, bus and taxi. Car rental facilities are also available, although driving in Paris is not recommended. For information on journey times and ticket prices between Paris's airports and the city centre, see the table opposite.

Airport Shuttle provides a door-to-door transfer service between all three airports and individual hotels. It costs €70 for one person, or €21–25 each for two or more people. Book at least 48 hours ahead, then call them after landing to confirm your journey.

The **RATP Roissybus** operates regular services from Charles de Gaulle, and RER trains (Line B) leave regularly every 5–15 minutes, calling at Gare du Nord, Châtelet-Les-Halles and several other major stations. **Le Bus Direct** runs a reliable service from both Charles de Gaulle and Orly.

A shuttle bus operates between Beauvais and Porte-Maillot. Trains run from Beauvais station to Gare du Nord, but the station is a 15-minute taxi-ride from the airport, and the train journey into Paris takes at least 1 hour 15 minutes.

Airport Shuttle
W airportshuttles.com
Le Bus Direct
W lebusdirect.com
RATP Roissybus
W ratp.fr/en/titres-et-tarifs/airport-tickets

Train Travel

International Train Travel

Regular high-speed trains connect Paris's six international railway stations to numerous major cities across Europe. Reservations for these services are essential, as seats get booked up quickly, particularly during peak times.

You can buy tickets and passes for multiple international journeys from **Eurail** or **Interrail**; however, you may need to pay an additional

Airport	Public Transport	Journey Time	Price
Charles de Gaulle	Le Bus Direct Line 2	45–70 mins	€17
	Le Bus Direct Line 4	1 hr 20 mins	€17
	RATP Roissybus	1 hr 10 mins	€12
	RER	25–30 mins	€10.30
	Taxi	25–45 mins	from €45
Orly	Le Bus Direct	20–60 mins	€12
	GOC	30 mins	€35
	RATP Orlybus	25–30 mins	€8.30
	Orlyval/RER	1 hr	€9.30
	Taxi	25–45 mins	from €25
Beauvais	Shuttle bus	1 hr 15 mins	€17
	Taxi	1 hr – 1 hr 30 mins	from €100

reservation fee depending on which rail service you travel with. Always check carefully before boarding that your pass is valid on the service you wish to use.

Eurostar runs a fast, regular and reliable service from London to central Paris via the Channel Tunnel.

Students and those under 26 can benefit from discounted rail travel both to and within France. For more information on discounted travel, visit the **Eurail** or **Interrail** website.

Thalys runs a high-speed service between Paris, Brussels and Amsterdam ten times a day, with a variety of special offers, package deals and half-price last-minute deals.

Eurail
W eurail.com
Eurostar
W eurostar.com
Interrail
W interrail.eu
Thalys
W thalys.com

Domestic Train Travel

Paris has a number of main train stations situated at various points across the city, all of which serve different regions.

The French state railway, **OUI SNCF**, has two services in Paris: the Banlieue suburban service and the Grandes Lignes, or long-distance service. The suburban services all operate within the five-zone network. The long-distance services operate throughout France. The TGV offers a reliable high-speed service which should be booked in advance.

Before boarding a train, remember to time-punch (composter) tickets to validate your journey; this does not apply for e-tickets. Tickets for city transport cannot be used on Banlieue trains, with the exception of some RER tickets to stations with both SNCF and RER lines.

OUI SNCF
W oui.sncf.com

PARIS'S MAIN STATIONS

Station	Destinations Served
Gare de Lyon	Southern France, the Alps, Italy and Switzerland
Gare de l'Est	Eastern France, Austria, Switzerland and Germany.
Gare du Nord	Northeast France, Britain and Northern Europe
Gare St-Lazare	Channel ports and Normandy
Gare d'Austerlitz	Southwest France, Brittany ports and Spain
Gare Montparnasse	Brittany ports and Spain

Public Transport

The Metro, RER, bus system and tramways are all run by **RATP** (Régie Autonome des Transports Parisiens).

RATP

W ratp.fr

Tickets

For the purpose of ticket pricing, the Paris metropolitan area is divided into five zones. Central Paris is zone 1, Charles de Gaulle airport is in zone 5, Orly airport and Versailles in zone 4. The Metro serves zones 1–3.

Ordinary Metro and RER tickets (called t+) can be bought either individually or as a group of ten. These tickets are also valid on trams and buses and can be used for transfers within 1 hour 30 minutes of first use.

Bus-only tickets can be purchased onboard from the driver. All bus tickets must be validated using the machine on the bus. Anyone travelling without a valid ticket may be fined.

Visitors can enjoy unlimited travel on the Metro, RER and Paris buses with a Paris Visite pass or a one-day Mobilis card, both valid for travel on most forms of public transport, and both available from RATP. There is also the **Passe Navigo Découverte**, a prepaid contactless smart card that costs €5.

Passe Navigo Découverte

W navigo.fr

Metro and RER

The Paris Metro has 14 main lines and two minor lines. The RER is a system of five lines of commuter trains that travel underground in central Paris and above ground in outlying areas. The two systems overlap in the city centre. Be aware that RER trips outside the centre require special tickets. Fares to suburbs and nearby towns vary.

Buses and Trams

Most buses must be flagged down at designated stops. A single ticket entitles the bearer to a single journey on one line only. If you want to make a change, you'll need another ticket. (Exceptions to this rule are the Balabus, Noctambus, Orlybus and Roissybus services, and lines 221, 297, 299, 350 and 351.)

There are 31 night bus lines, called Noctilien, serving Paris and its suburbs. The terminus for most lines is Châtelet.

There are three RATP tramways operating in Paris – T1 (Gare de St-Denis–Noisy le Sec), T2 (La Défense–Porte de Versailles), T3a (Pont du Garigliano–Porte de Vincennes) and T3b (Porte de Vincennes to Porte d'Asnières). The T4 (Aulnay-sous-Bois–Bondy) is run by SNCF and is a tram-train line.

Long-Distance Bus Travel

The main coach operator to Paris is **Eurolines**, based at the Gare Routière Internationale. Its coaches travel from Belgium, the Netherlands, Ireland, Germany, Scandinavia, the UK, Italy and Portugal. Low-cost alternatives are **Ouibus**, **Flixbus** and **Isilines**, all of which which connect Paris to other towns in France and to London, Brussels, Amsterdam, Milan and Barcelona.

Eurolines

W eurolines.eu

Flixbus

W flixbus.com

Isilines

W isilines.fr

Ouibus

W ouibus.com

Taxis

Taxis can be hailed in the street unless there is a taxi rank nearby. The meter will show an initial starting charge (around €2.50). If you order a taxi, the meter will show the charge from where the driver started their journey to collect you.

Vélo taxis are motorised tricycle rickshaws that offer a green alternative to traditional taxis. Taxi apps such as Uber and Taxify also operate in Paris. The following services can be booked by phone or online:

Citybird

W city-bird.com

Taxis G7

W taxisg7.com

Driving

Driving in Paris is not recommended. Traffic is often heavy, there are many one-way streets and parking is notoriously difficult, not to mention expensive.

Driving to Paris

Autoroutes (motorways) converge on Paris from all directions. For those travelling from Britain to Paris by road, the simplest way is to use the Eurotunnel trains that run between the terminals at Folkestone and Calais, which both have direct motorway access.

Paris is surrounded by an outer ring road called the Boulevard Périphérique. All motorways leading to the capital link in to the Périphérique, which separates the city from the suburbs. Each former city gate, called a *porte*, now corresponds to an exit onto or from the Périphérique. Arriving motorists should take time to check their destination address and consult a map of central Paris to find the closest corresponding *porte*.

To take your own car into France, you will need to carry proof of registration, valid insurance documents, a full and valid driving licence, and passport at all times.

Car Rental

To rent a car in France you must be 21 or over and have held a valid driver's licence for at least a year. You will also need to present a credit card to secure the rental deposit.

Driving licences issued by any European Union member state are valid throughout the EU. International driving licences are not needed for short-term visitors (up to 90 days) from North America, Australia and New Zealand. Visitors from other countries should check the regulations with their local automobile association before they travel.

Autolib' is a self-service electric car rental service that operates throughout Paris and the Paris region. You can pick up a car from one parking station, make your journey and park at any other station in the region. The service is open to everyone 18 years old or over who holds a valid driving licence.

Autolib'
w autolib.eu

Driving in Paris

Paris is a limited traffic zone and it is compulsory for all vehicles to display a Crit'Air sticker with a number ranging from 1 to 5, which denotes the level of pollution in ascending order. In the event of high pollution levels, vehicles with certain stickers may be banned from the road. The stickers can be purchased from the **Air Quality Certificate Service**.

Park in areas with a large "P" or *payant* sign on the pavement or road, and pay at the parking meter with *La Paris Carte* (available from any kiosk), a credit or debit card, or using the **PaybyPhone** app *(p315)*.

Paris has numerous underground car parks, signposted by a white "P" on a blue background.

Air Quality Certificate Service
w certificat-air.gouv.fr

Rules of the Road

Always drive on the right. Unless otherwise signposted, vehicles coming from the right have right of way. Cars on a roundabout usually have right of way, although the Arc de Triomphe is a hair-raising exception as cars give way to traffic on the right.

At all times, drivers must carry a valid driver's licence, registration and insurance documents. The wearing of seat belts is compulsory, and it is prohibited to sound your horn in the city. For motorbikes and scooters, the wearing of helmets and protective gloves is compulsory. In the city centre, it is against the law to use the bus lanes at any time of day. France strictly enforces its drink-drive limit *(p315)*.

Cycling

Paris is reasonably flat (with the exception of Montmartre), manageably small and has many backstreets where traffic is restricted. For details of the city's cycle lanes, download the free **Paris à Vélo** map.
Paris à Vélo
w paris.fr

Bicycle Hire

The **Vélib'** shared bicycle scheme is available 24 hours a day. The first half-hour is free, increasing by €1 for every additional half-hour up to €4. A one- or seven-day card is also available online.
Vélib'
w velib-metropole.fr

Bicycle Tours

Fat Tire Tours offer trips to Paris's most famous landmarks. **Paris à Vélo C'est Sympa!** runs multilingual tours to more offbeat locations.
Fat Tire Tours
w fattiretours.com
Paris à Vélo C'est Sympa!
w parisvelosympa.fr

Boats and Ferries

Arriving by Sea

The following companies run passenger and vehicle ferry services from the UK.

P&O Ferries runs services from Dover to Calais, **Condor Ferries** operates between Poole and St-Malo and **DFDS Seaways** runs routes between Newhaven and Dieppe. **Brittany Ferries** makes crossings from Plymouth to Roscoff, from Poole and Portsmouth to Cherbourg, and from Portsmouth to Le Havre and Caen. They also run an overnight service from Portsmouth to St-Malo.

Driving to Paris from Cherbourg takes about four hours; from Dieppe or Le Havre, about two and a half hours; and from Calais, two hours.

Brittany Ferries
w brittany-ferries.co.uk
Condor Ferries
w condorferries.co.uk
DFDS Seaways
w dfdsseaways.co.uk
P&O Ferries
w poferries.com/en/portal

Paris by Boat

Paris's river-boat shuttle service, the **Batobus**, runs every 20–45 minutes, with more frequent services in the spring and summer months. Tickets can be bought at Batobus stops, RATP and tourist offices.
Batobus
w www.batobus.com

PRACTICAL
INFORMATION

A little local know-how goes a long way in Paris. Here you will find all the essential advice and information you will need during your stay.

AT A GLANCE

EMERGENCY NUMBERS

GENERAL EMERGENCY	FIRE SERVICE AND AMBULANCE
112	**18**

POLICE	MEDICAL EMERGENCY
17	**15**

TIME ZONE
CET/CEST
Central European
Summer Time (CEST)
runs 31 Mar–27 Oct
2019

TAP WATER
Unless stated
otherwise, tap
water in France
is safe to drink.

TIPPING

Waiter	5–10%
Hotel Porter	€1 a bag
Housekeeping	€1 a day
Concierge	€1–2
Taxi Driver	Not expected

Personal Security

Paris is generally a safe city and most visits are trouble-free. However, beware of pickpockets on the Metro and on buses during the rush hour and in major tourist areas.

If you have anything stolen, report the crime as soon as possible to the nearest police station, and bring ID with you. Get a copy of the crime report in order to claim on your insurance.

When travelling late at night, avoid long transfers in Metro stations such as Châtelet-Les-Halles and Montparnasse. The last RER trains to and from outlying areas should also be avoided.

Contact your embassy if you have your passport stolen, or in the event of a serious crime or accident.

Health

If you fall sick during your visit, pharmacists are an excellent source of advice – they can diagnose many minor ailments and suggest appropriate treatment.

For English-speaking visitors, there are two private hospitals with bilingual staff and doctors: the **American Hospital of Paris** and the **Franco-Britannique Hospital**. The **Centre Médical Europe** is an inexpensive private clinic, which also has a dental practice.

All EU nationals holding a European Health Insurance Card (EHIC) are entitled to use the French national health service. Patients must pay for treatment and can then reclaim most of the cost from the health authorities. The process may be lengthy and travellers should therefore consider purchasing private travel insurance.

For visitors from outside the EU, payment of hospital and other medical expenses is the patient's responsibility. It is therefore important to arrange comprehensive medical insurance before travelling.

American Hospital of Paris
W american-hospital.org
Centre Médical Europe
W centre-medical-europe.fr
Franco-Britannique Hospital
W ihfb.org

Smoking, Alcohol and Drugs

Smoking is prohibited in all public places, but is allowed on restaurant, café and pub terraces, as long as they are not enclosed.

The possession of narcotics is prohibited and could result in a prison sentence.

Unless stated otherwise, alcohol consumption on the streets is permitted. France has a strict limit of 0.05 per cent BAC (blood alcohol content) for drivers.

ID

There is no requirement for visitors to carry ID, but in the event of a routine check you may be asked to show your passport. If you don't have it with you, the police may escort you to wherever your passport is being kept.

Local Customs

Etiquette (la politesse) is important to Parisians. On entering a store or cafe, you are expected to say "bonjour" to staff, and when leaving to say "au revoir". Be sure to add "s'il vous plaît" (please) when ordering something and "pardon" if you accidentally bump into someone.

The French usually shake hands on meeting someone for the first time. Friends and colleagues who know each other well greet each other with a kiss on each cheek. If you are unsure what's expected, wait to see if they proffer a hand or a cheek.

Visiting Churches and Cathedrals

Dress respectfully. Cover your torso and upper arms; ensure shorts and skirts cover your knees.

Mobile Phones and Wi-Fi

Free Wi-Fi hotspots are widely available in public spaces. Cafés and restaurants usually permit the use of their Wi-Fi on the condition that you make a purchase.

Visitors travelling to Paris with EU tariffs will be able to use their devices abroad without being affected by data roaming charges. Users will be charged the same rates for data, SMS and voice calls as they would pay at home.

Post

Stamps (timbres) can be bought at post offices and tabacs. Most post offices have self-service machines to weigh and frank your mail.

Taxes and Refunds

VAT is around 20% in France. Non-EU residents can claim back tax on certain goods. Look out for the Global Refund Tax-Free sign, where the retailer will supply a form and issue a détaxe receipt. Present the goods receipt, détaxe receipt and passport at customs when you depart to receive your refund.

Discount Cards

Entry to some national and municipal museums is free on the first Sunday of each month.

Visitors under 18 years of age and EU passport holders aged 18–26 years are usually admitted free of charge to national museums, and there are sometimes discounts for students and over-60s who have ID showing their date of birth.

The **Paris Pass** offers access to over 60 attractions for 2, 4 or 6 days. It also offers unlimited travel on the Metro, buses and RER within central Paris, and a ticket for a hop-on hop-off bus tour. It is worth carefully considering how many of the offers and discounts you are likely to take advantage of before purchasing.
Paris Pass
w parispass.com

WEBSITES AND APPS

en.parisinfo.com
The official tourist board website.
Le Fooding
No matter where you are in the city, find the nearest recommended restaurant in an instant.
PaybyPhone
Pay for on-street parking quickly and easily with this app.
RATP
The official app from RATP, the city's public transport operator.

INDEX

PHRASE BOOK

IN AN EMERGENCY

Help!	Au secours!	oh sekoor
Stop!	Arrêtez!	aret-ay
Call a doctor!	Appelez un médecin!	apuh-lay uñ medsañ
Call an ambulance!	Appelez une ambulance!	apuh-lay oon oñboo-loñs
Call the police!	Appelez la police!	apuh-lay lah poh-lees
Call the fire brigade!	Appelez les pompiers!	apuh-lay leh poñ-peeyay
Where is the nearest telephone?	Où est le téléphone le plus proche?	oo ay luh tehlehfon luh ploo prosh
Where is the nearest hospital?	Où est l'hôpital le plus proche?	oo ay l'opeetal luh ploo prosh

COMMUNICATION ESSENTIALS

Yes	Oui	wee
No	Non	noñ
Please	S'il vous plaît	seel voo play
Thank you	Merci	mer-see
Excuse me	Excusez-moi	exkoo-zay mwah
Hello	Bonjour	boñzhoor
Goodbye	Au revoir	oh ruh-vwar
Good night	Bonsoir	boñ-swar
Morning	Le matin	matañ
Afternoon	L'après-midi	l'apreh-meedee
Evening	Le soir	swar
Yesterday	Hier	eeyehr
Today	Aujourd'hui	oh-zhoor-dwee
Tomorrow	Demain	duhmañ
Here	Ici	ee-see
There	Là	lah
What?	Quoi, quel, quelle?	kwah, kel, kel
When?	Quand?	koñ
Why?	Pourquoi?	poor-kwah
Where?	Où?	oo

USEFUL PHRASES

How are you?	Comment allez-vous?	kom-moñ talay voo
Very well, thank you.	Très bien, merci.	treh byañ, mer-see
Pleased to meet you.	Enchanté de faire votre connaissance.	oñshoñ-tay duh fehr votr kon-ay-sans
See you soon.	A bientôt.	byañ-toh
That's fine.	C'est bon	say bon
Where is/are...?	Où est/sont...?	ooay/soñ
How far is it to...?	Combien de kilomètres d'ici à...?	kom-byañ duh keelo-metr d'ee-see ah
Which way to...?	Quelle est la direction pour...?	kel ay lah deer-ek-syoñ poor
Do you speak English?	Parlez-vous anglais?	par-lay voo oñg-lay
I don't understand.	Je ne comprends pas.	zhuh nuh kom-proñ pah
Could you speak slowly please?	Pouvez-vous parler moins vite s'il vous plaît?	poo-vay voo par-lay mwañ veet seel voo play
I'm sorry.	Excusez-moi.	exkoo-zay mwah

USEFUL WORDS

big	grand	groñ
small	petit	puh-tee
hot	chaud	show
cold	froid	frwah
good	bon/bien	boñ/byañ
bad	mauvais	moh-veh
enough	assez	assay
well	bien	byañ
open	ouvert	oo-ver
closed	fermé	fer-meh
left	gauche	gohsh
right	droite	drwaht
straight on	tout droite	too drwaht
near	près	preh
far	loin	lwañ
up	en haut	oñ oh
down	en bas	oñ bah
early	de bonne heure	duh bon urr
late	en retard	oñ ruh-tar
entrance	l'entrée	l'on-tray
exit	la sortie	sor-tee
toilet	les toilettes, le WC	twah-let, vay-see
free, unoccupied	libre	leebr
free, no charge	gratuit	grah-twee

MAKING A TELEPHONE CALL

I'd like to place a long-distance call.	Je voudrais faire un appel á l'étranger.	zhuh voo-dreh fehr uñ apel a laytroñ-zhay
I'd like to make a reverse charge call.	Je voudrais faire une communication en PCV.	zhuh voo-dreh fehr oon komoonikah-syoñ oñ peh-seh-veh
I'll try again later.	Je rappelerai plus tard.	zhuh rapeleray ploo tar
Can I leave a message?	Est-ce que je peux laisser un message?	es-keh zhuh puh leh-say uñ mehsazh
Hold on.	Ne quittez pas, s'il vous plaît.	nuh kee-tay pah seel voo play
Could you speak up a little please?	Pouvez-vous parler un peu plus fort?	poo-vay voo parlay uñ puh ploo for
local call	la communication locale	komoonikahsyoñ low-kal

SHOPPING

How much does this cost?	C'est combien s'il vous plaît?	say kom-byañ seel voo play
I would like ...	Je voudrais...	zhuh voo-dray
Do you have?	Est-ce que vous avez	es-kuh voo zavay
I'm just looking.	Je regarde seulement.	zhuh ruhgar suhlmoñ
Do you take credit cards?	Est-ce que vous acceptez les cartes de crédit?	es-kuh voo zaksept-ay leh kart duh kreh-dee
Do you take travellers' cheques?	Est-ce que vous acceptez les cheques de voyages?	es-kuh voo zaksept-ay leh shek duh vwayazh
What time do you open?	A quelle heure vous êtes ouvert?	ah kel urr voo zet oo-ver
What time do you close?	A quelle heure vous êtes fermé?	ah kel urr voo zet fer-may
This one.	Celui-ci	suhl-wee-see
That one.	Celui-là	suhl-wee-lah
expensive	cher	shehr
cheap	pas cher, bon marché	pah shehr, boñ mar-shay
size, clothes	la taille	tye
size, shoes	la pointure	pwañ-tur
white	blanc	bloñ
black	noir	nwahr
red	rouge	roozh
yellow	jaune	zhohwn
green	vert	vehr
blue	bleu	bluh

TYPES OF SHOP

antique shop	le magasin d'antiquités	maga-zañ d'oñteekee-tay
bakery	la boulangerie	booloñ-zhuree
bank	la banque	boñk
bookshop	la librairie	lee-brehree
butcher	la boucherie	boo-shehree
cake shop	la pâtisserie	patee-sree
cheese shop	la fromagerie	fromazh-ree
chemist	la pharmacie	farmah-see
dairy	la crémerie	krem-ree
department store	le grand magasin	groñ maga-zañ
delicatessen	la charcuterie	sharkoot-ree
fishmonger	la poissonnerie	pwasson-ree
gift shop	le magasin du cadeaux	maga-zañ duh kadoh
greengrocer	le marchand de légumes	mar-shoñ duh lay-goom
grocery	l'alimentation	alee-moñta-syoñ
hairdresser	le coiffeur	kwafuhr
market	le marché	marsh-ay
newsagent	le magasin de journaux	maga-zañ duh zhoor-no
post office	la poste, le bureau de poste, le PTT	pohst, booroh duh pohst, peh-teh-teh
shoe shop	le magasin de chaussures	maga-zañ duh show-soor
supermarket	le supermarché	soo pehr-marshay
tobacconist	le tabac	tabah
travel agent	l'agence de voyages	l'azhoñs duh vwayazh

SIGHTSEEING

abbey	l'abbaye	l'abay-ee
art gallery	la galerie d'art	galer-ree dart
bus station	la gare routière	gahr roo-tee-yehr
cathedral	la cathédrale	katay-dral
church	l'église	l'aygleez
garden	le jardin	zhar-dañ

library	la bibliothèque	beebleeo-tek
museum	le musée	moo-zay
railway station	la gare (SNCF)	gahr (es-en-say-ef)
tourist	les renseignements	roñsayn-moñ
information	touristiques, le	toorees-teek, sandee-
office	syndicat d'initiative	ka deenee-syateev
town hall	l'hôtel de ville	l'ohtel duh veel
closed for	fermeture	fehrmeh-tur
public holiday	jour férié	zhoor fehree-ay

STAYING IN A HOTEL

Do you have a	Est-ce que vous	es-kuh voo-zavay
vacant room?	avez une chambre?	oon shambr
double room,	la chambre à deux	shambr ah duh
with double bed	personnes, avec	pehr-son avek un
	un grand lit	groñ lee
twin room	la chambre à	shambr ah
	deux lits	duh lee
single room	la chambre à	shambr ah
	une personne	oon pehr-son
room with a	la chambre avec	shambr avek
bath, shower	salle de bains,	sal duh bañ,
	une douche	oon doosh
porter	le garçon	gar-soñ
key	la clef	klay
I have a	J'ai fait une	zhay fay oon
reservation.	réservation.	rayzehrva-syoñ

EATING OUT

Have you	Avez-vous une	avay-voo oon
got a table?	table de libre?	tahbl duh leebr
I want to	Je voudrais	zhuh voo-dray
reserve	réserver	rayzehr-vay
a table.	une table.	oon tahbl
The bill	L'addition s'il	l'adee-syoñ seel
please.	vous plaît.	voo play
I am a	Je suis	zhuh swee
vegetarian.	végétarien.	vezhay-tehryañ
Waitress/	Madame,	mah-dam,
waiter	Mademoiselle/	mah-demwahzel/
	Monsieur	muh-syuh
menu	le menu, la carte	men-oo, kart
fixed-price	le menu à	men-oo ah
menu	prix fixe	pree feeks
cover charge	le couvert	koo-vehr
wine list	la carte des vins	kart-deh vañ
glass	le verre	vehr
bottle	la bouteille	boo-tay
knife	le couteau	koo-toh
fork	la fourchette	for-shet
spoon	la cuillère	kwee-yehr
breakfast	le petit	puh-tee
	déjeuner	deh-zhuh-nay
lunch	le déjeuner	deh-zhuh-nay
dinner	le dîner	dee-nay
main course	le plat principal	plah prañsee-pal
starter, first	l'entrée, les hors	l'oñ-tray, or-
course	d'oeuvre	duhvr
dish of the day	le plat du jour	plah doo zhoor
wine bar	le bar à vin	bar ah vañ
café	le café	ka-fay
rare	saignant	say-noñ
medium	à point	ah pwañ
well done	bien cuit	byañ kwee

MENU DECODER

apple	la pomme	pom
baked	cuit au four	kweet oh foor
banana	la banane	banan
beef	le boeuf	buhf
beer, draught	la bière, bière	bee-yehr, bee-yehr
beer	à la pression	ah lah pres-syoñ
boiled	bouilli	boo-yee
bread	le pain	pan
butter	le beurre	burr
cake	le gâteau	gah-toh
cheese	le fromage	from-azh
chicken	le poulet	poo-lay
chips	les frites	freet
chocolate	le chocolat	shoko-lah
cocktail	le cocktail	cocktail
coffee	le café	kah-fay
dessert	le dessert	deh-ser
dry	sec	sek
duck	le canard	kanar
egg	l'oeuf	l'uf
fish	le poisson	pwah-ssoñ
fresh fruit	le fruit frais	frwee freh
garlic	l'ail	l'eye
grilled	grillé	gree-yay

ham	le jambon	zhoñ-boñ
ice, ice cream	la glace	glas
lamb	l'agneau	l'anyoh
lemon	le citron	see-troñ
lobster	le homard	omahr
meat	la viande	vee-yand
milk	le lait	leh
mineral water	l'eau minérale	l'oh meeney-ral
mustard	la moutarde	moo-tard
oil	l'huile	l'weel
olives	les olives	leh zoleev
onions	les oignons	leh zonyoñ
orange	l'orange	l'oroñzh
fresh orange juice	l'orange pressée	l'oroñzh press-eh
fresh lemon juice	le citron pressé	see-troñ press-eh
pepper	le poivre	pwavr
poached	poché	posh-ay
pork	le porc	por
potatoes	les pommes de terre	pom-duh tehr
prawns	les crevettes	kruh-vet
rice	le riz	ree
roast	rôti	row-tee
roll	le petit pain	puh-tee pañ
salt	le sel	sel
sauce	la sauce	sohs
sausage, fresh	la saucisse	sohsees
seafood	les fruits de mer	frwee duh mer
shellfish	les crustaces	kroos-tas
snails	les escargots	leh zes-kar-goh
soup	la soupe, le potage	soop, poh-tazh
steak	le bifteck, le steack	beef-tek, stek
sugar	le sucre	sookr
tea	le thé	tay
toast	pain grillé	pan greeyay
vegetables	les légumes	lay-goom
vinegar	le vinaigre	veenaygr
water	l'eau	l'oh
red wine	le vin rouge	vañ roozh
white wine	le vin blanc	vañ bloñ

NUMBERS

0	zéro	zeh-roh
1	un, une	uñ, oon
2	deux	duh
3	trois	trwah
4	quatre	katr
5	cinq	sañk
6	six	sees
7	sept	set
8	huit	weet
9	neuf	nerf
10	dix	dees
11	onze	oñz
12	douze	dooz
13	treize	trehz
14	quatorze	katorz
15	quinze	kañz
16	seize	sehz
17	dix-sept	dees-set
18	dix-huit	dees-weet
19	dix-neuf	dees-nerf
20	vingt	vañ
30	trente	tront
40	quarante	karoñt
50	cinquante	sañkoñt
60	soixante	swasoñt
70	soixante-dix	swasoñt-dees
80	quatre-vingts	katr-vañ
90	quatre-vingt-dix	katr-vañ-dees
100	cent	soñ
1,000	mille	meel

TIME

one minute	une minute	oon mee-noot
one hour	une heure	oon urr
half an hour	une demi-heure	oon duh-mee urr
Monday	lundi	luñ-dee
Tuesday	mardi	mar-dee
Wednesday	mercredi	mehrkruh-dee
Thursday	jeudi	zhuh-dee
Friday	vendredi	voñdruh-dee
Saturday	samedi	sam-dee
Sunday	dimanche	dee-moñsh

ACKNOWLEDGMENTS

DK Travel would like to thank the following people whose help and assistance contributed to the preparation of this book

Karissa Adams, Elizabeth Byrne, James Davis, Sarah Dennis, Matt Dobbin, Bridget Fuller, Pauline Giacomelli-Harris, Meryl Halls, George Hamilton-Jones, Catherine Hetherington, Debbie James, Chris Rushby, Mike Sansbury

Cartographic Data ERA-Maptec Ltd (Dublin) adapted with permission from original survey and mapping by Shobunsha (Japan)

PICTURE CREDITS

The publisher would like to thank the following for their kind permission to reproduce their photographs:

Key: a-above; b-below/bottom; c-centre; f-far; l-left; r-right; t-top

123RF.com: Jon Bilous 18tc, 114-5cl; Francesco Bucchi 303br; Nattee Chalermtiragool 32br; Christian Mueller 267bl; Inna Nerlich 89cra.

4Corners: Antonino Bartuccio 6-7c; Pietro Canali 11crb; Susanne Kremer 4.

Alamy Stock Photo: Todd Anderson 186cr; Andrzej Gorzkowski Photography 299bl; ART Collection 60bl; Peter Barritt 185cr; Martin Beddall 303bl; Piere Bonbon 24tl, 262-3; Eden Breitz 219cb; Helen Cathcart 119tr; Chronicle 70br, 131tr; Daisy Corlett 49b; Crowdspark / Newzulu / Dan Pier 134tc; De Rocker 156cra; Delmarty / Alpaca / Andia 26crb; Directphoto Collection 23tl, 234-5; Beth Dixson 189tr; Chad Ehlers 302cla; Everett Collection Inc 283cr; PE Forsberg 99tc; Giovanni Guarino Photo 46-7b; GL Archive 60br, 131ca; Granger Historical Picture Archive 62cr; hitandrun / Greg Meeson / © Succession Brancusi - All rights reserved. ADAGP, Paris and DACS, London 2018 *Brancusi's studio being exhibited at the Pompidou Centre in Paris* 91crb; Hemis / Arnaud Chicurel 232bl, 247tl; Bertrand Gardel 36b, 36-7t, 43tr, 213tl, 221cra, 221crb, Henri Bouchard *Apollo* © ADAGP, Paris and DACS, London 2018 222tr; Gilles Rigoulet 270bl; Pascal Ducept 28bl; René Mattes 28crb, 289tl; Sylvain Sonnet © Succession Picasso / DACS, London 2018 *Femmes à leur toilette (Women washing)* 88-9b; Bertrand Gardel 8-9cr, 106-7b, 143tr; Bertrand Rieger 137br, 245br; Sylvain Sonnet 96tl; Heritage Image Partnership Ltd / The Print Collector 61tl; Peter Horree 187br; IanDagnall Computing 131crb; Iconotec / Arthur Leroy 120b; JaiHoneybrook 294cr; Boris Karpinski 8cla; John Kellerman 92-3b, 121t, 165br, 242b, 242-3t; Keystone Pictures USA 131br; Elena Korchenko 297t; Lautaro 221bl; Lebrecht Music and Arts Photo Library 104br; Iugris 105; Centre Pompidou in Paris: Studio Piano & Rogers; courtesy of Fondazione Renzo Piano and Rogers Stirk Harbour + Partners / Luciano Mortula 90-1b; National Geographic Creative 83tl; Niday Picture Library 61bc; John Norman 28cr; Paris 94crb; Pawel Libera Images 300-1t; William Perry 26t; Photo 12 / Gilles Targat 136cr, 176bl; PhotoAlto / Laurence Mouton 58cla; Photononstop / Christophe Lehenaff 42-3b; Daniel Thierry 270-1; Pierre Pochan 136t; Henri Cochet Statue outside Roland Garros; Paris / Paul Quayle 293br; National Museum of Modern Art in the Pompidou Centre, Paris / Mervyn Rees Xavier Veilhan © Veilhan / ADAGP, Paris and DACS, London 2018 *Le Rhinocéros* 91cra; Robertharding / Godong 33ca; Peter Schickert 96-7b; Science History Images 61cla; Shawshots 219crb; SJH Photography 301bl; Sergey Skleznev 267cr; Splash News/ Lionel Urman 41tl; William Stevens 40b; Street Art 18bl, 126-7; Claude Thibault 121br; / Tuul and Bruno Morandi © Succession Picasso / DACS, London 2018 *Head of a Woman* 88tr; Perry van Munster 48tc; Frédéric Vielcanet 51br; Don White 84-5cb; Tracey Whitefoot 287br; John G. Wilbanks 44-5b; Gari Wyn Williams 274bc.

AWL Images: Jon Arnold 1; Tour eiffel- Illuminations Pierre Bideau 21t,

196-7cl; Jan Christopher Becke 8clb, 173cla, 239tr; Walter Bibikow 39cr; Danita Delimont Stock 297cl; Bertrand Gardel 12-3bc; Carlos Sanchez Pereyra 17t, 84-5.

Candelaria: Fabien Voileau 53b.

Cité Des Sciences et de L'industrie: EPPD CSI / JP 145bl; E Luider 144-5t.

La Cuisine Cooking: 8cl.

Depositphotos Inc: packshot 299clb, wjarek 209br.

Disneyland® Paris: 303t; © Disney / Pixar: 301clb, 301br.

Dorling Kindersley: Neil Lukas 283clb, © Succession Brancusi - All rights reserved. ADAGP, Paris and DACS, London 2018 *The Kiss* 282br; Musee Marmottan / Susanna Price 304tr; Alphonse Terroir *Denis Diderot* (1925) / Neil Lukas / CNHMS, Paris 253tr; Jules Selmes 77t, 233crb; Valerio Vincenzo 208b.

Dreamstime.com: Adisa 82bl, 258-9b; Georgios Alexandris 43cl; Andersastphoto 193b; Andrey Andronov 191tr; Antoine2k 51tr, 118-9b, 306-7b; Apn68140 55cla; Valentin Armianu 13cr, 22tc, 190-1, 214-5; Astormfr 16c, 66-7; Bargotiphotography 218; Christian Bertrand 11tc; Ilona Melanie Bicker 30t; Lembi Buchanan 133t, 209t; Michal Cervenansky 284b; Christianm 176tc; Ionut David 24cb, 278-9; Maurizio De Mattei 184-5t; Nicolas De Corte 159t; Digikhmer 210-1b; Matthew Dixon 206b; Yury Dmitrienko 41cr; Dennis Dolkens 75cr, 124-5b, 296-7b; Chris Dorney 230bl; Viorel Dudau 173tr; Evolove 220-1t; Fayethequeen93 146crb; Ruslan Gilmanshin 172-3b; Gornostaj 167cra; Ioana Grecu 225bl; Alberto Grosescu 13br; Guillohmz 119cla, 298crb; Bensliman Hassan 146b, 275bl; Dieter Hawlan 302b; Infomods 229t; Javarman 269tr; Valerijs Jegorovs 174-5b; Jeromecorreia 194bl; Joymsk 158bl; Aliaksandr Kazlou 131tl; Kmiragaya 286-7t; Sergii Kolesnyk 30bl, 173tl; Maryna Kordiumova 185crb; Denys Kuvaiev 135br; Liudmila Laurova 46-7tl; Bo Li 185bl; José Lledó

30crb; Madrabothair 76b, 132bl, 132-3b. 177t; Tomas Marek 10ca, 282-3t; Meunierd 293crb; Minacarson 113br, 261tl; Daniel Buren © DB-ADAGP Paris and DACS, London 2018 *Les Deux Plateaux, Palais Royal* 188-9bl; Luciano Mortula 23cb, 248-9; MrFly 200clb; Neirfy 2-3; Nui7711 94-5t; William Perry 74bl, 75tr, 79tr; Kovalenkov Petr 109b, 224t; Mathias Pfauwadel 25tc, 290-1; Photofires 298-9t; Photogolfer 225br, 305tr; Ekaterina Pokrovsky 13tc; John Queenan 12clb; Redlunar 254bl; Eq Roy/ Architect Dominique Perrault © ADAGP, Paris and DACS, London 2018 *The Bibliotheque Nationale de France* 274-5t; Jozef Sedmak 192tr; Dmitry Shishkin 57cr; Siraanamwong 239cla; Smontgom65 28t; Alena Sobaleva 256b; Spytsekouras 255b; Darius Strazdas 17bl, 100-1, 104clb, 107tc, 130-1b; Petr Švec 32-3tl; Worakan Thaomor 204br; Tupungato 207tr; Ukrphoto 238cra; Valio84sl 12tc; Dennis Van De Water 266-7, 268bl; VanderWolfImages 20t, 168-9; Ivan Varyukhin 303clb; Vitalyedush 253tl, 257t, 304b; Vvoevale 78-9bc, 160t; Dirk Wenzel 285tl; Jason Yoder 73bl; Zatletic 75c.

Getty Images: AFP / Eric Feferberg 58cl, 59tr; Kenzo Tribouillard 59bl; Lionel Bonaventure 58bl; Atlantide Phototravel / Stefano Amantini 33bc, / Massimo Borchi 204cl; Bettmann 283br; BSIP 285br; Centre Pompidou in Paris: Studio Piano & Rogers; courtesy of Fondazione Renzo Piano and Rogers Stirk Harbour + Partners / Busà Photography 91c; Guillaume Chanson 238-9b; Christophel Fine Art 45cl, 62tl; Corbis / VCG / Robert Holmes / 48-9tc; Corbis Documentary / P Deliss 73cra; Ian Cumming 48bl; Bruno De Hogues 10-11bc, 26bl, 276bl; De Agostini / Biblioteca Ambrosiana 219bl; C. Sappa 70bl; Stephane De Sakutin 267br; Simona Dumitru 292-3t; Neil Farrin 288cl; Owen Franken 56b, 195tl; Gallo Images / Ayhan Altun 73cr; Bertrand Guay 108tr, 213br; Francois Guillot 41br; Daniel Haug 59br; Heritage Images 219cra; Boris Horvat 219cl; Hulton Archive 200bl; Corbis Historical 61tr, 70fbl; John Sones Singing Bowl Media 98bl; Julian Elliott Photography 246bl; Keystone 283cb; Lo Chun Kit 58br; Pascal Le Segretain 40tl; Philippe Le Tellier 63bl; Lonely Planet Images /